THE HEALING POWER OF
GEMSTONES

GANESHA MANTRA

गजाननम् भूत गणादि सेवितम्

कपित्य्य जम्बू फल चारु भक्षणम्

उमा सुतम् शोक विनाश कारकम्

नमामि विघ्नेश्वर पाद पंकजम्

THE HEALING POWER OF

GEMSTONES

IN TANTRA, AYURVEDA, AND ASTROLOGY

BASED ON TRADITIONAL
KNOWLEDGE OF THE HINDUS

by

HARISH JOHARI

DESTINY BOOKS
Rochester, Vermont

Destiny Books
One Park Street
Rochester, Vermont 05767

Library of Congress Cataloging-in-Publication Data
Johari, Harish, 1934-
   The healing power of gemstones.

   Includes index.
   1. Precious stones—Therapeutic use. 2. Tantrism.
3. Medicine, Ayurvedic. 4. Astrology. I. Title.
RM666.P825J64 1988   615.8'56   88-30912
ISBN 0-89281-215-X
Cover photograph by John Taylor.
Printed and bound in the United States

10 9 8 7 6 5 4 3 2 1

Destiny Books is a division of Inner Traditions International, Ltd.

Distributed to the book trade in the United States by Harper and Row
Publishers, Inc.

Distributed to the book trade in Canada by Book Center, Inc., Montreal,
Quebec

ODE TO AGNI

अग्निमीले पुरोहितं यज्ञस्य देवम् ।
ऋत्विजं   होतारं रत्नधातमम् ॥
ऋु.वे.

AGNIMĪLE PUROHITAM YAGYASYA DEVAM,
RITUAJAM HOTĀRAM RATNADHĀTAMAM.
RIG VEDA.

We worship Agni, the fire god,
He who always does good to others
As lord of sacrifice
(He gives all gods their share)
And as progenitor of seasons
And beholder of gems.

Contents

Author's Note

IN THE YEAR 1974 my first book, entitled *Dhanwantari,* was published by Rams Head Inc., California. In it there was a chapter "Why Jewelry for Health" to explain the use of jewelry as a tool for balancing the psychophysiological system. This chapter dealt with gems, their relationship with planets, and their use in medicinal remedies, but the information was not enough to be of practical use. The necessity of writing a detailed description of gems and their cosmic power was always in my head. After almost fourteen years this wish is fulfilled. Here is a unique combination of information derived from three different sources— astrology, Ayurveda, and Tantra—to provide a methodology for using the power stored in gems.

According to *Rig Veda,* the oldest existing scripture, gems are produced by intense heat, that is, fire (known as Agni in Vedic language) and tectonic pressure within the earth. They are crystallizations of the ions of elements and elemental compounds formed in the process of purification and concentration of the most essential forms of matter. Gems have great potential to absorb, reflect, and radiate different frequencies of light and to transfer light in the form of ions to the lymphatic fluids and blood plasma, which contains electrolytes.

Man is a universe inside a universe. His body—like the body of the universe—is composed of cells connected with each other by an electromagnetic force, which works through electrolytes present in each cell. Individual consciousness is a product of Ego and Mind, and all pleasure and pain exists because of this Ego-Mind combination. It is because of this eternal pair of Ego and Mind that we have uncountable desires and we need an unlimited amount of energy to fulfill them. Unfulfilled desires cause illness and pain, and methods of curing disease and pain are always necessary. This book is written to help meet the human need for healing; its proper study will help in overcoming pain and bring happiness and inspiration to life.

Because the information comes from Ayurveda and Tantra it may be difficult for Western readers to understand Ayurvedic preparations of medicinal remedies or Tantric methods of invoking planetary energy through worship and rituals. But, as I wrote in the introduction of my book *Dhanwantari,* ". . . man must make full use of whatever tools exist, drawing on all peoples and all cultures from the dawn of creation through the latest refinements of the present. He cannot alienate himself from Truth, wherever it exists, be it in laboratories, universities, tribal cultures, or in the homilies and folk sayings."

Some credit for the knowledge of gems also goes to my family name Johari, which literally means "the one who knows about Jawharat (gems)." I remember that when I was a very young boy, Maulvi Abul Hasan, my Urdu and Persian teacher, recited a Persian verse whenever and wherever he saw me:

> *"Qadre Hira Shah vadanad*
> *Ya vadanad Jauhari."*

> "The value of a diamond is known to a king,
> or the Jauhari knows it."

I always smiled and thought, "Maybe one day I will really know it and will prove worthy of my family name and become a real Johari."

I am indebted to all those whose knowledge has benefited me, especially the sages and seers of ancient times who left behind them an inexhaustible treasure of knowledge. Their knowledge of the use of gems for physical, psychological, and spiritual benefits requires many lifetimes to understand.

I am thankful to Lamberta Stheeman for providing diapositives of my original paintings of Rahu and Ketu from her private art collection.

I am thankful to Heidegret Rauhut for her patience and labor in preparing the typed manuscript of the present edition.

I am thankful to all those Western friends who used gems, gem pendulums, and gem powders and pills and gave me positive feedback useful in preparing the present edition.

I am thankful to Peter my student for preparing illustrations for the gajput (gem oxide) talismans, and numerical yantras.

I am sure the knowledge contained in these pages will help those who will use it, as it has helped those who used it for many millennia.

Om. Shanti Shanti Shanti

Harish Johari
363 Punjab Pura
Bareilly, U.P. INDIA

About the Cover

The cover of *The Healing Power of Gemstones* shows a cluster of clear rock quartz crystal that has been engraved with the Tantric mandala, Shri Yantra. This yantra is known in the Hindu tradition to represent the form of the cosmos as well as the form of the human body. The quartz cluster contains rutilated tourmalines, or crystals within the crystal, which appear as black fibers crossing one another. Tourmalated quartz crystal of this kind is valued for its strong healing and psychic vibrations.

Approximately three to four thousand years old, the crystal measures eight inches wide, eleven inches high, and four inches thick. It was unearthed in Africa and has been vertically slab-cut and lap-polished. Because of its many inclusions, it was particularly difficult to engrave. The artists chanted throughout the engraving process, during which a small amount of prehistoric water was released.

This piece is the work of David Sugar and Carol Iselin, an artistic team whose crystal engravings have been placed in seven major museums throughout the world, including the Smithsonian Institution in Washington, D.C., and the Victoria and Albert in London. Some of their engravings, such as a piece created for the American space program, have documented major historic events.

Part *I*

Introduction

श्री गणेषाय नमः

SHRI GANESHAYE NAMAH

I pay my homage to Lord Ganesha.

1
Gems and the Human Race

FROM THE VERY DAWN of civilization man has been fascinated by brilliant, shiny, colorful shells, stones, and crystals. Their possession made him more important than others. Some of those who collected them also felt their power. Those who benefited by possessing gems prescribed them to others . . . and an oral tradition of sorts grew around their use. Archaeological excavations done around the world show that man collected gems everywhere and somehow knew their use. There is evidence of the systematic mining of gems in Egypt, and about seven thousand years ago gems were mined in the Oxus valley of Afghanistan. These mines still produce lapis lazuli—worth millions of rupees every year.

THE ORIGIN OF THE RELATIONSHIP BETWEEN GEMS AND THE HUMAN BODY

The whole process of evolution is a constant interplay of the eternal pair of opposites, Sun and Moon, or Agni (fire) and Soma (water). The Vedic concept of Hiranyagarbha, the Golden Embryo on the eternal water, clearly indicates the formation of the phenomenal world by the two—fire and water—representing male and female principles.

3

Fire somehow seems to be the beginning of the world of names and forms. It flowed in the form of lava, carrying with it all the minerals and the elemental force of nature, which later developed into organic matter through the process of condensation. The condensation and crystallization of minerals produced colorful rocky crystals known as gems. All gems, with the exception of coral and pearls, are the purest and finest consolidation of minerals that were formed due to extreme heat and pressure inside the body of the molten Earth. All gems are therefore energy in crystalline form. They are highly sensitive and radioactive. They absorb and transmit energy as frequencies because they are composed of minerals that emit electrical charges in increased pressure, that radiate in low heat, and that glow from inside after the light source is removed and in the presence of ultraviolet light in darkness.

Gems are composed of the following minerals: aluminum, beryllium, calcium, carbon, copper, fluorine, hydrogen, iron, manganese, oxygen, potassium, phosphorus, sulphur, sodium, silicon, tin, zirconium, zinc, and others.

Nine out of these eighteen are the main components of the nine major gems: aluminum, beryllium, carbon, calcium, fluorine, hydrogen, oxygen, silicon, and zirconium; three of these are common in all gems: aluminum, oxygen, and silicon.

These three form the bulk of the outermost surface of our planet Earth. Oxygen and silicon are found on almost 75 percent of Earth's surface. Aluminum makes up over 8 percent of Earth's crust.

The chemical nature of gems brings them in close contact with man. They are crystals of clear and purified chemicals that are also found in the human body. Their electromagnetic field influences the environment in a very subtle manner; their clarity makes them a pure source of energy. They serve as valuable agents of the electromagnetic energy that influences the electrochemical nature of the human organism. In addition to this they serve as ionizers— creating ionic balance inside and outside the organism. Their contact with the electromagnetic field of the body becomes easy when they are embedded in pure electrolytes like copper, silver, and gold and used as rings worn between two joints of the ring finger. Joints are naturally the most active parts of the body, where the network of nerve fibers and the lymphatic fluid is the most concentrated. The nerve fibers and the lymphatic fluid together serve as the assimilators of energy emitted by the gems. With their slight and constant contact with the skin they bring changes in body chemistry by their interaction with the body's energy field, which is permeated by a complex electromagnetic field. The energy that operates in the human organism is physicochemical in nature and works through the nerves, tissues, and fibers. In addition to this, pranic energy also works through its own channels, known as nadis, which are different from the nerves of the nervous system. The body is permeated more by pranic energy than by nerves.

Gems work with both kinds of energy—physicochemical, i.e., electrochemical; and pranic, i.e., the vital life force—whether they are used as jewelry or taken orally as pastes or oxides.

This view explains the process through which gems are formed; how they operate in absorbing and transmitting light frequencies and electromagnetic energy; their ability to create ionic balance, and so forth, but it does not link them with our emotional self. It lacks the human quality, which makes it easy for us to accept them. Another view comes from folklore, religious scriptures, and tradition. Ancient scriptures from across the world have praised gems as powerful agents of energy that influence human fate and destiny, induce good energy, and expel the negative energy that produces sickness, suffering, and psychosis. Gems have also been regarded as bringers of peace, prosperity, and happiness. Favorable gems bring about name, fame, and power and make life easier. In the *Rig Veda* the beneficial aspect of using gems is mentioned in the tenth mantra of the nineteenth sutra of the sixth mandala. The Puranas (ancient Indian stories), in their own allegorical method, tell the origin of gems and correlate them with various organs of the human body and the nine planets of our solar system. Among these scriptures are: *Devi Bhagwat* (8.11.12), *Mahabharata* (tenth mandala), *Vishnu Dharmotter Purana, Bhava-Prakash, Tantra Sara, Agasthyamat (Ratna Prakash), Arth Shastra* of Kautilya, *Shukraniti, Budha Bhatta, Surminti, Chandreshwar, Brihat Samhita* of Varahmihir, *Agni Purana,* and *Kurma Purana.* These texts mention gems as powerful agents to help the human organism, but offer no mention of their medical properties or their uses as oxides, pastes, or powders; this information was accumulated in the later tradition of Ayurveda.

It was the tantriks (the practitioners of the science of Tantra) who used gems as oxides and powders and introduced this way of using the gems to Ayurvedacharyas (adepts of the Ayurveda). Later, proper research on the chemical nature of gems and their powders (pastes) and oxides was conducted by these tantrik alchemists. All of the scriptures mentioned above, with the exception of *Tantra Sara,* deal with gems as agents of absorbing and transmitting the energy linked with the seven or nine planets—and as decorative objects that absorb negative energy and produce healthy energy for the body and mind. They all recommend the use of gems to help create a favorable environment.

Tantriks treated gems as storehouses of divine energy and began to use gems for carving objects of worship, idols, rosaries, talismans (yantras), amulets, pendulums, and so forth. They were also used for the construction of chauk (a quadrangular pattern used for invocation of the deities, or the nine planets), mandalas, and pots used for offering the holy water or keeping the offerings for consecration. Lingams made of sphatik mani (quartz) and moonstone are still popular in India. Yantras made of sphatik mani in pyramid shape are still available in abundance in the antique shops of India and Nepal. Tantriks believed that yantras carved in metals and rosaries made of precious stones give siddhi (power to achieve desired goal) quicker than a rosary made from other beads—with the exception of rudraksha, which is a special bead obtained from the rudraksha tree, sacred to the shaiva, believers in the lord Shiva.

Offering gemstones in fire worship (yagya) is purely tantrik, and using the oxides as prasad (consecrated food) is most probably the origin of gem therapy.

In *Tantra Sara,* a major tantrik scripture, the human body is stated to be an island of nine gems. These nine gems correspond with the nine dhatus (ingredients) of which the human body is composed. The description of these nine dhatus is found in Ayurvedic texts. These nine ingredients are as follows:

1. Mans — Flesh
2. Loma — Hair
3. Twacha — Skin
4. Rakta — Blood
5. Asthi — Bone
6. Majja — Marrow
7. Medha — Fat
8. Shukra — Semen
9. Prana — Vitality (life force)

The nine gems known as nav-ratnas are related to these nine dhatus. Ayurvedic texts mostly mention sapt-dhatus, the "seven ingredients," which are:

1.	Raja	Clay or Earth
2.	Rasa	Fluids
3.	Rakta	Blood
4.	Asthi	Bone
5.	Medha	Fat
6.	Majja	Marrow
7.	Mans	Flesh

Shukra is considered to be the eighth dhatu, which comes from the essence of every dhatu. But in some scriptures nine dhatus are also mentioned, which we have given in the table of nine dhatus above. The *Tantra Sara* gives a clear statement of their correspondence to the nav-ratnas, which is very helpful in understanding the relationship of gems with the human organism.

The gems related with the nine ingredients (dhatus) are:

1.	Flesh	Pushparaga	Yellow or white sapphire
2.	Hair	Neel mani	Blue Sapphire
3.	Skin	Vaidurya mani	Cat's-eye
4.	Blood	Prawal	Coral
5.	Bone	Vajra	Diamond
6.	Marrow	Markat	Emerald
7.	Fat	Gomed	Hessonite or cinnamon stone
8.	Semen	Mukta	Pearl
9.	Vitality	Padmaraga	Ruby

Wearing these gems influences the dhatus and the psychophysical well-being. The Puranas present beautiful stories about the origin of gems and through these stories convey some of the utility of the gems. The *Kurma Purana* states that gems were created from the seven different kinds of rays of light emanating from the seven major planets of our solar system. These rays were transmitted in the seven colors of the rainbow: violet, indigo, blue, green, yellow, orange, and red. These seven rays of light are responsible for all material existence in the solar system, including the human body. Colors are frequencies of light in different bands, and therefore they are energy in a different form, which directly influences human form and consciousness. There are hot and cold colors and colors that are neutral (neither hot nor cold). Hot colors increase heat, which results in arrogance and anger; cold colors calm the system. The neutral colors produce pleasant feelings and joy.

Another Purana says that these seven rays of light emanate from the divine body of the lord of the universe known as Jagdishwara (jagat = universe, ishwara = lord; together they become Jagdishwara, or Jagdish). The divine light is perceived by human eyes as the seven-colored light. According to this theory the divine light is the creator and preserver of the entire universe. Through this light the seven planets get their nourishment, and the planets transmit this light to our planet, where these rays give nourishment to the gems. The gems also repeat the same process. They absorb the energy from the planet, assimilate it, and transmit it to the environment, and if they are in contact with the human organism then they also provide this energy there, as well. This view connects the human body with the planets (Sun, Moon, Mars, Mercury, Jupiter, Venus, and Saturn) and with the gem related to each planet.

The writer of the scripture *Brihat Samhita* states:

रत्नानि बलादैत्याद्धिचितोन्ये वदन्तिजातानि
केचित भुवः स्वाभावाद्वैचित्र्यं प्राहुरुपलानाम्

The gems were formed from the body of a demon called Bali; some writers trace their origin from the body of a great sage, Dadhichi.

—Varahamihir

The Agni Purana presents an apt story that is very popular in India: Indra, the lord of forty-nine kinds of Maruts (winds), thunder, clouds, rains, lightning, and heaven, was defeated by a demon known as Vrittasura and became disheartened. Gods and demigods living in Swarg Loka (heaven) were turned out of heaven and Indra was dethroned. He approached Brahma, the lord of creation, to save the gods and demigods from this powerful demon. Brahma advised Indra to approach the great sage Dadhichi, who spent nearly all of his time in meditation, and remained almost constantly in a state of *samadhi* (trance). If the sage Dadhichi would agree to give his spine, and he (Indra) could get a vajra (thunderbolt) made from the spine, the demon Vrittasura would be destroyed. Indra then approached the sage and told him what Brahma had said. Dadhichi, who was a great ascetic and completely disinterested in his physical body, readily agreed to give his spine, and advised Indra thus: get a black cow, apply salt to his (Dadhichi's) body while he sat in samadhi, and let the cow lick the salt from his body. This would cause the flesh to come off of the body and then the spine could be easily taken out of its skeleton without harm. Indra agreed to the proposal and obtained his undamaged spine, which he gave to the celestial architect Vishwakarma for carving a vajra (thunderbolt). When Vishwakarma was carving the vajra some unused pieces of the spine fell on the earth at four different spots. From these, four diamond mines originated. This is also one of the reasons why the diamond is also known by the name vajra. Other gems were created by other pieces of the spine which fell on earth while Vishwakarma was chiseling the vajra.

Another story from the Puranas states that at one time gods, demigods, and demons made a combined effort to churn the Ocean of Milk (Ksheer Sagar) in order to get elixir—the water of life—from the ocean. They made Mount Meru (meru = spine) their churning stick, and the serpent king Vasuki their rope. Vishnu in the form of a turtle held Mount Meru on his back and the ocean was churned by gods and demons together. After twelve precious objects came out of the ocean the divine medicine man Dhanwantari came out with a pot of amrit (elixir). Vishnu, assuming the form of a beautiful woman (Mohini), took the job of distributing elixir equally to the gods and the demons—but he gave liquor (*varuni*) to the demons and amrit to the gods. When the demons realized that they were being tricked by the beautiful woman they tried to grab the Amrit Kumbh (the pot of elixir) from her and a quarrel between gods and demons arose. Jayant, the son of Indra, got hold of the pot and ran away with it. During the quarrel some drops of elixir fell on the earth and were converted into the precious gem mines. Thus the origin of gems is with drops of the elixir.

The *Garuda Purana* gives a different story about the origin of gems. It tells about the demon king Bali, who became invincible because of his austerity and good conduct. He once defeated all the gods and demigods who lived in heaven. Indra then assumed the form of a brahmin (priest) and went to Bali as a begging priest, because Indra knew that Bali had achieved his power because of his good deeds. Indra disguised as a brahmin asked Bali alms, which he agreed to give. Indra, however, had not told him specifically what he wanted. When Bali asked him—after giving his word to give him whatever he wanted—the disguised Indra said that he wanted to perform his sacrificial rites and that he wanted him (Bali) to become the animal to be sacrificed. Bali in his generosity accepted Indra's request and assumed the form of the animal (buffalo) to be sacrificed. Then the gods and demigods sacrificed him. Because Bali offered his body for a noble deed and with benevolence, he became pure and his body was converted into the nine gems of eighty-four types. Of these, twenty-one are of special importance and nine gems are particularly well known and precious. The story says that wherever the pieces of the body of Bali fell, gems related to that part of the body originated:

येतु रावण गंगायां जायन्ते कुरुबिन्दुव:
पद्मरराग धनं रागं विभ्राणास्फटिकार्चिष:।"

द्राबवधिपते: पित्तमाद्याय मुजगाधिप.......
सहसैव मुमोच तत्फणीन्द्र: सुरक्साभ्यक्त तुरुष्क पाढ पायाम्,
वरमाणिक्य गिवे रूपत्यकाया'

• Wherever his bones fell on earth mines of diamonds originated.
• Wherever his teeth fell pearls originated. Eight different sources of pearls are (1) oysters, (2) conch, (3) fish (whales), (4) snakes, (5) wild boar, (6) elephants, (7) clouds, and (8) bamboo. Out of these eight

sources oysters are the only readily available source; pearls from the other seven sources are extremely rare.

- His blood was evaporated by sunlight. Ravana, powerful demon king of Singhal Dweep (Sri Lanka), stopped it from going upward and compelled it to fall into a river in his country. The river was named Ravan Ganga from that day, and from the bed of that river came rubies.

- His bile was being carried by Vasuki, the king of snakes, and the eagle god Garuda attacked him and forced him to drop it on Earth, which is the origin of emeralds.

- His eyes fell on Earth and became blue sapphires.

- His skin fell on the Himalayas and became yellow and white sapphires.

- His sound turned into cat's-eye.

- His arms and other parts of the body became other precious and semiprecious gemstones.

- His semen turned into hessonite, or cinnamon stone.

- His intestines became coral.

- His fat became quartz.

- The rest of his body was turned into agate.

After the formation of these gems the nine planets distributed them among themselves, as follows:

Pearl Ring may bring eye problem

Sun selected Ruby (Manikya) — *Topaz too unsuitable for many*
Moon selected Pearls (Mukta)
Mars selected Coral (Prawal) *9, 18, 27*
Mercury selected Emerald (Markat)
Jupiter selected Yellow sapphire (Pushpraga)
Venus selected Diamond (Vajra)
Saturn selected Blue sapphire (Neelmani)
Rahu selected Hessonite (Gomed)
Ketu selected Cat's-eye (Vaidurya)

Thus the gems got their relationship with the nine planets. It is interesting that a scripture on healing, *Anubhut Yogmala*, lists these gems and states that they can cure the parts of the body and the diseases related to these parts when they are used orally as fine powders, or oxides. The parts of the body of Bali, the demon king, are also mentioned with the gems. The following chart can be very helpful in gem therapy:

Table 1

Gems That Came From the Body of Bali and the Diseases for Which They Can Be Used

Gem	Part of the body of the demon king Bali	Diseases that could be cured
Diamond	Bones of Bali	Diseases of bones
Pearl	Teeth	Pyorrhea
Ruby	Blood	Diseases of the blood; purifies blood
Emerald	Bile	Diseases of bile
Blue sapphire	Eyes	Eye troubles
Cat's-eye	Sound	Diseases connected with speech; disorders of vocal cords
Yellow and white sapphire	Skin	Skin diseases; leprosy
Tourmaline	Nails	Diseases of the nails
Hessonite	Semen	Seminal diseases
Lapis lazuli	Radiance	Cures jaundice; improves sight
Agate	All other parts of the body	Gives lustre to the body
Quartz	Fats	Debility, tuberculosis, diseases of the spleen, etc.

Use of these gems as gemstone pendulums, amulets, rings, and necklaces, along with their oral use as paste, powders, and oxides brings better results and helps in early recovery. One thing should not be forgotten: food plays an important role in curing diseases and one should always consult a dietary expert in order to use only those grains, vegetables, and fruit that will help the organism in recovery. If proper attention is not paid to diet, the gems or any medicine will not help as quickly as they could when proper food is taken.

(1) Turquoise bring wisdom, philosophy etc / may bring good luck or fortune

(2) Pearl / created eye problems / water pouring out from one eye — tested — not for me

(3) Zirconia — lethargic luck not a big one.

(4) Moonstone good

(5) Blue Sapphire not good for me $900 Ring brought only bad luck / Returned the Ring.

2
Gems and Astrology

THE NATURAL INSTINCT of man to know the unknown is the mother of all sciences, including astrology. The Vedic seers realized that by meditation, contemplation, and research one could know the mysteries of matter and mind. It only requires true understanding of the laws of nature, because from the gross material reality to the subtlest frequencies, all is a part of one single continuum of vibrations. Everything is interrelated and interdependent. The man and the universe surrounding him are all the products of the same law through which creation is begun, preserved, and destroyed. Keen observation, right attitude, imagination guided by right knowledge, and systematic thinking can solve all mysteries. Truth is truth at all levels; matter and mind are not separate, they are two sides of the same coin. Ignorance creates mystery, bad body chemistry creates negative thoughts and wrong attitude. Right food, austerity, and penance can connect man with the divine, which is pure knowledge.

Vedic seers like Narada, Bhrigu, Garg, Shaunik, Parashar, and Shuk through their austerity and penance developed this divine insight and wrote scriptures on astrology.

Astrology studies man as a microcosm and considers him to be an indivisible part of the macrocosm; it is based on the assumption that the human body and psyche are influenced by celestial bodies, the stars and planets of our solar system. Through the help of horoscope (the natal chart) an astrologer can understand the psychophysical nature of any individual. He can assess his latent potential, role in life, health, wealth, friends and foes, ups and downs, life span, diseases, kinds of obstacles or problems one can have, the relationship of the individual with his or her father and mother, brothers and sisters, superiors and subordinates, wife or husband and partners, and so forth.

Planets, too, have friends and foes. They are exalted in one sign and debilitated or exiled in another. Their placement in the twelve houses of the natal chart plays an important role. To make this statement clearer, I present the following chart.

Astrologers and gem therapists use gems to compensate for the loss of energy caused by the weak planets (i.e., debilitated, exiled, badly-aspected), to provide missing chemicals and reestablish electrochemical balance, or to provide more strength to the exalted favorable planets. Gems can enhance the benevolent effect of the malignant planets. This quality of gems has made them the favorites of astrologers, priests, tantriks, and gem therapists.

In the *Jatak Parijat* there is a verse that assigns the nine gems to the nine planets:

मानिक्यं दिननायकस्य.विमलं मुक्ताफलम शीतगोः।
माहेयस्यच विद्रुमं मरकतं सौमस्य गारुत्मकम ॥
देवज्यस्य चपुष्पारागम् सुराचार्यस्य वज्र शनैः ।
नीलं निर्मलमन्ययोश्च गोदंत गोमेद वैडूर्य के: ॥

MANIKYAM DINNAYAKASYA, VIMALAM MUKTAPHALAM
SHITGOH, MAHEYASYA CHA VIDRUMUM MARKATAM
SOMYASYA GARUTMAKAM DEVEJYASYA CHA PUSHPRAGAM
SURACHARYASYA VAJRAM SHANAIH NEELAM NIRMALMANYA
YOSHCH GEEDATE GOMED VAIDURYAKEH

Ruby is the gem of the Lord of the Day (the Sun)
Glowing pearl is the gemstone of the cool Moon
Red coral is the gem of Mars
Emerald is the gem of the noble Mercury
Yellow sapphire is the gem of Jupiter, the teacher of the gods
Diamond is the gem of Venus, the teacher of demons
Blue sapphire is the gem of Saturn
Hessonite is the gem of Rahu
and Cat's-eye is the gemstone of Ketu.

Table 2

Relations Among the Planets*

Planet	Friend	Enemy	Exalted	Debilitated	Exiled	Sign	Color	Weekday	Gemstone
Sun	Moon, Mars, Jupiter	Saturn, Rahu, Ketu, Mercury	Aries	Libra	Aquarius	Leo	Gold, orange, light brown	Sunday	Ruby
Moon	Sun, Mars, Jupiter	Saturn, Rahu, Ketu, Mercury, Venus	Taurus	Scorpio	Capricorn	Cancer	Silver, light blue	Monday	Pearl
Mars	Sun, Moon, Jupiter	Saturn, Venus, Mercury	Capricorn	Cancer	Libra, Taurus	Aries, Scorpio	Red (all shades)	Tuesday	Coral
Mercury	Saturn, Rahu, Ketu	Sun, Mars	Virgo	Pisces	Sagittarius, Pisces	Gemini, Virgo	Green, light grey	Wednesday	Emerald
Jupiter	Moon, Mars	None	Cancer	Capricorn	Gemini, Virgo	Sagittarius, Pisces	Yellow	Thursday	Topaz
Venus	Saturn, Mars, Moon	Mercury	Pisces	Virgo	Aries, Scorpio	Libra, Taurus	White	Friday	Diamond
Saturn	Mercury, Rahu, Ketu	Moon, Mars	Libra	Aries	Leo, Cancer	Aquarius, Capricorn	Black, Turquoise	Saturday	Blue sapphire
Rahu (north node)	Saturn, Ketu, Mercury	Sun, Moon	Taurus	Scorpio	—	—	Black, dark green	—	Amethyst
Ketu (south node)	Saturn, Rahu, Mercury	Sun, Moon	Scorpio	Taurus	—	—	Black	—	Cat's-eye

Houses: Generally, planets sitting in houses 1, 4, 7, 9, and 10 are considered to be strong. Planets residing in 6, 8, and 12 are weakened in their powers. In evaluation of the strength of a planet it should also be taken into account that Sun, Moon, Mars, and Venus are stronger in the first halves of signs, while Saturn, Jupiter, Mercury, Rahu, and Ketu are stronger in the higher half of a zodiac sign.

Aspects: First, all planets *see* seven houses; i.e., any planet sitting in the opposite sign is *seen.* Second, conjunction means sitting in the same sign. Saturn also sees third and tenth houses; Mars, fourth and eighth; Jupiter, fifth and ninth. Planets under aspects of friends will be strengthened; planets seen by an enemy are weakened.

This assignment is the same as that in the story of Bali from the *Garuda Purana.* There is, however, no mention of gems ruled by planets in the *Brihat Samhita* of Varahamihir. The *Ratnapariksha* of Agasthya, the *Agni Purana,* the *Devi Bhagwat,* and the *Mahabharata* of Vedvyasa agree with the assignment of the same gems to the nine planets. The *Jatak Parijat* and the *Phal Deepika* specify the same list as the *Garuda Purana.* These gems are called nav-ratna in Indian languages.

The nav-ratna (nine gems) are divided into two groups: (1) maha-ratna (maha = great, ratna = gem) = precious; and (2) up-ratna (up = sub, ratna = gem) = semiprecious. In the first group of maha-ratna there are five gems: diamond, pearl, ruby, blue sapphire, and emerald. In the second group of up-ratna there are four gems: hessonite, yellow sapphire, cat's-eye, and coral.

This division is based neither on the market value of the gems nor on their brilliance, lustre, or durability, but on their utility and their influence on the human psyche, body chemistry, and electromagnetic field.

There is no disagreement in the relationship of gems to planets. The list of gems with the planets with which they are assigned is consistent within the Sanskrit scriptures, but there are many popular views about their use by astrologers, gem therapists, and tantriks. Most Indian astrologers, gem therapists, and tantriks agree on the use of the gemstone related to the moon sign (rashi). (The moon sign means the placement of Moon in a particular sign of the Zodiac, e.g., Moon in Aries makes Aries the moon sign.) Because Moon governs psyche it holds a very important place in the life of an individual, and that is why the use of the gemstone according to the rashi is very popular in India. This way of selecting a gemstone, however, is too general. We have also to consider whether the Moon is rightly placed in the natal chart. If Moon is sitting in Aries in the sixth, eighth, or twelfth house, use of a coral ring, which is related to Mars, the ruler of Zodiac sign Aries, will not help. A tantrik, a gem therapist, and a good astrologer will suggest instead a pearl ring, which is the ring for that rashi. Similarly, if Moon is sitting with Sun (which only happens when an individual is born on the fourteenth or fifteenth day of the descending moon cycle), Moon even in Taurus—its sign of exaltation—becomes debilitated and needs support. Pearls will be the only choice, and not the diamond, which is related to the Moon sign Taurus, ruled by Venus. This shows that the general law of selecting a gemstone with the rashi is not correct.

The other, less popular view is that the gemstone related to the ascendant should be used. Ascendant is known as lagna in Sanskrit and is always the first house in the natal chart. This house is supposed to be very powerful and to rule the body. According to the advocates of this view the ascendant has the maximum influence on an individual's life. It governs the atmosphere in which the newborn baby takes its first breath. It is the starting point. It is connected with the body chemistry of the individual, which designs the thought patterns, emotional behavior, and ideas. The gem of the lagna is as important as the gem related to the rashi. The only good point of this system is that the lagna (ascendant) is always placed in the first house, whereas rashi (Moon) can be placed in any of the twelve houses. The problem with this system is that the lord of the lagna (ascendant) is not always placed in the first house. It could also be in any of the twelve houses. It could be exalted, debilitated, exiled, or weak. Thus we see that a general law in use of gems with rashi or lagna cannot always be helpful, and a careful observation of the natal chart is necessary. If the lord of the ascendant is exalted, sitting in a friendly sign, is conjunct, or seen by friendly planets, the gemstone related to the ascendant will help and vice versa.

Like gems, the planets are also divided into two groups: (1) Benefic (shubh grah): Moon, Mercury, Jupiter, and Venus belong to this group, which is lunar in nature; and (2) Malefic (kroor grah): Sun, Mars, Saturn, Rahu, and Ketu belong to this group, which is solar in nature.

If the ascendant belongs to the benefic group (shubh grah), the use of gemstones will enhance lunar qualities of benevolence, nobility, creativity, and gentleness.

If the ascendant belongs to the malefic group (kroor grah), the use of gems will enhance male qualities of arrogance, roughness, self-destruction, and coarseness.

But if the lord of the ascendant is sitting in the first, fourth, seventh, or tenth house with friendly planets in a friendly sign, it will help the individual in achieving name, fame, wealth, good health, and cooperation from friends and subordinates.

There are exceptions: Saturn, Rahu, and Ketu, which belong to the malefic group of planets, when placed in the third, sixth, or eleventh house act like shubh grah, benefic planets, and become powerful. If they are in a friendly sign they become more beneficial.

The eighth and twelfth houses are not supposed to be good for benefic planets in any way. It might be good for malefic planets to sit there because they become weak in these houses. The exception is only for the malefic planets sitting in the eleventh house. Thus, the eleventh house is only good for the malefic planets. This clarifies our statement that it is not always beneficial to select gemstones only because they are related to rashi (Moon sign) or lagna (ascendant).

To wear a gem is to add the energy of the planet related to the gem. If the planet is badly aspected it will only add to one's problems.

Some astrologers and gem therapists believe that the use of a gem will please the planet creating trouble and make the troublemaker friendly and favorable. This may sound true, but logically, increasing energy of an ill-aspected planet will only create problems; the negative energy will become more powerful. Tantriks suggest that donating the gem related to a malefic or ill-aspected planet is helpful. This view deserves consideration. Donating always helps. If the donation is made to a deserving candidate who could benefit by its use, the planet will become favorable. The author has tried it in many cases and gained favorable results.

Another criterion for wearing gems is to wear those related to the planets whose major period (mahadasha) is influencing the individual. This period is calculated by observing the constellation (nakshatra) of the Moon. There are twenty-seven nakshatras, known as the twenty-seven wives of the Moon in Indian mythology. The Moon rotates in these constellations in a particular order, as follows: (1) Ashvini, (2) Bharni, (3) Kritika, (4) Rohini, (5) Mrigshira, (6) Adra, (7) Punarvasu, (8) Pushya, (9) Ashlekha, (10) Magha, (11) Purva-Phalguni, (12) Uttra-Phalguni, (13) Hast, (14) Chitra, (15) Swati, (16) Vishakha, (17) Anuradha, (18) Jyeshtha, (19) Mul, (20) Purvakshad (also known as Purvakhad), (21) Uttrakhad, (22) Shravan, (23) Dhanishtha, (24) Kshatbhikha, (25) Purva Bhadrapad, (26) Uttra Bhadrapad, (27) Revati.

Each nakshatra is divided into four steps (charan). The astrologers in India look to see in which step of which nakshatra the individual is born. The lord of the nakshatra determines the major period, and the step in which one is born determines the time or duration of the major period. The major period is always ruled by one of the nine planets. The nakshatra only gives a clue to the astrologer to find out the planet under whose major period the individual is born. The steps give a clue as to how much time from the major period has already passed and how much longer the major period will last. For example, an individual is born in the final part of the second step of a nakshatra called Bharni. This individual will be born under the major period (mahadasha) of the lord of Bharni Nakshatra, which is Venus. The time of the major period is twenty years. Because the individual is born in the end of the second charan (step) the astrologer will divide twenty by four. This means that one step equals five years. Two steps are gone, thus ten years are gone, and the individual will have ten years of mahadasha (major period) of Venus—or in other words, up until ten years of age he will be influenced by the planet Venus. After ten years of age the mahadasha of the next planet in order will begin. There is also an order in which major periods operate, which is as follows:

1. Sun . . . . The duration of the mahadasha is 6 years
2. Moon . . . . The duration of the mahadasha is 10 years
3. Mars . . . . The duration of the mahadasha is 7 years
4. Rahu . . . . The duration of the mahadasha is 18 years
5. Jupiter . . . . The duration of the mahadasha is 16 years
6. Saturn . . . . The duration of the mahadasha is 19 years
7. Mercury . . . . The duration of the mahadasha is 17 years
8. Ketu . . . . The duration of the mahadasha is 7 years
9. Venus . . . . The duration of the mahadasha is 20 years

After Venus the major period of Sun starts again and the same order is repeated. Some people get the mahadasha of the same planet twice, and those who live longer than 100 to 120 years can get the mahadasha (major period) of the same planet twice. After the mahadasha of Venus the mahadasha of Sun will start. After Sun, the mahadasha of Moon will start, and all the mahadashas will come one after another in the order given above. During this period the use of the gemstone related to the planet which is the lord of the mahadasha will benefit the individual. Again, if the planet is well-aspected the gem will be favorable; if the planet is debilitated, exiled, or seen by a powerful enemy planet it will not be so useful. It is always necessary to consult a natal chart before selecting a gem to wear or to donate. Knowledge of astrology is therefore necessary for gem therapists and tantriks advising clients to use gems, although medicine men who study Ayurveda and administer gem oxides and powders are not required to study it.

Table 3

Nakshatra Chart No. 1
Chart to determine one's major period (mahadasha):*

Name of Nakshatra	Steps (Charan)	Month	Lord of Nakshatra	Period of Mahadasha
Ashvini	IIII	21st of April	Ketu	7 years
Bharni	IIII	to	Venus	20 years
Kritka	I	20th of May	Sun	6 years
Kritka	III	21st of May	Sun	6 years
Rohini	IIII	to	Moon	10 years
Mrigshira	II	20th of June	Mars	7 years
Mrigshira	II	21st of June	Mars	7 years
Adra	IIII	to	Rahu	18 years
Punarvasu	III	20th of July	Jupiter	16 years
Punarvasu	I	21st of July	Jupiter	16 years
Pushya	IIII	to	Saturn	19 years
Ashlekha	IIII	20th of August	Mercury	17 years
Magha	IIII	21st of August	Ketu	7 years
Purva Phalguni	IIII	to	Venus	20 years
Uttra Phalguni	I	20th of September	Sun	6 years
Uttra Phalguni	III	21st of September	Sun	6 years
Hast	IIII	to	Moon	10 years
Chitra	II	20th of October	Mars	7 years
Chitra	II	21st of October	Mars	7 years
Swati	IIII	to	Rahu	18 years
Vishakha	III	20th of November	Jupiter	16 years
Vishakha	I	21st of November	Jupiter	16 years
Anuradha	IIII	to	Saturn	19 years
Jyeshtha	III	20th of December	Mercury	17 years
Jyeshtha	I	21st of December	Mercury	17 years
Mul	IIII	to	Ketu	7 years
Purvashad	IIII	20th of January	Venus	20 years
Uttrashad	I		Sun	6 years

(Table 3, continued)

Name of Nakshatra	Steps (Charan)	Month	Lord of Nakshatra	Period of Mahadasha
Uttrashad	III	21st of January	Sun	6 years
Shravan	IIII	to	Moon	10 years
Dhanishtha	II	20th of February	Mars	7 years
Dhanishtha	II	21st of February	Mars	7 years
Kshat Bhikha	IIII	to	Rahu	18 years
Purva Bhadrapad	III	20th of March	Jupiter	16 years
Purva Bhadrapad	I	21st of March	Jupiter	16 years
Uttra Bhadrapad	IIII	to	Saturn	19 years
Revti	IIII	20th of April	Mercury	17 years

* The steps or charan can be easily ascertained if one knows the degrees. We are giving a chart of nakshatras that works with degrees.

In each major period (mahadasha) comes a subperiod, and the same planets repeat themselves in the subperiod in the same order, except that their period is one-tenth of the period of a mahadasha. This subperiod is called the antardasha. In each mahadasha the antardasha starts with the mahadasha; that is, with the beginning of the mahadasha of Venus, the antardasha of Venus will start. The major period of Venus is twenty years, and the antardasha of Venus is only two years. So for two years Venus will be ruling both mahadasha and antardasha.

After the antardasha of Venus in Venus the antardasha of Sun will begin; then the antardasha of Moon, Mars, Rahu, Jupiter, Saturn, Mercury, and Ketu will come within the twenty-year period of the mahadasha of Venus. The same will happen in the subperiod within the two years of the antardasha of Venus in the mahadasha of Venus: the sub-subperiod of Venus will come for two months—this is called pratyantardasha—and then all the planets will come in the two-year period of antardasha in the same order, but for a short duration. There are further divisions and subdivisions, known as sookshmdasha and pranadasha, through which the astrologer can know the influence of any planet at a given moment.

According to the sages antardasha has more influence because it is a brief period, and if one can use gems related to the lords of mahadasha and antardasha there will be more benefit.

We will add a nakshatra chart here for our readers to find out their major period (mahadasha):

Table 4

Nakshatra Chart No. 2*

Name	Degrees— Minutes From	Degrees— Minutes To	Period of Mahadasha	Lord
Ashvini Nakshatra	00° 00	13° 20	7 years	Ketu
Bharni Nakshatra	13° 20	26° 40	20 years	Venus
Kritika Nakshatra	26° 40	40° 00	6 years	Sun
Rohini Nakshatra	40° 00	53° 20	10 years	Moon
Mrigashira Nakshatra	53° 20	66° 40	7 years	Mars
Adra Nakshatra	66° 40	80° 00	18 years	Rahu
Punaryasu Nakshatra	80° 00	93° 20	16 years	Jupiter
Pushya Nakshatra	93° 20	106° 40	19 years	Saturn
Ashlekha Nakshatra	106° 40	120° 00	17 years	Mercury
Magha Nakshatra	120° 00	133° 20	7 years	Ketu
Purva Phalguni	133° 20	146° 40	20 years	Venus
Uttara Phalguni	146° 40	160° 00	6 years	Sun
Hast Nakshatra	160° 00	173° 20	10 years	Moon
Chitra Nakshatra	173° 20	186° 40	7 years	Mars
Swati Nakshatra	186° 40	200° 00	18 years	Rahu
Vishakha Nakshatra	200° 00	213° 20	16 years	Jupiter
Anuradha Nakshatra	213° 20	226° 40	19 years	Saturn
Jyeshtha Nakshatra	226° 40	240° 00	17 years	Mercury
Mula Nakshatra	240° 00	253° 20	7 years	Ketu
Purvashad Nakshatra	253° 20	266° 40	20 years	Venus
Uttrashad Nakshatra	266° 40	280° 00	6 years	Sun
Shravana Nakshatra	280° 00	293° 20	10 years	Moon
Dhanishtha Nakshatra	293° 20	306° 40	7 years	Mars
Kshata Bhika Nakshatra	306° 40	320° 00	18 years	Rahu
Purva Bhadrapad Nakshatra	320° 00	333° 20	16 years	Jupiter
Uttara Bhadrapad Nakshatra	333° 20	346° 40	19 years	Saturn
Revti Nakshatra	346° 40	360° 00	17 years	Mercury

*The 360 degrees of zodiac are divided by 27 nakshatras, or lunar mansions, comprised of 13 degrees and 20 minutes each. These 27 constellations of Moon consist of 3 groups of 9; each of the 9 nakshatras is ruled by one of the nine planets including Rahu and Ketu. The year in the Indian calendar starts on the 21st of April and at 00° 00 to 13° 20 Ashvini nakshatra remains, that is, from sunrise of 21st of April to 4th of May. Twenty minutes after sunrise the nakshatra Ashvini will rule and influence the natives born during this period— and because it is ruled by Ketu they will be born in mahadasha of Ketu. From this time up to 17th of May, 40 minutes past sunrise, the next nakshatra bharni will rule, and the persons born during this period will be born in the mahadasha of Venus, who rules bharni, and so on.

The farmers in India know the utility of this system and they sow seeds only in favorable nakshatras. Medicine men pick herbs only in the proper nakshatra and most of the time they do it only in Pushya nakshatra. Tantriks prepare amulets and yantras only in favorable nakshatras. Knowledge of nakshatras is therefore necessary for astrologers, vaidyas (medicine men), and tantriks. As we have mentioned, there are many views among astrologers about their use, but most astrologers agree that gems related to the lord of the major period (mahadasha) is helpful if that lord is well placed in the natal chart. The next point on which most of them agree is that gems can help weak planets, that is, a planet that is lacking in degrees, or one in the last part (after 25 degrees).

The Use of Nav-Ratnas (Nine Gems)

There is one more way of using gems—making a ring in which all the nine gems are set in a particular order, as follows:

Emerald	Diamond	Pearl
Yellow Sapphire	Ruby	Coral
Cat's Eye	Blue Sapphire	Hessonite

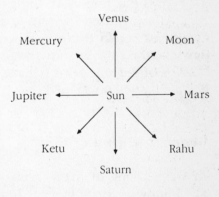

A pendulum made with these nine gems worn like a necklace is also useful. The size of the gems in a ring becomes too small, but in a pendulum they can be set in any size, and very beautiful shapes can be created. A double row of the same gems also can be used to make the pendulum more effective.

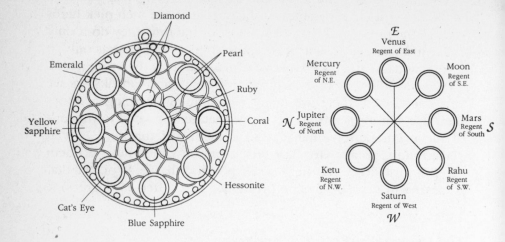

This type of setting is basically tantrik in origin, and the same diagram is made in tantrik worship. The diagram is made with wheat flour, and beans the color of the planet are used to fill the squares. The diagram is commonly used in all auspicious ceremonies for Navgrah Poojan (invocation of the nine planets).

There is one important thing about the nine-gem pendulum or ring. All gems used for setting should be flawless and of a good quality to obtain maximum benefit from it. If all gems are not flawless, the ruby at least should be large, lustrous, and flawless. If a ring of the nine gems is made, the corners should be rounded—not purely square-shaped.

Wearing a Ring of Gems

To wear a ring of many gems set in any order is inauspicious. The following list of inauspicious combinations should be kept in mind—and these gems should never be set together: (1) ruby and diamond; (2) ruby and blue sapphire; (3) pearl and blue sapphire; (4) pearl and cat's-eye; (5) blue sapphire and yellow sapphire; (6) yellow sapphire and emerald; (7) ruby and hessonite; (8) ruby and cat's-eye. Substitute gems should not be used in a nav-ratna ring or pendulum.

Here is a list of substitute gems.

Table 5

Substitute Gems

Gem	*Substitute Gem*
1. Ruby	garnet, star ruby, red spinel, red zircon, red tourmaline, rose quartz.
2. Pearl	moonstone, quartz
3. Coral	sang moongi, carnelian, red jasper
4. Emerald	aquamarine, peridot, green zircon, green agate, jade, green tourmaline
5. Yellow Sapphire	yellow pearl, yellow zircon, yellow tourmaline, topaz, and citrine
6. Diamond	white sapphire, white zircon, white tourmaline
7. Blue Sapphire	blue zircon, amethyst, blue tourmaline, lapis lazuli, blue spinel, neeli
8. Hessonite	hessonite garnet
9. Cat's-eye	tiger's-eye

The gemstones of the planets that are lords of the sixth, eighth, or twelfth houses should not be worn—except during the mahadasha of Saturn, Rahu, and Ketu if they are sitting in the sixth house.

The gems of the planets that are lords of the sixth, eighth, or twelfth houses should be donated on their respective days.

A list of the day associated with the planets is given in the table of relationships of the planets in the beginning of this chapter (Table 2, page 17). The author would like to present some clarification of this assignment.

The reason a day is named after a planet is based on the fact that the first hour before sunrise is ruled by the planets with whom the day is associated. The planet starts the day—and the energy of that planet sets the body chemistry for that day. For example, Sun rules the first hours before sunrise on Sunday.

METALS ASSOCIATED WITH GEMS AND PLANETS

In the *Brihat Samhita* of Varahamihir and in the *Jatak Parijat* there is a mention of metals associated with the planets. We are giving a table of gems, the metals in which they should be set, and the weights of gems that are supposed to be effective. A gem can be heavier than the prescribed weight, but it should not be lighter.

Table 6

Gems, Metal, and Required Minimum Weight

Name of Gem	Name of Planet	Metal	Minimum Weight Required
Ruby	Sun	7 parts gold and 1 part copper	2½ carats minimum 1.77m carats
Pearl	Moon	silver	2, 4, 6 or 11 carats
Coral	Mars	3 parts gold and 4 parts copper	6 carats
Emerald	Mercury	silver, white gold, platinum, bronze	3 carats
Yellow Sapphire	Jupiter	gold	3 carats
Diamond	Venus	silver, white gold, platinum	1½ carats
Blue Sapphire	Saturn	iron, steel, or a mixture of iron and silver	5 carats
Hessonite	Rahu	five metals in equal proportion (iron, silver, copper, gold, zinc) or Ashth Dhatu (eight metals)	5 carats
Cat's-eye	Ketu	five metals, as in Rahu, or Ashth Dhatu (eight metals)	5 carats

Important Note: For the best results the gems should be bought on the day assigned to the planet to which they are related, i.e., ruby on Sunday, pearl on Monday, coral on Tuesday, emerald on Wednesday, yellow sapphire on Thursday, diamond on Friday, and blue sapphire, hessonite, and cat's-eye on Saturday. They should be given to the jeweler on the same day. The ring or locket—whatever is to be made—should be made on that day; if not, at least the gem should be set on the same day as mentioned above and one should get the ring from the jeweler on the day related to the gem and its planet. The ring should be washed in milk and Gangawater and then worn on the same day.

Some astrologers advise their clients to wear the rings of different gems on different fingers. As a general rule the ring finger is
the best for wearing rings, but as each finger is related to a planet,
the ring should be worn on the finger connected with the planet.
This belief is quite popular and sometimes we see people wearing
rings on many fingers. There is also a distinction between the right
and left hand: the right hand is solar and the left hand, lunar.
(There is much tantrik literature available on this subject.) If a
person wearing rings is seeking balance in his life, the gems related with Sun, Mars, Saturn, Rahu, and Ketu should be worn on
the left hand (i.e., solar gems on lunar hand)—and the gems related with Moon, Mercury, Venus, and Jupiter should be worn on
the right hand. But if one wants to enhance solar energy in one's
system, such gems as ruby, coral, blue sapphire, hessonite, and
cat's-eye should be worn on the right hand.

Diagram Showing Planets and Gems
Related to the Fingers

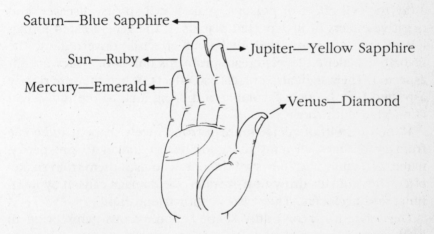

Saturn—Blue Sapphire

Sun—Ruby

Mercury—Emerald

Jupiter—Yellow Sapphire

Venus—Diamond

There are many ways gems can be used: in rings, lockets, chains
or necklaces, nose posts, earrings, amulets, pendulums, and objects
of use in which the gem touches the hand or the body (pens,
knives, cups and plates, idols, lingams, and so forth).

Aside from the maha-ratnas (important gems) and up-ratnas (less
important gems) there are other semiprecious stones that are used

as substitutes for the nav-ratnas (nine gems) by astrologers, gem therapists, and tantriks since time immemorial:

1. Sunstone
2. Garnet
3. Moonstone
4. Quartz
5. Lapis lazuli
6. Amethyst
7. Opal
8. Peridot
9. Amber
10. Onyx
11. Topaz of many kinds and colors
12. Citrine
13. Kidney stone
14. Spinel of many colors
15. Bloodstone
16. Aquamarine
17. Jade (green and white)
18. Carnelian
19. Star ruby
20. Agate of many colors
21. Star stone, asterias, or goldstone
22. Tourmaline of many colors
23. Neeli

According to *Agastya Mat* (1–9) the gems have the power to take away the evil effect of poisons, snakes, evil spirits, diseases, and negative effects of ill-aspected planets. If the gems related to malefic planets are worn, their malignant effect is converted into the favorable. Malefic planets create problems only when they are ill-aspected. Their sight also creates bad effects. When they are rightly aspected they become favorable and bring luck to the individual connected with them.

If they are without defects, are lustrous, nicely shaped, and come from good mines, all gems give good health, longevity, prosperity, name, and fame, and they save the one who uses them from snakebite, wild animals, drowning in water, the damage caused by lightning, and accidents. They also benefit friendship.

Defective, badly or oddly shaped, nonlustrous gems bring ill luck, sorrow, and maladies.

Besides astrologers, gem therapists, tantriks and medicine men, jewelers in India and abroad also know about the power of gems. They know which mines produce the highest quality gems. They also know about the flaws of gems and prescribe use of gems for their customers. Jewelers also are of great help in finding good-quality gems.

PRECIOUS AND SEMIPRECIOUS GEMS

The use of precious and semiprecious gems has been popular in Eastern and Western countries and in the Middle East. Plato believed in the correspondence of gems with the planets of our solar system. Throughout the world gems have been used not only as ornament but as agents of energy and storehouses of occult power.

Coral, pearls, ruby, rock crystal, onyx, amethyst, jade, and agate have been more popular in the West than the East. Amber and rock crystals are mentioned in the Holy Bible. In Germany amber beads in the form of a necklace are given to children to help them in teething; many people use amber to save themselves from rheumatism. The Turks used amber for the mouthpiece of their smoking pipes to prevent infection. In India sadhus wear amber beads or necklaces to save them from disorders of the stomach, intestines, and liver.

In Rome, the use of coral is older than the use of pearl. Romans used coral not only as jewelry (rings, necklaces, etc.) but also as amulets and charms against fire, lightning, whirlwind, sorcery, charms, poison, and shipwreck. Coral was also used to help children in teething.

Amethyst was the favorite stone of the Greeks. They used it for good dreams, valor, chastity, and safety from thieves.

Nowadays there is a strong interest in wearing lucky stones according to the sun sign. It began in the West but is also quite popular in India. The difference in the lucky stones of the Western world and India is that Indians use lucky stones that correspond to their rashi (Moon sign) and, as stated before, Westerners use them according to their sun sign, which is determined by the month in which they are born. The list of gems corresponding to planets is very different, and there is also a difference in the metals in which the gems should be set.

There are many books by Western authors which are based on the science of gemology. Among these authors are Andre Cailleux, Joel Arem, Frederick H. Pough, Edward H. Kraus, Walter F. Hunt, Lewus S. Ramsdel, P. Herbert, and Max Baur. Pliny, Helen Souter, and Sir Hugh Platt have written works that deal with the occult power of gems. Pliny the Younger's magnum opus, *Historia Naturalis,* contains gem lore of the ancient Romans and discusses the use of talismans and amulets. *Curious Lores of Precious Stones* by George Frederick Kunz, who knew many languages and traveled around the world, is an interesting book, because it covers many aspects of gems and presents gem lore not found in other books. Also of interest is *History and Mystery of Precious Stones,* by William Jones. It is a highly entertaining Victorian compilation.

The following tables are only included to show the difference between the Eastern and Western assignment of gems to planets, zodiac signs, months, and days of the week. The author, it must be noted, does not agree with the Western assignments and finds them confusing.

Table 7

Precious Stones and Their Metals

Gem	Planet	Metal According to the Western System	Metal According to the Phala Deepika
Blue Sapphire	Sun	Gold	Copper
Rock Crystal	Moon	Silver	Alloy
Diamond	Mars	Iron	Copper
Bloodstone	Mercury	Silver	Lead
Carnelian	Jupiter	Alloy	Gold
Emerald	Venus	Copper	Silver
Onyx	Saturn	Lead	Iron

Table 8

Birthstones—According to the Western System

Month of Birth	Birthstone
January	Garnet
February	Amethyst
March	Bloodstone/Aquamarine
April	Diamond
May	Emerald
June	Pearl/Moonstone
July	Ruby
August	Sardonyx/Peridot
September	Sapphire/Chrysolite
October	Opal/Tourmaline
November	Topaz
December	Turquoise/Lapis Lazuli

Table 9

**Gems According to Sun Sign—
According to the Western System**

Date of Birth	Sun Sign	Birthstones
21 March to 19 April	Aries	Diamond, Bloodstone, Aquamarine, Emerald
20 April to 20 May	Taurus	Emerald, Diamond
21 May to 21 June	Gemini	Pearl/Moonstone, Agate, Emerald
22 June to 22 July	Cancer	Ruby, Emerald
23 July to 22 August	Leo	Sardonyx/Peridot, Ruby Onyx, Turquoise
23 August to 22 September	Virgo	Opal/Tourmaline, Sardonyx, Peridot
23 September to 23 October	Libra	Opal/Tourmaline, Yellow Sapphire, Topaz, Chrysolite
24 October to 21 November	Scorpio	Yellow Sapphire/Topaz, Opal, Aquamarine
22 November to 21 December	Sagittarius	Turquoise/Hessonite, Garnet, Topaz
22 December to 19 January	Capricorn	Pyrope Garnet, Turquoise
20 January to 19 February	Aquarius	Amethyst, Garnet, Onyx, Ruby, Diamond, Jade
19 February to 20 March	Pisces	Aquamarine/Bloodstone, Amethyst, Jasper

Table 10

Table of Gems According to the Day of the Week— According to the Western System

Days	*Gems*
Sunday	Ruby
Monday	Pearl/Opal
Tuesday	Bloodstone/Amethyst
Wednesday	Olivine/Jade/Agate
Thursday	Emerald/Sapphire
Friday	Lapis Lazuli/Turquoise
Saturday	Onyx

Part *II*

The Precious Gemstones and Their Ruling Planets

The Sun is male, assertive, independent, disciplined, illuminating, and purifying. It is the source of all existing phenomena on earth—the protector and preserver of life—and ruler of the intellect. The sun rides a chariot pulled by seven horses, representing the seven visible rays of light and the seven colors. He holds the lotus of purity in three hands and grants fearlessness with his fourth hand.

3

The Sun
and Its
Gemstone, Ruby

दीवाकरस्तस्य महामहीम्नो महासुखस्योत्तम रक्तबीजम् ।
असृग्गृहीत्वा, चर्वितुं प्रतस्थे......."

तत्सिंहली चारुनितम्ब बिम्ब विक्षोभिता गाघ महा हृदायाम ।
पूगद्रुमाबृद्ध तट द्वयायां मुमोच सूर्यः सविंदुत्तमायाम् ॥

T HE SUN, according to the Vedas, is the parent of all existing phenomena in the solar system. One of its names
is Aditya ("first born"); it is also called Bhutasya Jatah (creator
or father of all bhutas, i.e., objects and ingredients from which
objects assume form). He is the ruler of all the planets that rotate
around him. The Sun is considered to be the soul of Kala Purusha
(Kala = time, Purusha = being; combined, it means the being
that binds himself to Time).

The Sun represents the male or father principle.

Its color is bloodred, its nature is bile-dominated, and it is the
lord of the direction East.

It is the ruler of the zodiacal sign Leo, and is exalted in the sign Aries, debilitated in Libra, and exiled in Aquarius. The Moon, Mars, and Jupiter are its natural friends, and Venus, Saturn, Rahu (dragon's head, or the north node of the Moon), and Ketu (dragon's tail, the south node of the Moon) are its natural enemies. Mercury is neutral. Nakshatras Kritika, Uttra Phalguni, and Uttra Khad are ruled by the Sun.

It is regarded as a kroor-grah (malefic planet), but it is actually an auspicious planet. It is powerful when placed in the seventh house from the ascendant. In six signs after Capricorn it is moving toward exaltation and is powerful. Its friendship with Jupiter is sattvik (pure, as Jupiter is the teacher of the Sun); with the Moon, rajasik (energetic and active, as the Moon is the opposite and counterpart of the Sun); and with Mars, tamasik (angry, combative, and obstinate, as Mars and the Sun are both fiery).

The Sun gives us vitality and the power of resistance and immunity. It is responsible for our physical makeup—the body's constitution. The Sun gives life force, the power of will, intellect, brilliance, prosperity, success in worldly affairs, wealth, personal conduct, activity, cheerfulness, good fortune, wisdom, ambition, fame, the understanding of the phenomenal world, and the knowledge of medicine. It also governs our relationship with temples and holy places.

When the Sun is not rightly placed in the natal chart, that is, ill-aspected or afflicted by a malefic planet, it brings pessimism, sorrow, quarrels, humiliation, and poverty.

The human spine is specially influenced by the Sun. Pingala Nadi, which represents the Sun, originates at the base of the spine on the right side, is solar in nature, and terminates in the right nostril. The Sun is connected with the right eye in men and the left eye in women. The Sun rules the heart, liver, lungs, head (brain), nerves, and bones.

The Sun also represents kings, government officials, rich and famous people, personnel of royal families, gemologists, artists, dramatists, jewelers, and creative people. Copper is its metal but it rules over gold, almonds, peanuts, coconut, mustard seeds, wool, red flowers, red sandalwood, and what in India are called "red" cows. It shows its influence from twelve to twenty-four years of age.

An afflicted and ill-aspected Sun gives low and high blood pressure, indigestion, jaundice, cholera, fever, diabetes, appendicitis, hemorrhage, cardiac thrombosis, eruptions on the face, typhoid, tuberculosis, mental problems caused by thinking too much, diseases of the head, epilepsy, and disorders caused by aggravated bile. *Fasting on Sundays helps in befriending the Sun.*

The gemstone related to the Sun is ruby. When the Sun is debilitated, exiled, or afflicted by malefic planets or is ill-aspected, wearing a flawless, good-quality ruby helps. It is advised that if the ascendant is Virgo, Capricorn, or Pisces, one should not wear ruby, but use substitutes for ruby.

THE RUBY

Ruby is a gemstone of the corundum family and is attractive because of its brilliance, if it is crystal clear and transparent. It is found in a variety of crimson and scarlet red colors ranging from pink to a deep ruddy violet color. It has the smooth and delicate lustre of clarified butter. The gemstone is solid and possesses high specific gravity (3.9–4.1), its hardness is 9 on a scale of 1–10. Its refractive index is 1.76 to 1.77, and its main ingredients are aluminum and oxygen. The red tint in ruby comes from a light combination of iron and chromium. The finest quality ruby has a delicate rose color, similar to the eye of a living cuckoo. The molecular structure of ruby is linear, following the crystal axis. When light is refracted in the ruby it is arranged in parallel horizontal waves.

QUALITIES OF A GOOD RUBY

1. smoothness
2. transparence
3. lustre
4. brilliance
5. hardness
6. heaviness in weight, high density
7. silky or milky inclusions
8. color: transparent carmine red with bluish tint like pigeon blood
9. regular shape

FLAWS OF RUBIES

1. dullness—gives problems with brothers
2. brittleness—gives problems in having a son
3. flimsiness—gives problems with lightning
4. cracks—gives bad luck
5. bubbles—makes the gem ineffective
6. feather—gives bad luck
7. dirty—ineffective
8. spotty (spots of black or honey color)—gives restlessness, problems in having children
9. slit, cavity, hole—bad luck, diseases, weakness
10. bluishness in color—gives stomach problems
11. honey color, milky color—destroys animals and pets (Pashudhan)
12. lack of water and fire (brittle, dull, opaque, lacking glitter)—gives bad luck
13. not homogeneous—brings troubles for father and for self
14. irregular lines inside—domestic quarrels, disturbance
15. blackish or whitish tint—loss of wealth; bad reputation
16. forms similar to shape of trident, triangle, or cross—troubles in having children; bad name; loss of wealth; early death
17. two colors—restlessness, obstacles, disease, and problems for father and self
18. smoky color—divine obstacles, bad luck

IDENTIFICATION OF REAL RUBIES

1. If you place a real ruby on an unopened lotus bud it will open up and become a blossoming lotus in a short time.
2. If you place a real ruby in a glass jar, a red hue of light will be seen to emit from the jar.
3. If pearls are put together with a real ruby in a silver plate and placed in sunlight, the silver plate will appear blackish, the pearls will have a red hue, and the ruby will shine like the Sun.
4. If a ruby is placed in a silver plate and seen in sunlight the plate will reflect a reddish tint.
5. If a ruby is placed in cow's milk in a glass jar, the milk will appear of rosy color, whereas normally it has a yellowish tint.
6. A ruby will appear dark red from one angle and pale when viewed from the other side.
7. A real ruby is heavier and more dense than an imitation or a similar stone.

8. A crack in a real ruby will not shine and will have a zigzag quality, whereas in an imitation ruby a crack is shiny, straight, and clearly visible.
9. Bubbles in a real ruby are rarely found; they are not round and have the same color as the gem, but in an imitation stone bubbles are round, bare, white, and sometimes hollow.
10. If the silky spot, which remains stationary, has a bluish tint and does not emit flickering light, the gem is an imitation.
11. A real ruby, when placed on the eyelids, remains cool longer than an imitation does because of its compact molecular structure. A piece of glass or imitation gem, that is, a synthetic ruby, gets warm quickly.
12. Layers of a real ruby are linear and straight, whereas in an imitation they are circular.
13. The color in a natural real ruby is not uniform, whereas in an imitation the color is homogeneous.
14. An imitation ruby appears orange when placed under an ultraviolet lamp.
15. A real ruby continues shining after it has been x-rayed, but an imitation shines only as long as the source of light is shining on it.

Imitation rubies are produced by fusing powdered alumina and chromic oxide by a hydrogen-oxygen flame at 2100° centigrade. Because all the gas used in this process is not consumed, round bubbles arranged in a semicircular fashion appear around the center, and sometimes white particles in powder form are visible if the lower part of the synthetic stone is included in the cut and polished gem.

Another variety of synthetic ruby is produced by a hydrothermal process. It is difficult to distinguish them from real rubies, but because they are very expensive they cannot be marketed easily.

CLASSIFICATION OF RUBIES

The classification of rubies in four castes (varnas) is the same as the classification of man in four castes, according to the Vedas:

1. Brahmin
2. Kshatriya
3. Vaishya
4. Shudra

The Puranas say that from the head of the creator, Brahma, brahmins were created; that is why they are devoted to learning and to the higher ideals of life. From this caste come the priests and sages who compiled scriptures.

From the hands of Brahma, kshatriyas were created. They protect humanity, fight evil, and establish the atmosphere in which dharma (laws) can be practiced; from this caste come the rulers.

From the stomach of Brahma, vaishyas were created. They care for the physical well-being of society. From this caste come the merchants and tradesmen.

Shudras were created from the feet of Brahma. Shudras serve the above-mentioned three Varnas (castes), just as feet serve the body.

Rubies of the Brahmin Varna are of rose color, light in tint, transparent, and radiant, and are best suited for spiritually inclined, learned people.

Rubies of the Kshatriya Varna are of bloodred color, transparent, radiant, and lustrous, and are best suited for rulers.

Rubies of the Vaishya Varna are of crimson red tint, resembling the color of pigeon's blood, are transparent and radiant, and are best suited to people of the merchant class.

Rubies of the Shudra Varna have a dirty reddish or bluish tinge, are less transparent, are of mixed color, are less radiant, and are best suited for the serving class.

According to their color and texture rubies are classified in the classical texts as follows:

Padmaraga is the ruby of finest grade, radiating like the morning sun, glowing like fire, soft and smooth-looking in texture, and is of the tint of molten gold.

Saugandhik is the ruby shining like the eyes of a stork or chakor (a legendary night bird), its red color is like the seeds of a Kundhari pomegranate or palash flower (when the palash tree flowers in the forest it appears that the forest is on fire), it glows like fireflies and is soft and smooth in texture.

Neelgandh is the ruby of scarlet red tint with a bluish hue, like the hue found in lotus petals.

Kuruvind is the ruby similar to padmaraga and saugandhik in hue, but it is more lustrous and smaller in size.

Jamuniya is the ruby with a violet tint resembling the color of the jambu fruit or the red kaner flower.

RITUALS FOR WEARING A RUBY

A ruby should be bought on a Sunday, Monday, or Thursday in the ascending moon cycle. Ideally, it should be bought, set, and worn when the Sun is in Leo and it is Pushya Nakshatra. In case the nakshatra is not Pushya, the nakshatras ruled by the Sun, i.e., Kritika, Uttra Phalguni, and Uttrakhad, are also suitable for it.

The weight of the gemstone ruby should not be less than 3 rattikas, or 1.77 metric carats, and the gemstone should be flawless. It is better if it is 2½ carats in weight.

The stone should be given to the jeweler on the same day and it should be set and the ring should be polished on the same days as mentioned above. The stone should be mounted in an open-backed ring made of a mixture of gold and copper. The gemstone should touch the skin of the wearer's finger.

The best time to wear a ruby ring is sunrise.

Before wearing the ring it should be kept immersed for some time in raw cow's milk. Then it should be washed with Ganga-water (if Ganga-water is not available rainwater or water kept in a copper pot can be used). After it has been washed the ring should be kept on a red cloth, on which a Sun yantra is drawn with either red sandalwood paste or roli, a mixture of turmeric powder and a pinch of calcium hydroxide (powdered limestone), which has been fired. An engraved copper yantra of the Sun god or an idol of the Sun god made in gold and placed on an asana (seat) made of 50 grams of silver should be set. The idol needs proper worship and a priest to perform the specific Sun rituals.

A yantra needs no priest, and the person who wants to wear the ring can do the rituals himself. The ring should be placed in front of the idol or engraved copper yantra, on the red cloth, on which the numerical yantra of the Sun is drawn. Flowers and incense should be offered to the engraved copper yantra, and the yantra and the gemstone mounted in the ring should be worshiped, reciting the mantra of the Sun god:

ॐ ह्रीं हंसः सूर्याय नमः ॐ

AUM HRING HAMSAH SURYAYE NAMAH AUM

Ruby/Sun: Who Should Wear A Ruby

Ascendant/Ruler	Sun is Natural Ruler of	Relationship of the Sun with the Ruler of the Ascendant	Nature of the House Ruled by the Sun	Suitability/Unsuitability of the Ruby & its Effects
Aries/Mars	5th house	Friend	Auspicious	Suitable—Gives intelligence, honor, & progeny. Helps spiritual development. Special benefits in the major or subperiod of Sun.
Taurus/Venus	4th house	Enemy	Auspicious	Suitable only in the major/subperiod of Sun, or if Sun is in the 10th house.
Gemini/Mercury	3rd house	Friend	Auspicious	Not suitable. Wear only if Sun is in the 3rd house, during the major or subperiod of Sun.
Cancer/Moon	2nd house	Friend	Auspicious	Suitable. For best results, wear in the same setting with pearls.
Leo/Sun	1st house Ascendant	Sun Himself is the Ruler	Auspicious	Suitable and beneficial. Ruby is a must for those with Leo ascendant. Gives vitality, health, long life, and success in material world.
Virgo/Mercury	12th house	Friend	Inauspicious	Not suitable. Wear only if Sun is in the 12th house or in major/subperiod of Sun, along with an emerald ring on the other hand.
Libra/Venus	11th house	Enemy	Auspicious	Always suitable. Gives health & long life, especially if Sun is in the 11th house. Ruby will bring fame, wealth, and honor.
Scorpio/Mars	10th house	Friend	Auspicious	Suitable. Bestows honor, status, and power. If Sun is in the 10th house, it gives special power in the political field.

Sign/Ruler	House	Relation	Aspect	Description
Sagittarius/Jupiter	9th house	Friend	Auspicious	Suitable. Brings honor, power, and status. Especially beneficial if Sun is in the 9th house.
Capricorn/Saturn	8th house	Enemy	Inauspicious	Not suitable. Wear only if Sun is in the 8th house, during the major or subperiod of Sun.
Aquarius/Saturn	7th house	Enemy	Auspicious	Not suitable. Wear only if Sun is in the 7th house, during the major or subperiod of Sun.
Pisces/Jupiter	6th house	Friend	Inauspicious	Not suitable. Wear only if Sun is in the 6th house, during the major or subperiod of Sun.

The 2nd and 7th houses are both auspicious but also death-inflicting houses, especially during the major or sub-periods of the planets that rule them. If the ruling planet is benefic and a friend of the ruler of the ascendant, that aspect can be lessened.

The Mantra should be recited 108 times and then the wearer should meditate on the gemstone as a symbol of the Sun god. After meditation the ring should be worn on the ring finger of the right hand.

If an idol of the Sun god instead of a Sun yantra engraved on a copper plate is used, then Homa (fire worship) with the same mantra and a complete worship by a competent priest is needed. Then the idol and its silver asana with some coins must be donated to the priest.

If an engraved yantra is used, no Homa is required, and the yantra can either be donated to a priest or it can be kept in a shrine. The yantra used for drawing on the cloth and the one engraved on a copper plate is mostly a numerical yantra.

The yantra to be drawn on red cloth with red sandalwood paste or roli is as follows:

6	1	8
7	5	3
2	9	4

The following yantra engraved on a copper plate should be placed or seated on the cloth asana on which the above yantra is written with red sandalwood paste or roli:

6	32	3	34	35	1
7	11	27	28	8	30
19	14	16	15	23	24
18	20	22	21	17	13
25	29	10	9	26	12
36	5	33	4	2	31

The worship of the yantra engraved on copper should be done facing east sitting on a red asana made of wool. First the yantra is honored by a tilak (a mark usually put on the forehead) of red sandalwood paste or roli, then the flowers and incense should be offered, and then the ring should be placed in front of the copper yantra. It should also be honored by a tilak after it is washed and dried, as stated before. Then flowers and incense should be offered to the gemstone and then the mantra should be recited either 108 times or 7000 times. Then the wearer should meditate—and after meditation the ring should be worn.

A ring worn by this method brings good luck, peace, and prosperity.

Then the yantra should be wrapped in the red cloth on which the yantra is made with red sandalwood paste or roli—and it should either be donated to a priest or kept in a shrine.

MEDICINAL UTILITY OF THE RUBY

The Ayurvedic text *Rasa Tantra Sar* states that to make an oxide (bhasma) or a paste (pishthi) of ruby, the stone should first be purified by boiling fine pieces of ruby in lemon juice in a daula yantra for twenty-four hours.

Daula yantra is a device in which the gemstone remains immersed but suspended in the liquid in which it is boiled. The following diagram can help in understanding the method of boiling:

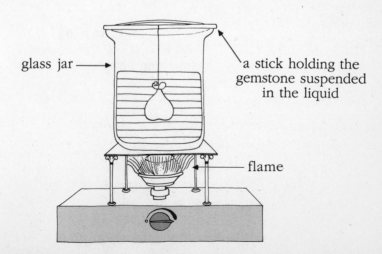

glass jar

a stick holding the gemstone suspended in the liquid

flame

If bhasma (oxide) is to be made, the purified ruby is powdered and placed in a mortar made of simak stone (porphyry) and ground with a mixture of sulphur, mansel, and hartal in equal proportions, in the juice of a jackfruit. The mixture should be ground for twelve hours and converted into a fine powder. Then a tablet of the whole mixture is made and dried in the sun. After the tablet is dry two earthen pots, which can cover each other,

are taken and the tablet is kept inside. The pots are

put together and sealed with fine clay and dried.

After they are dry they are wrapped with a cloth

soaked in clay and allowed to dry again. Then the

ball-like structure is fired in 2 kg. of cowdung cakes. Firing the ball many times converts ruby into a fine oxide. The two earthen pots are known as sarava yantra or sarava samput. These earthen pots should be taken from a goldsmith who has used them to heat sohaga (borax).

Gajput: The Process for Making the Gem Oxide.

Break the gemstone into very fine pieces with a cast iron or metal mortar and pestle.

Grind the gemstone pieces in a stone mortar with the required liquid.

Gajput (cont'd.)

Make a kiln underground and line the walls with raw clay bricks.

Then fill the kiln with cow dung cakes and place the sarva yantra in the center.

Cover the kiln with cow dung cakes and fire.

After the fire cools the ball is taken out and the oxide of the gem is obtained. Sometimes the same process is repeated because the oxide required for medicinal purposes is not yet ready.

If pishthi (paste) is to be made, pieces of ruby that have been purified in daula yantra should be washed and dried and placed in a mortar made of simak stone. The paste should be made by grinding the powdered and purified ruby in rosewater for fifteen days. Some Unani hakims (doctors who follow the Greek system of medicine) make a mixture of kewrawater—sandalwater and rose water in equal proportions—heat the ruby pieces on a piece of mica, dip them into the mixture ten to twenty times, and then grind them in the same mixture. (One rattika = .59 carat or ¹/₈ gram.)

Dosage: ½ to 1 rattika with cream of milk (malai) once or twice a day, or ½ to 1 rattika of pishthi with goldleaf and ½ tsp. honey twice a day.

In the Ayurveda text *Rasa Tantra Sar* there is a mantra that says:

रत्नां शोधनं श्रेष्ठं,मारणम्नगुण प्रदम ।
भस्मानांवीर्यहानि स्यात्तस्मात्तानि विशोधयेत् ॥

This translates as:

> The purification of gems is ideal but their oxide is less so,
> because in making an oxide there is a loss of vital life force—
> the veerya of the gemstone. In pishthi the essential chemical
> nature of the gem remains the same and the vital life force,
> the veerya, remains intact.

This oxide of ruby or the paste (pishthi) of ruby is medically
used for impotence, loss of semen, heart troubles, troubles of
aggravated bile and wind (pitta and vata), loss of blood, tuberculosis, diminished vision, indigestion, prolonged fevers, loss
of appetite, diabetes, high or low blood pressure, mental problems,
chronic dysentery, dry cough, problems created by aggravated
mucus (kapha), pain in limbs, poisoning, debility, and fear.

To prepare bhasma (oxide) or pishthi (paste), flaws in the ruby
do not matter, although the ruby should have fine color, fire, and
water (lustre). The paste is not to be used as paste but as a powder,
so after the paste is made it should be dried and kept in a glass
bottle, preferably of red color, and stored in a dry place. The lid
should be sealed with pure beeswax.

SOURCES OF RUBIES

Ruby mines are found in Burma, Thailand, Sri Lanka, Kabul (Afghanistan), Tanganyika, and South India.

Rubies found in the mines of upper Burma in a location in
Mogok are supposed to be of the highest quality and are found
in various tints of crimson red.

Rubies found in Thailand are of an inferior quality.

Rubies found in the Ratnapur mines of Sri Lanka are lustrous but
have less fire and radiance in comparison to Burmese Mogok rubies.

Kabul rubies are brittle, with white spots, though they have a fine color. Sometimes good, lustrous, brilliant rubies are found in Kabul also—and they are better in quality than Burma rubies—but this is rare.

Tanganyika rubies are brittle. They are of two kinds: rubies of red color with a dark tint, and rubies of reddish yellow color.

Rubies found in South India at Kangiyan are of a dull red color and dirty with dark blue and pale tint. Both transparent and translucent rubies are found here. Sometimes very fine, clear, lustrous rubies are also found here.

Rubies found in Alipur, Hyderabad are opaque and translucent, though some lovely, lustrous, transparent rubies are also found here.

The Moon is feminine, imaginative, receptive, sensitive, intuitive and subject to change. It acts as a large crystalline transformer, converting solar energy into life-giving, magnetic, mothering energy which it reflects to the planet Earth. The Moon rules over our psyche, which is represented by the deer on which he rides. In one hand he is holding the disc (chakra) of Vishnu to remove obstacles, and in another hand a conch (symbol of primordial sound) whose sound leads to liberation from the cycle of birth and rebirth. In his third hand he holds a lotus of purity, and in his fourth hand the reins of the deer (psyche).

4
The Moon and Its Gemstone, Pearl

नक्षत्र मालेव दिवो विशीर्णादन्तावलि स्तरस्य महासुरस्य,
विचित्र वर्णेषु विशुद्ध वर्णापयः सुपत्युः पयसांपपात।

THE FAMOUS Vedic verse Purusha Sukta, describing the cosmic man, states, *"chandrama manso jatah"*: "Moon was born from the mind of the cosmic man," i.e., Virat Purusa, or Kal Purusa.

Moon is the presiding deity of the element water, and rules over the tides of the sea. The sphere of the Moon is the reservoir of rainwater and thus Moon is the ruler of plants and the vegetable kingdom.

Moon represents the mother or female principle, the energy that creates and preserves.

The color of Moon is white. Its nature is mucus-dominated, tender-hearted, wise, and learned. It rules peace of mind, comfort, general well-being, and also the fortune of a person. It shows its influence around twenty-four to twenty-five years of age. The Moon gives illumination, sense of purpose, intuitive nature, sensuality, taste, youth, love of poetry, fine arts and music, love of jewelry, attractive appearance, wealth and good fortune. It makes us moody, emotional, and sensitive. It rules milk, grains, liquids,

53

growth, fertility, impregnation, and conception. It influences the infant stage of an individual, which guides his behavior in the later part of his life. It is cold and moist. It also influences childbirth and rules the left nostril, the Ida Nadi, eyesight, the breasts, and the brain (memory). Moon influences travelers, hunters, fishermen, prostitutes, cooks, nurses, and caterers.

It rules over the zodiacal sign Cancer, is exalted in the zodiacal sign Taurus, and is debilitated in Capricorn. The sign of its fall is Scorpio. Sun, Mars, and Jupiter are the Moon's natural friends, and Mercury, Venus, and Saturn are its natural enemies. In Rohini, Hast, Shravan, Punarvasu, Vishakha, and Purva Bhadrapad nakshatras it gives good and beneficial effect. It also gives favorable effects if it is in Kritika, Uttra Phalguni, Ashlekha, Jyestha, Uttra Khad, and Revati nakshatras. It is powerful if it is placed in the fourth house of the natal horoscope of an individual.

The Moon is powerful from the tenth day of the ascending Moon cycle to the fifth day of the descending Moon cycle and is regarded as a benefic planet (shubh graha).

It is auspicious (benefic) for those who are born in the ascending Moon cycle and malefic for those who are born in the descending Moon cycle.

For persons whose Moon is not rightly placed in their natal chart or is ill-aspected, success becomes difficult; sometimes it even becomes difficult to achieve a comfortable life on earth. It makes such people weak or sick in their early years.

An afflicted, debilitated, exiled, or weak Moon causes cold, cough, fever, eye ailments, lunacy, paralysis, epilepsy, hysteria, colic pains, beriberi, intestinal disorders, throat troubles, bronchitis, dysentery, neurosis, typhoid, and cancer.

The gemstone related to Moon is pearl, and its metal is silver.

Wearing a pearl ring mounted in silver in such a way that the pearl touches the skin helps strengthen a weak or afflicted Moon. It attracts lunar energy, which is lacking in such cases.

THE PEARL

Formation of a pearl inside a pearl oyster is thought to occur because of the presence of foreign material inside the body of the oyster. To save itself from the undesired material the mollusk coats the object with layer after layer of nacre. It takes many years for a mollusk to produce a pearl of substantial size. The process through which the pearls are formed inside the body of the mollusk is very delicate, and a little disturbance at any stage of development of a pearl can influence its shape and lustre. The finest pearl is that which has no foreign matter in its core.

There is a common belief among tantriks that when Svati Nakshatra rain comes to earth it produces pearl in pearl oysters. The mollusk is then said to open its mouth to receive the first raindrops. When these same raindrops fall into the mouth of a cobra, it produces venom. The same raindrops also produce camphor in the banana plant, go-lochan (go-rochan or calcium) when they fall in the horn of a cow, and bansh-lochan and bansh-mukta (or bamboo pearl) when they fall inside a bamboo shoot. Bansh-lochan is known as Calcium bamboana and is very much used in Ayurvedic medicines.

The pearls thus produced by the raindrops of Svati Nakshatra are the finest and have no foreign matter in them.

Pearls are said to be obtained from eight sources:

द्विपेन्द्र जीमूत वराह शंख मत्स्यादि शुक्त्युद्भव वेणुजानि,
मुक्ताफलानि प्रथितनि लोके तेषां च शुक्त्युद्भव मेव भूर्वि।

1. *Sky pearl,* known in Sanskrit as megh-mukta and akash mukta: It is said that when it rains under the influence of Pushya or Shravan nakshatra on a Sunday or a Monday, this pearl comes to earth with raindrops. It is formed in clouds and is brilliant yellow or sky-grey color with yellow tint. It is round in shape and emits sparkling light similar to the lightning in the clouds. A common belief is that before it comes to earth it is taken away by gods, and whenever gods are pleased with somebody they allow it to come to earth—and then it is found by the one who is blessed by the gods. Megh mukta fulfills the desires of its owner and he finds hidden treasures from inside the earth many times in his life.

2. *Cobra pearl,* known as sarp-mukta or sarp-mani: This pearl also develops in the cobra hood of a king cobra when raindrops influenced by Svati Nakshatra fall into the mouth of the king

cobra. But it only happens in the cobra who has passed one hundred years of life on earth. After the pearl originates in its hood, the cobra achieves the magical power of transforming itself into any form it desires, and the older the snake becomes the more the mani (gem) grows in size and lustre. It is a moon-like pearl of blue tint, very radiant, and it emits light in darkness. It is perfectly round in shape. The snake keeps the gem in its mouth and only takes it out in darkness to play with it and to search for its prey in its light. If one is lucky and finds it one obtains wealth, property, progeny, and the fulfillment of all desires. The gem destroys all negative influences. It is said that after the gem is separated from the cobra, the snake dies.

3. *Bamboo pearl,* known as bansh mukta: Bansh mukta is found in the hollow of the bamboo. It is of greenish tint and elliptical in form like a berry. Its birth in bamboo is related to the rain of the Svati Nakshatra. The rain in Pushya and Shravan nakshatras also produces this pearl in the hollow of the bamboo. This pearl cannot be drilled and so cannot be used as a bead in a necklace. It is different from bansh-lochan or Calcium bamboana, which is pure white in color and irregular in shape, but is also produced in the hollow of the bamboo and is used in Ayurvedic medicines. It is said that the bamboo in which this pearl is found makes a sound when the wind blows through the bamboo groves, and the sound resembles the chanting of Vedic mantras in low pitch. Only a lucky person can find this pearl, which brings good luck, name, fame, respect, peace, and prosperity to its owner.

4. *Hog pearl,* known as shookar mukta: Hog pearl is found in the head of a hog. It is quite large, like the bamboo pearl. It is round and mustard yellow. This pearl, like the sky pearl, cobra pearl, and bamboo pearl, is also rare. It is supposed to have many powers, which it provides to the one who possesses it. It gives vak siddhi—the power of speech: whatever its owner says comes true—and swar siddhi—command over musical voices: one becomes a musician of high grade and can produce rain, clouds, and fire by singing certain ragas. If a pregnant woman wears it she gives birth to a son of high qualities. It also increases the power to memorize.

5. *Elephantine pearl,* known as gaj mukta: This pearl orig-

inates in the temple of the elephants of Airawat breed, which is born under the influence of Pushya or Shravan nakshatra on a Monday or a Sunday. The size of this pearl is almost equal to the size of an amla fruit. It is perfectly round in shape, of moonlike hue, and is less lustrous than an oyster pearl, but it gives peaceful vibrations and a cool feeling to the eyes. Gaj mukta is famous for removing obstacles and bestowing peace and prosperity on its owner.

6. *Conch pearl,* known as shankh mukta: This pearl, also rare, is found inside a conch shell. It is oval in shape and as large as an egg in size. It is found in ochre brown, light yellow, white, and light blue shades. It is not radiant like other pearls, but is pleasantly smooth and well shaped. Sometimes there are three stripes on it (such a conch pearl exists in the collection of Shri Raj Roop Tank, a renowned gemologist of Jaipur). Shankh mukta gives peace, prosperity, progeny, and stable wealth. It destroys poverty and sin and fulfills all the desires of the one who owns it. This pearl cannot be drilled.

7. *Fish pearl,* also known as meen mukta: Nurtured in the stomach or womb of a fish, this pearl is small (equal to the size of a small sweet pea) and yellowish white. It is regarded as a gem of power, it can cure tuberculosis and other diseases, and it is believed to give the power to see underwater.

Note: All of the above-mentioned varieties of pearls are rare, but as Shri Raj Roop Tank, in his book *Indian Gemology,* claims to have seen all these varieties in the collection of Shri Dhanroop Mal, the renowned jeweler of Ajmer, they should exist.

8. *Oyster pearl,* known as shukti mukta: This pearl is formed inside the body of pearl oysters from alternating layers of aragonite and an organic compound, conchiolin. Tantriks claim that it is produced by the first raindrop of Svati Nakshatra, and assumes five different forms, according to the dominance of the elements. If the pearl is formed:

1) under the influence of the akasha element, it has no lustre and is light in weight
2) under the influence of the air element, it has a bluish hue and emits waves of light in the presence of light

3) under the influence of the fire element, it takes on a reddish or rose-colored tint and emits reddish light in the presence of light
4) under the influence of the water element, it is brilliant white. It is the most lustrous of pearls, and it shines like a star in the blue sky. Its shimmering glow and delicate play of surface color, its smoothness, spotlessness, and globular shape make it delightful and agreeable to the eyes. The gleam of circulating water can be clearly seen in its form
5) under the influence of the earth element, it is heavy in weight and not as high in quality as the pearl formed under the influence of the water element

Whenever a reference to a high-quality shukti mukta (oyster pearl) is made, it is always a description of pearls formed under the influence of the water element. These are the pearls that are the gemstone of the Moon.

A genuine pearl is supposed to have the following qualities:

1. Moonlike, shining white color
2. Perfectly round, globular shape and size
3. Compactness, which gives it a high specific gravity
4. Lustre, soft glamor, attractiveness, and brilliance of reflection
5. Smoothness, which gives an agreeable sensation to the eyes
6. Spotlessness and freedom from blemishes (dents, scratches, ridges) and impurities

One who wears or possesses a pearl with all of the above-mentioned qualities enjoys good fortune and is blessed by the goddess Lakshmi (the goddess of prosperity), lives long and becomes sinless, and obtains vitality and intelligence. He achieves high position by his wisdom and becomes famous.

A pearl with a yellow lustre brings prosperity. Red-tinted pearls make one intelligent, shining white pearls bring fame, and a pearl with a bluish hue brings good fortune.

A pearl devoid of lustre, that is, dirty, broken, having no gleam of circulating water, black or copper colored, partly white and partly colored, irregular, odd in shape, having holes, dents, or spots is defective and should be avoided.

FLAWS OF PEARLS

1. cracks or ridges—wearing of such a pearl is injurious to one's health
2. wavy thin line on the surface—brings misfortune
3. dents—bring loss of wealth
4. protrusion like the beak of a bird—harmful to progeny; brings humiliation
5. a juncture line or a girdle—induces fear and is injurious to physical well-being
6. a mole-like formation on the surface layer—brings sadness and disease
7. tiny spots like the marks of smallpox—harmful to progeny
8. a blister or swelling—injurious to wealth; brings bad luck
9. a stain on the surface—brings humiliation and is harmful to progeny
10. dullness or absence of lustre—brings poverty or financial crisis; shortens one's life
11. sheathy, having a thin epithelium and woodlike material inside—is inauspicious
12. dusty, having clay or sand particles inside—is devoid of any good or bad effect
13. dome-shaped, in which the lower half is composed of foreign material—brings bad luck
14. hole or pouchlike formation—causes leprosy
15. fish-eye spot, spot looking like the eye of a fish—loss of progeny
16. having three corners (triangular in shape)—causes impotence, brings bad luck
17. square shape and flat—harmful to one's spouse
18. copper tint—harmful to brothers and sisters
19. oval and long in shape—makes one foolish
20. broken—loss of job, wealth, and earnings
21. coral-like appearance—brings misfortune and poverty

Nowadays with modern technology, defective (asymmetrical and irregular) pearls can be made round, shapely, and flawless. Pearls without lustre can be made lustrous, but even then it is not possible to refine all pearls with defects. Only those in which the possibility of refinement exists can be refined.

In ancient days jewelers used simple methods to increase the lustre of pearls, but they could not refine the asymmetrical, irregular, and oddly shaped pearls. There are several methods to increase the lustre or to bring lustre back to a pearl that has lost it because of a chemical reaction caused by vinegar, fruit juices, lemon juices, or acidic body perspiration:

1. Wash pearls in a solution of soapnut (dried soapberry) powder
2. Make a hole in a radish root and put the pearl inside. Fill the hole with powdered raw sugar and leave it for some time. After a few hours the pearl is taken out and washed
3. Heat some rice with water (not to the boiling point), then strain the water and wash the pearl in it
4. Feed a pearl that is dirty and without lustre to a pigeon and wait for twenty hours. After twenty hours the pearl will come out in the excreta of the pigeon. It is then taken out and cleaned with a soft cloth. Through this process the pearl becomes somewhat thinner and lighter in weight, but it brings the lustre back to a pearl that otherwise cannot be refined.

Because pearls can be refined chemically, these techniques are rarely used today.

CULTURED PEARLS

Cultured pearls have been on the market for at least seven hundred years, but they have not always been as easily available as they are now. The Chinese are supposed to have been pioneers in this field, but for a few decades the Japanese have been the major suppliers of cultured pearls.

Cultured pearls are also a natural growth inside the pearl oyster, but they are created by human surgical skill. The Japanese once estimated that about 45 percent of the mollusks died in this process of producing cultured pearls because it is difficult to introduce foreign matter into the body of a mollusk.

A good pearl produced by this process has the same qualities as a genuine pearl—and it is difficult to distinguish between the two. Sometimes very nice and beautiful pearls can be obtained from these industrial procedures. Astrologers, gem therapists, Ayurvedic doctors, and tantriks have to accept them in place of genuine pearls which are rare nowadays. They believe that they have a similar effect on the human organism as genuine pearls had—and prescribe them to their clients in the absence of genuine pearls.

Yet the one who is buying a pearl for Moon energy should make sure that the pearl he buys has none of the above-mentioned flaws.

Natural pearls also exist on the market. These are not genuine pearls—they are artificially created as are cultured pearls, but the material that is introduced is natural mother-of-pearl. Natural pearls that are made in fresh water have a bluish tint. The difference between cultured and natural pearls becomes evident when they are drilled because the foreign material introduced into the natural pearls during their creation comes out and they become hollow. Otherwise they are very similar in radiance and weight to genuine pearls, whereas cultured pearls have a ball of foreign matter resembling glass, which can be seen while drilling. This ball sometimes becomes loose in drilling and can be felt moving around. Natural pearls are better than cultured pearls.

IDENTIFICATION OF GENUINE, CULTURED, AND IMITATION PEARLS

1. Difference in the bore: There is uniformity in the bore of genuine pearls, whereas in cultured pearls it is thin at the starting point and wide in the middle.
2. Difference in structure: In genuine pearls the structure is concentric, whereas in the cultured pearl it is parallel, as it is in the mother-of-pearl bead introduced into the mollusk to produce a cultured pearl.
3. Difference in epithelium: It is hard in cultured pearls and soft in genuine pearls.
4. Difference in lustre: When cultured, imitation, or artificial pearls are treated with a mixture of cow's urine and saltpeter for twenty-four hours, their lustre decreases. Genuine pearls retain their lustre after such treatment.
5. Differences can also be detected with the help of a pearl illuminator, but this detection is only possible in the case of drilled pearls. Another method used for undrilled pearls is to x-ray them.

Imitation pearls are cheap decorative items produced with glass bells and the scales of freshwater fish dissolved in ammonia; they are no substitutes for genuine or cultured pearls.

Gem therapists, astrologers, and tantriks prefer Basra pearls from the Persian Gulf; Venezuela pearls are equally good. Genuine Basra are the best, if available.

For Ayurvedic medicines beads of pearls that are very small and cannot be used in jewelry are used. These pearls are known as seed pearls and are very effective for medical use. Genuine, lustrous but broken and misshapen pearls or powder obtained from the drilling of genuine pearls can also be used, although in *Ras Tantra Sar* it is forbidden to use defective pearls. The powder obtained from drilling genuine pearls and broken genuine pearls is less effective, and the sheathy pearls are not used at all, but in the absence of small seed pearls they can be used. The use of cultured or natural pearls is prohibited for medical purposes. The epithelium of genuine, natural, and cultured pearls is destroyed if they are treated with hydrochloric acid, whereas in the imitation pearls it is not destroyed. Natural and genuine pearls produce bubbles and a foamlike substance when treated with acid, as cultured pearls do, but imitation wax pearls do not. Natural and cultured pearls can be used for jewelry, as they are the only pearls available on the ordinary market.

CLASSIFICATION OF PEARLS

The classification of pearls follows the system of the four varnas (castes):

1. Brahmin—pearls of this varna are white and are best suited for spiritually inclined and learned people.
2. Kshatriya—pearls of this varna are rosy and they make the wearer intelligent and powerful.
3. Vaishya—pearls of this varna are yellow and are supposed to bring material prosperity.
4. Shudra—pearls of this varna are black. They are rare and are available only in the United States and Mexico.

RITUALS FOR WEARING A PEARL

A pearl should be bought on a Monday in the ascending moon cycle. Sunday and Thursday are also prescribed as good days for buying a pearl, but Saturday is not a good day in any way for it. It would be ideal to buy the pearl on a Monday of an ascending cycle when the Moon is in Pushya, Rohini, Hast, or Shravan nakshatra. If these nakshatras are on a Thursday or Sunday of the ascending cycle the pearl can be purchased on any of these days.

The weight of the pearl should not be less than two rattikas (approximately $1/_8$ gm or .59 carat). It is best when it is four rattikas, but if one desires to have a larger pearl one can buy one of six or eleven rattikas or two, four, six, or eleven carats. Seven and eight are the numbers prohibited for the weight of the pearl, so it should not be seven or eight rattikas or carats in weight. The pearl should be genuine and flawless.

The pearl should be given to the jeweler on the same day, and the ring should be constructed and polished on the same days as mentioned above under the influence of the same nakshatras. The pearl should be mounted in silver. The setting should be open-backed so that the pearl touches the skin of the finger.

The best time to wear a pearl ring is evening, or when the Moon is rising.

Before wearing the ring for the first time, immerse it in raw cow's milk for some time. Then it should be washed with Ganga-water, rainwater, spring water, or water kept in a copper pot. After it has been washed the ring should be placed on a white cloth on which a Moon Yantra has been drawn with white sandalwood paste. An engraved Moon Yantra or an idol of the Moon god made in silver, weighing forty-eight or eighty-four grams, should be placed on this white cloth and worshiped. For the worship of an idol a priest is required but for the worship of a yantra no priest is needed—and the person who will wear the ring can do the worship himself. The ring should be placed in front of the silver-engraved yantra, on the white cloth on which the yantra is written with white sandalwood paste. Flowers and incense should be offered to the engraved silver yantra and the pearl mounted in the ring should be worshiped by reciting the mantra of Moon god:

ॐसों सोमाय नमः ॐ

AUM SOM SOMAYE NAMAH AUM

The mantra should be recited 108 or 11,000 times, and one should meditate on the gemstone as a symbol of the Moon god. After meditating, one should place the ring on the left hand, either on the ring finger or the little finger.

Pearl/Moon: Who Should Wear A Pearl

Ascendant/Ruler	Moon is Natural Ruler of	Relationship of the Moon with the Ruler of the Ascendant	Nature of the House Ruled by the Moon	Suitability/Unsuitability of the Pearl & its Effects
Aries/Mars	4th house	Friend	Auspicious	Suitable. Brings freedom from mental & psychological problems, favor from mother success in education, and inheritance of property. Good in general but especially in the major and subperiods of Moon.
Taurus/Venus	3rd house	Enemy	Auspicious	Not suitable. Wear only if Moon is in the 3rd house, during the major or subperiod of Moon.
Gemini/Mercury	2nd house	Enemy	Auspicious	Not suitable. Wear only if exalted Moon is in 9th, 10th, 11th, or 12th house. Wear only in major or subperiod of Moon.
Cancer/Moon	1st house Ascendant	Moon Himself is the Ruler	Auspicious	Suitable & beneficial. Those with Cancer ascendants should wear pearl all their lives. Brings ease of living, freedom from mental problems, good health, and long life.
Leo/Sun	12th house	Friend	Inauspicious	Not suitable because Moon is the ruler of the 12th house. If Moon is in the 12th house, pearls can be worn during the major & subperiods of Moon.
Virgo/Mercury	11th house	Enemy	Auspicious	Suitable if Moon is in Taurus in the 9th house or Moon is afflicted in the chart. Beneficial only during the major & subperiods of Moon.
Libra/Venus	10th house	Enemy	Auspicious	Suitable. Especially beneficial if Moon is in the 10th house and during the major & subperiods of Moon. Brings good name, fame, honor, wealth, & luck.

Sign/Ruler	House	Relation	Nature	Remarks
Scorpio/Mars	9th house	Friend	Auspicious	Beneficial. Brings religious nature, purity of mind, good health, and life (to one's father). Should be worn with coral.
Sagittarius/Jupiter	8th house	Friend	Inauspicious	Not suitable because Moon is the ruler of the 8th house. Can only be worn in the major & subperiods of Moon or if Moon is in the 8th house.
Capricorn/Saturn	7th house	Enemy	Auspicious	Not suitable. But can be worn during major & sub-periods of Moon or when Moon is in Cancer in the 7th house.
Aquarius/Saturn	6th house	Enemy	Inauspicious	Not suitable. Same as above.
Pisces/Jupiter	5th house	Friend	Auspicious	Suitable & beneficial. Brings good name, fame, good fortune, & progeny. More beneficial in major & sub-periods of Moon.

The 2nd and 7th houses are both auspicious but also death-inflicting houses, especially during the major or sub-periods of the planets that rule them. If the ruling planet is benefic and a friend of the ruler of the ascendant, that aspect can be lessened.

If one uses an idol of the Moon god instead of an engraved yantra, Havan or Homa (fire worship) should be performed, and for this job one needs a competent priest. The idol also should be offered an asana (a seat) made of silver (at least four or seven grams in weight) and after the worship is finished the idol, its silver asana, some silver coins, and some sweets made of milk, rice, and coconut powder should be donated to the priest. If a yantra is worshiped, the engraved yantra on silver with the white cloth on which the yantra is drawn with white sandalwood paste should be kept in a shrine. The yantra used for drawing on the cloth and the yantra engraved on silver are numerical yantras generally known as magic squares. The yantra to be drawn on cloth with white sandalwood paste is as follows:

7	2	9
8	6	4
3	10	5

The yantra to be engraved on silver is as follows:

37	78	29	70	21	62	13	54	5
6	38	79	30	71	22	63	14	46
47	7	39	80	31	72	23	55	15
16	48	8	40	81	32	64	24	56
57	17	49	9	41	73	33	65	25
26	58	18	50	1	42	74	34	66
67	27	59	10	51	2	43	75	35
36	68	19	60	11	52	3	44	76
77	28	59	20	61	12	53	4	45

The worship of both the yantra and the idol should be done facing northwest, sitting on a straw mat or the skin of an antelope. First the yantra should be washed and dried with a clean white cloth and then it should be honored with a tilak (a mark on the top of the yantra) with white sandalwood paste. The flowers and incense should be offered, and then the ring should be placed in front of the idol or yantra. The pearl in the ring should also be honored by a tilak, and flowers and incense should be offered to it. Then the mantra should be recited 108 or 11,000 times, and after finishing the mantra one should meditate and pray. After meditation and prayer a sweet dish made from rice, milk, and coconut should be offered, and this should be followed by an offering of water. The sweet dish and water could be offered to a ghee lamp, which is lighted in the beginning of the worship. After completing the whole process one may wear the ring.

A ring worn in this manner brings good luck, neutralizes problems caused by the Moon, gives mental peace, progeny, and financial gains, fulfills the desires of the one who wears it, and cures ailments caused by a weak and afflicted Moon.

MEDICINAL UTILITY OF PEARLS

As stated in the *Rasa Tantra Sar,* pearls with lustre should be used to make either oxide or paste (powder). Pearls that break down during the process of drilling become useless for jewelry, but they are not useless for making medicinal preparations. Oddly shaped, lustrous pearls and the dust obtained from drilling holes in pearls can also be used. Cultured and artificially made pearls should not be used.

After being drilled, the pearls should be purified. There are several ways to do this:

1. Boil them in the juice of jayanti (jasmine) for three hours in a daula yantra. According to *Dhanwantari Nighantu* (a treatise on the teachings of the medicine god) in *Bhav Prakash,** a concentrated solution (kwath) of jasmine leaves and twigs should be made by boiling them together in water. When the water is reduced to one-third by boiling, the concentrated extract should be strained and used to boil the pearls in a daula yantra.

*Motram Banarsi Dass, publisher. Delhi/Banaras

2. Boil them in cow's milk for three hours in a daula yantra.
3. Add four parts water to one part fresh lemon juice and soak the pearls in this mixture for twelve hours. Then clean the pearls with fresh water.

Mukta Bhasm (Pearl Oxide)

Any of the three above-mentioned methods can be used to purify pearls, but after each (boiling or soaking) treatment they should be washed with pure water. (Tap water that is treated with chlorine or any other chemical should not be used.) After washing the pearls dry them on a clean, dry cloth.

The best pearls for medical preparations are the small, shiny seed pearls. The dust obtained from drilling the holes in pearls also should be purified by the same method.

After the pearls are dried, they should be ground in a mortar made of simak stone, kasauti (basanite), or agate. The juice of ghee kunwar (a cactus) should be added to the purified pearls, and the mixture should be ground for twelve hours. Then a tablet should be made from the ground mixture and dried in the sun. After the tablet is completely dry, two clay bowls of the same size should be taken, and the tablet should be placed in one pot and covered with the other pot. This is called sarva samput, in the Ayurveda. The pots should be sealed with fine clay and the cloth soaked in clay and dried. The tablet sealed in the pots should then be fired in two kilograms of cowdung cakes. The pots will become red-hot. After they are cool take out the tablets and grind again in cow's milk and again make a tablet from the ground mixture. Seal them again in two earthen pots, and fire again in two kilograms of cowdung. After they have been fired, the pots should be allowed enough time to cool. The oxide is ready. The pots should be carefully opened. Nice, white, fine, and soft oxide will now be ready in the clay pots. This is called mukta bhasm or pearl oxide.

Dosage: ½ to 1 rattika twice a day with milk, honey, rock sugar candy powder, malai (cream skimmed from milk), sweet butter, or chyavan prash (a preparation made from the amla fruit, available in Indian spice shops).

Usage: Cough, aggravated bile, tuberculosis, asthma, low digestive fire, burning sensation in any part of the body, madness of any kind, diseases caused by aggravation of wind (vayu), and impotence.

Mukta bhasm provides strength and longevity.

Mukta Pishthi (pearl paste or powder)

Pishthi (paste) of pearls is far better than the oxide. The true qualities of pearls are at their best in the pishthi.

To make the pishthi, the pearls should be purified by any of the above-mentioned methods. The best is to boil them in cow's milk, because treating pearls with lemon juice spoils their lustre. After the purification, the pearls should be ground in rose water for twenty-one days, or 168 hours (one day means eight hours of normal work). The grinding is done in a special manner: *no force to crush* the pearls should be applied. The hand should move gently in a very slow rhythm. The grinding of pearls is a kind of meditation. Gently, the hands should move to and fro, with equal light force. Experts of pishthi say that you should just hold the pestle and move it to and fro—the pestle has enough weight to pulverize the pearls. After they have been ground for some time, the pearl fragments deposited on the side walls of the mortar should be removed with rose water. At least three liters of rose water should be consumed during the process of grinding 150 grams of pearls. After the powdered pearls become as fine as finest dust the paste should be allowed to dry. The powder should be so soft and without particles that it could be safely used as surma (an eye remedy) on the eyelids. If there are any particles and the powder is not finely ground, it will hurt the eyes. Before testing, it can be felt by rubbing it between the fingers. It should be as smooth as talcum powder. Then it can be used on the body.

Dosage: ½ to 1 rattika with either milk, gulkand (a jam made of rose petals and sugar, available in Indian spice shops), sandalwood sherbet, rose sherbet, sitopiladi powder (see glossary for formula), silver leaf, or honey.

Usage: Eye troubles, general debility, tuberculosis, chest troubles, weakness of heart, cough, low-grade fever, hiccups, illusions of ghosts or evil spirits, nosebleed, weakness of mind, and urinary troubles. The use of pearls subdues bilious temperament and acidity. It improves eyesight (in India a wide variety of surma, in which powdered pearls are used, is available).

Pearl paste is considered sheet veerya (cool in essence) and diuretic, and cures a burning sensation in the urinary tract. It induces sleep and can be given when the patient suffers from insomnia. It cures disgust, anger, stress, strain, problems caused by waking too much, stressed mind, problems created by eating hot and spicy foods, heatstroke, sunstroke, lethargy, inability to think, high-pitched voice, roughness in touch (body texture), bad odors from the mouth and body, harsh voice, and short temper.

Pearl paste helps in recovering from shocks, especially mental shocks caused by the sudden demise of someone near and dear, mental problems caused by liquor, hemp, marijuana, astromonium (dhatura or devil's weed), or other drugs. In the case of schizophrenia, mukta pishthi (pearl paste in powdered form) should be given with the oxides of marcasite, pyrites, the oxide or paste of coral, or a jam made from kushthmand (a Chinese squash that grows as big as a pumpkin, has green skin, is white inside, and is astringent in taste). One can also use the jam made from brahmi (a creeper of the clover family that grows at an altitude of 4,000 to 6,000 feet near water in the Himalayas), or brahmi ghee.

In cases where a patient is possessed by a ghost or evil spirit and becomes violent, mukta pishthi is very helpful.

Pearls also help the body's immune system. They provide resistance and strengthen the nerves. Pearls are the highest quality calcium, and as calcium is a neuromotor transmitter and an electrolyte, it is food for the nerves.

After suzak (venereal disease of the male organ), after a poisonous bite, food poisoning, or any kind of poisoning when the bile is aggravated and a burning sensation in the urinary tract is experienced, pearls should be administered. Pearls are also an effective way to stop bleeding.

For red eyes, heat felt in the eyes, hot tears, and frequent eye troubles, pearls used orally or in surma are soothing. Special surma with pearls is available in shops that deal especially with surma.

Pearl pishthi is especially helpful for women during their menstrual cycle, in pregnancy, after delivery when there is much loss of blood, and for mothers who are breast-feeding.

Pearl pishthi is good for patients with heart palpitations. For tuberculosis, restlessness, high fever, boils, and diabetes, pearls are very helpful.

Pearl pishthi is ideal for providing immediate relief for breathlessness due to obesity and for burning sensations inside the stomach.

In bleeding piles when a burning sensation is felt in the anal region, pearl pishthi with fresh warm milk (warm from the body temperature of the cow, not heated on a flame) serves as a relief.

In debility caused by constant dysentery, when the stools create a burning sensation in the anus and the mouth becomes sore and red, pearls are very helpful when taken with sandalwood sherbet. They help revive strength by strengthening the seven dhatus, and they provide vitality. They help fluids, blood, muscle, fiber, tissue, skin, bone, hair, liver, spleen, heart, and endocrine glands, and they delay old age.

CHIEF SOURCES OF PEARLS

Gulf of Manar in Sri Lanka: The famous classical Indian gemologist Varahamihir states that the best pearls were found in the Indian Ocean. Their color, as observed by him, was as white as a swan, and they were lustrous and smooth. He praises the pearls from the Gulf of Manar. The pearls found in Manar, however, are slightly smoky in tinge and lighter in weight than their competitors, the pearls found in the Persian Gulf. Most probably during his time the pearls found in Ceylon (Sri Lanka) were the best, as other sources have also said that Ceylon pearls were exported to ancient Rome. Indian gem dealers nowadays believe that the best pearls are found in the Persian Gulf.

The Persian Gulf: The most lustrous and durable pearls are found on the banks of the Bahrain Islands in the Persian Gulf. They are famous as Basra pearls in India and jewelers, gem therapists, and Ayurvedic doctors prefer them over any other variety found today. They are highly prized because they resist wear and tear and are brilliant with a good epithelium. Their color, though, might not be as clearly silver in tone as some of the pearls found in the widespread sites of the Indian Ocean. Basra pearls are also becoming less available since the oil industry has spoiled the sites from Oman to Qatar.

Bay of Bengal: The pearls obtained from the Bay of Bengal are globular, rose-colored, and very attractive. But they are softer than Basra pearls and so are less durable. They lose their rose tinge when worn—becoming white—because of the chemical reaction with perspiration. They are treated with chemicals to make them even and white looking in color, but a little negligence in washing destroys their lustre. The chemical treatment also makes them less durable.

South Indian Fisheries: Pearls are also found in southern India and in Tamil Nadu and Andhra Pradesh. Tuticorin in South India has been a famous source of pearls for several centuries. Pearls found in Tuticorin are similar to Basra pearls from the Persian Gulf.

Darbhanga: These pearls are similar to pearls found in the Bay of Bengal but are of inferior quality and are mostly used for medicinal purposes.

Gomti: These pearls are similar to pearls found in Darbhanga fisheries, but they are very soft and lose their lustre when rubbed on ordinary cotton cloth. They also become light in weight. Such pearls are also found on Oran Island, Bombay.

Venezuela: These pearls are similar to the pearls obtained from the Persian Gulf, but they are whiter than the Basra pearls and are not round, like pearls from Basra. A good globular-shaped pearl is rare. Venezuela also yields a good amount of the rare black pearls.

Mexico: These pearls are known as kagavasi in India. They are black, shiny smooth, and globular in shape. White pearls also are found on the coast of Mexico and have been available for many centuries.

Australia: These pearls are hard and shaped like teeth. Although they are white they are not attractive and thus are not highly priced.

The best pearls are found in salt water, but many varieties of pearls are reared in fresh water. Pliny calls them *unio*. Unio mussels sometimes produce very good varieties of pearls that are as well-shaped, smooth, shiny, and attractive as pearls found in the Indian Ocean.

Pearls were also found in Europe, but industrial waste dumped into the rivers has destroyed many of the fine freshwater pearl fisheries.

Note: Pearls are very delicate, and it is advised not to place them in cotton, because cotton can produce scratches, waves, and cracks in their surface. One should avoid also damp, moist storage places.

One should not wear oddly shaped pearls. China produces many such pearls commercially. They are cheap, but they bring bad luck, for all pearls, if they are oddly shaped, bring bad vibrations.

Mars is masculine, authoritative, aggressive, and courageous. It is regarded as a warrior and the commander in chief of the assembly of gods. It governs our muscular system, blood, and behavior. Mars rides a ram, symbolizing muscular strength, combative nature, and fire. In his hands he holds a sword of control, a shield of security, a lotus of purity, and a mace of strength.

5

Mars and Its Gemstone, Coral

आद्रायश्रेषं स्तक्स्यात्र बलक्य केक्लादिषु-'विद्रमाक्सुमहागुणा।

MARS IS A masculine, dry, and fiery planet. It is said to be the commander-in-chief of the assembly of the nine planets. It is also personified as the god of war. Mars is a warrior by nature—bile-dominated in temperament—and it rules over courage, bravery, patience, self-confidence, leadership abilities, physical strength, forcefulness, violence, animal nature, cattle, land as property, earth, fire, saffron, musk, mercury (the metal), cuts, burns, bruises, anger, hatred, impulsive nature, and insensitivity.

Mars makes its natives short-tempered; argumentative; lovers of weapons, guns, and explosives; commanders; generals; soldiers; and policemen. It also gives them great technical and mechanical abilities and makes them builders, designers, engineers, and good surgeons.

Mars is fond of law and order—and arrangement. It gives energy, drive, determination, a strong sense of purpose, great administrative ability, and independent spirit.

Mars is regarded as a malefic planet in astrology and gives its natives the ability to put their own desires above those of others. It makes them prone to illegal ventures and illicit love affairs. Mars is capable of harming any or all of its associations.

Mars gives its best effect from twenty-seven to twenty-eight and up to thirty-two years of age. Its metal is copper; its day is Tuesday.

Mars is known in Sanskrit as Kuja or Rudher, which means relating to the blood. It is related with the blood, muscular system, and bone marrow (which is formed from the essence of blood).

Mars is red in color and the ruler of the direction South. It is best placed in the tenth house, where it gets directional strength (dik-bala). It is tamasik in nature, which makes its natives tend toward laziness and inactivity. It is exalted in Capricorn and the sign of its fall is Cancer. Mars functions well in Aries and Scorpio, the zodiacal signs over which it rules. Sun, Moon, and Jupiter are its natural friends, Venus and Saturn are neutral in friendship, and Mercury, Rahu, and Ketu are its enemies. It is powerful in Pisces and Aquarius. Mrigshira, Dhanishtha, and Chitra are its nakshatras. Leo, Sagittarius, and Pisces are friendly zodiacal signs and Gemini, Taurus, Libra, and Virgo are enemy zodiacal signs. Its friendship with Jupiter is sattvik, with the Sun is rajasik, and when it is seated with the Moon it becomes powerful. In the second house Mars becomes weak, but it becomes powerful in the third, sixth, and eleventh houses, in addition to the tenth house, where it is most powerful.

If Mars is afflicted or weak, it causes troubles; it makes its natives cruel, violent, aggressive, rough, and rude. It causes eczema, rashes, disorders of the blood and bile, cuts, wounds, electric shocks, gunshots, knife wounds, burns, bruises, anger, hatred, psychic disturbances, poverty, infections, smallpox, plague, tuberculosis, thirst, piles, ulcers, fevers, poisoning, surgical operations, and diseases of the stomach, liver, lungs, nose, and ears. Afflicted Mars gives lack of ambition and motivation, and success in life becomes difficult.

When Mars is weak or afflicted, people are advised to wear on Tuesdays a coral in a copper and gold ring with an open back, which enables the stone to touch the skin of the finger.

Those born on the ninth, eighteenth, or twenty-seventh day of any month are ruled by Mars.

Coral, known as *prawal* in Sanskrit and *moonga* in Hindi, is formed by plants and animals in warm seas. Coral is also known as aragonite when found in the lining of seashells and is counted as a calcite by mineralogists. Coral is a calcareous, skeleton-like deposit of the coral polyp—a tiny invertebrate that dwells in quiet waters and is found at depths ranging from 20 to 1,000 feet. Just as ants prepare anthills, the insect *Isis nobiles* produces a plant-like structure with branches and dwells in it. Usually these are not very thick or high and are found standing erect on rocks in the sea; but sometimes they become as tall as man and quite thick in diameter. These large, thick pieces are sometimes used to make idols, sculptures of deities, and handles for swords, but as its usual size is not large, and its diameter does not usually exceed one inch, most of it is consumed in making round beads and oval pieces for rings, amulets, and pendants.

Coral is composed of successive rings of thin, concentric deposits of calcium and the secretions from the body of *Isis nobiles* and is found as a colony. Sometimes such colonies cover a whole rock. The color of coral depends on the depth at which it is found— below 160 feet its color is light. The best-colored corals are found between depths of 100 and 160 feet. Its red color is due to the presence of iron oxide.

It is found in many shades of red and pink. The color usually ranges from white to pink to vermilion red and deep scarlet. It is devoid of lustre in its natural condition, and the raw material is mostly opaque. Semi-transparent corals also are available, but they also have opaqueness. Corals of yellow ocher, cream, chocolate, and black color are also available. The chemical composition of the black coral is different from white, rose, pink, red, yellow, cream, and chocolate-colored corals. Coral reefs are attacked by worms and sponges, which create holes in them and destroy their color. Coral tends to have uniformity in color, and variation in shade in a single piece is rare. Temperature plays an important role in its color and growth, and immature coral reefs have a lighter color and disintegrate quickly. It requires many years for a coral reef to mature and become suitable for use in jewelry. The season suitable for taking the reefs out of the sea is from March to October.

A good coral that is related to the planet Mars and recommended by astrologers, gem therapists, and jewelers is a deep red coral, which resembles well-ripened bimb fruit or an unripe cherry. *Shukra Niti* praises a blood-red coral, which is a mixture of vermilion with a touch of carmine or scarlet red. In *Aaine Jawahar,* coral of deep red color is held as the most effective gem for an afflicted or weak Mars. *Ratna Pariksha* says it should be of the color of bimb fruit. Most Hindu scriptures on the subject agree that red coral is useful as jewelry and for pleasing the planet Mars, but the use of white corals is more popular in Bengal, where people also use it for Mars energy. In any case, the best gem should have the following qualities:

1. deep red color
2. regular shape and even surface
3. round or oval shape
4. shininess and the quality of emitting honey-like, lovely, and delicate splendor
5. free of dents, holes, or perforations
6. large, with proportionate thickness
7. smooth
8. heavier than average corals of its size.

Even the corals that are vermilion—similar to the color of mercury oxide or red like the color of rust (iron oxide) or brownish red—give good energy if they possess the above-mentioned characteristics. One who wears or possesses such coral enjoys good fortune and is never possessed by evil spirits or bothered by ghosts, bad vibrations, nightmares, storms, or lightning. Illusions of ghosts or evil spirits cannot affect the wearer, and he will never suffer the ill effects of the evil eye. Japa (constant repetition of a mantra or a name of God) done with a coral mala (rosary) with 108 beads brings siddhi (power).

FLAWS OF CORAL

1. A coral having holes, according to the shastras, is harmful for the health of the one who wears it.
2. A coral having perforations gives pain in the body and migraine.
3. A coral with dents increases suffering and is bad for marital relationships.
4. A coral that is broken or has a cutting mark is harmful to peace, prosperity, and progeny.
5. A coral having a crack on the surface or the body brings injuries from sharp-edged weapons.
6. A coral having many shades in one piece destroys comfort, wealth, and peace of mind.
7. A coral having black spots brings accidents and is sometimes fatal.
8. A coral having white spots worsens disease and destroys mental peace.
9. A coral uneven in thickness increases suffering.

10. A coral similar to the color of lacquer (dark brown) gives fear of weapons and thieves.
11. A coral that is very light in weight brings misfortune.

In general the shastras prohibit the use of whitish yellow, smoky, or thin coral, coral having marks, dents, holes, or perforations, or one that is broken, uneven in thickness, and not having splendor or a regular shape.

White coral is also prohibited, although its use is common in Bengal and other parts of the world, namely, Europe, the United States, and Mexico.

Black coral is not desirable according to the shastras.

A thin coral is also not good to wear.

A coral that is stained to improve its natural color also is not good.

IDENTIFICATION OF REAL CORAL

1. If real coral is placed in a glass of cow's milk, the color of the milk will appear pink or take on a red tinge. Imitation coral will not affect the whiteness of milk.
2. If a coral is dropped in blood, blood will thicken around it.
3. A synthetic coral has higher specific gravity than a real coral; it is heavier in weight.
4. An imitation coral produces a distinct sound when rubbed, which resembles the sound of glass being rubbed.
5. An imitation coral shows granules in its texture when examined under a magnifying glass.
6. An imitation coral turns a piece of turmeric root-red when rubbed against it.
7. A true coral changes color according to the physical well-being of the wearer. It fades before the disorder in physical health is noticeable and resumes its original color when physical health is restored.

CLASSIFICATION OF CORAL

1. Brahmin: Corals of vermilion color. They are best suited for spiritually inclined, learned persons.
2. Kshatriya: Corals of scarlet-red color. They are best for politicians, officers, army people, and policemen.
3. Vaishya: Corals of orange red or ocher color. They are best for businessmen and people who desire material prosperity.

4. Shudra: Dark and dull corals. They are best for the working class, for manual laborers, and people who have Rahu, Ketu, or Saturn conjunct with Mars in their horoscope.

RITUALS FOR WEARING A CORAL

A coral should be bought on a Tuesday when the Moon is in Aries or Scorpio, when any of the four nakshatras Mrigshira, Chitra, Anuradha, or Dhanishtha is present. The coral should be bought between sunrise and 11:00 A.M. and should be given to the jeweler within this time. The jeweler should set it on a Tuesday when the Moon is in any of the four nakshatras mentioned above, between the same hours. The stone should be set so that it touches the skin. The coral's weight should be no less than 6 carats. Coral of nine, eleven, or twelve rattikas or carats is preferable. It should not be five or fourteen rattikas in weight in any case. The metal used should be a mixture of copper and gold—any other metal should not be used in the mixture. Preparing a ring on a Tuesday when the Moon is in Capricorn is very auspicious. The best time to wear a coral ring is one hour after sunrise or up until 11:00 A.M., as mentioned above.

Before wearing the ring for the first time, immerse it in raw cow's milk and wash it in Ganga-water, rainwater, spring water, or water kept in a copper pot for some time. After being washed, the ring should be placed on a red cloth on which a numerical Mars Yantra is drawn with red sandalwood paste, gorochan (a red calcium from cowhorn), saffron, or roli. An engraved yantra of Mars on copper, or an idol of Mars made in copper should be placed on the red cloth and worshiped. Flowers and incense should be offered after the yantra engraved on copper or the idol is bathed. If an invocation of Mars energy in an idol is necessary, proper worship by a priest is required. In the case of a yantra, the one who has to wear the ring sits facing east, lights a lamp, and offers flowers, incense, tilak, and sweets to the yantra. The yantra and the gemstone set in the ring should be worshiped by reciting the mantra of Mars:

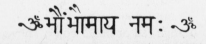

ॐ भौं भौमाय नमः ॐ

AUM BHAUM BHAUMAYE NAMAH AUM

The mantra should be recited 108 or 10,000 times, and then the wearer should meditate on the gemstone as a symbol of Mars. After meditation the ring should be worn on the ring finger of the right hand.

The yantra to be drawn on red cloth with red sandalwood paste or with ground saffron paste made thin like an ink is as follows:

8	3	10
9	7	5
4	11	6

The yantra to be engraved on a copper plate is as follows:

11	24	7	20	3
4	12	25	8	16
17	5	13	21	9
10	18	1	14	22
23	6	19	2	15

After worship the yantra should be wrapped in the red cloth on which the other yantra is drawn and it should either be donated to a priest or kept in a shrine.

MEDICINAL UTILITY OF CORAL

Coral needs to be purified before an oxide (bhasma) or a paste (pishthi) can be made from it.

For making medicinal preparations one does not need the coral

Coral/Mars: Who Should Wear Coral

Ascendant/Ruler	Mars is Natural Ruler of	Relationship of Mars with the Ruler of the Ascendant	Nature of the House Ruled by Mars	Suitability/Unsuitability of Coral & its Effects
Aries/Mars	1st house Ascendant, 8th house	Mars Himself is the Ruler	Auspicious, Inauspicious	Suitable & beneficial. Coral should be worn throughout life. Gives health, courage, good name, and fame.
Taurus/Venus	12th house, 7th house	Enemy	Inauspicious, Auspicious	Not suitable. Wear only if Mars is in the 7th or 12th house, during the major & subperiods of Mars.
Gemini/Mercury	6th house, 11th house	Enemy	Inauspicious, Auspicious	Not suitable. Can be worn only in the major & sub-periods of Mars or when Mars is in the 6th or 11th house.
Cancer/Moon	5th house, 10th house	Friend	Auspicious, Auspicious	Suitable & beneficial. Brings good luck, good name, fame, honor, success, and children. Red coral should be worn with pearls during major & subperiods of Mars.
Leo/Sun	4th house, 9th house	Friend	Auspicious, Auspicious	Suitable & beneficial. Brings honor, good luck, good name, fame, land & property. Red coral with ruby proves more beneficial during major & subperiods of Mars.
Virgo/Mercury	3rd house, 8th house	Enemy	Auspicious, Inauspicious	Not suitable. Wear only if Mars is in the 3rd or 8th house, during the major or subperiods of Mars.
Libra/Venus	2nd house, 7th house	Enemy	Auspicious, Auspicious	Not suitable, but if Mars is in the 7th house coral will be very beneficial, especially during the major & sub-periods of Mars.

Sign/Ruler	House	Mars Relationship	Status	Remarks
Scorpio/Mars	1st house 6th house	Mars Himself is the Ruler	Auspicious Inauspicious	Suitable & beneficial. Red coral should be worn for good health, courage, good name, fame, and wealth.
Sagittarius/Jupiter	5th house 12th house	Friend	Auspicious Inauspicious	Suitable & beneficial. Brings good luck, children, good name, and fame. Especially beneficial during the major & subperiods of Mars.
Capricorn/Saturn	4th house 11th house	Enemy	Auspicious Auspicious	Beneficial in major and subperiods of Mars. Brings acquisition of land, property, domestic happiness, and harmonious relationship with one's mother.
Aquarius/Saturn	3rd house 10th house	Enemy	Auspicious Auspicious	Beneficial only in major & subperiods of Mars. Especially beneficial when Mars is in the 10th house.
Pisces/Jupiter	2nd house 9th house	Friend	Auspicious Auspicious	Suitable & beneficial. Use of coral with a yellow sapphire is especially recommended. Brings success and many other great benefits.

The 2nd and 7th houses are both auspicious but also death-inflicting houses, especially during the major or sub-periods of the planets that rule them. If the ruling planet is benefic and a friend of the ruler of the ascendant, that aspect can be lessened.

used in jewelry; one should select deep red coral. White coral is not used for preparing oxide or paste. Coral branches slightly heavier in weight than normal branches of the same size and thickness should be carefully selected. They should be steamed in the juice of jasmine twigs and leaves in a daula yantra for about three hours and then washed with fresh mineral water, spring water, or rainwater.

Another method is to soak coral branches in buttermilk that is not too sour for about three hours, and then wash them with hot water.

After the branches are purified and dried in the shade they are ready for making bhasma (oxide) or pishthi (paste).

To Make Coral Oxide

Take 160 grams of purified coral reef, powder it, and add 48 grams of kajjali (a mixture of mercury and sulphur used in Ayurvedic medicine) mixed in ghee kunwar (cactus juice—aloe vera). Grind it in a mortar made of kasauti (basonite) for twelve hours. Make a tablet of the paste and dry it in the sun. Then take two earthen pots of the same size, put the tablet in one and cover it with the other—this is known as sarvasamput—and then seal the pots with clay. After the pots are sealed take cloth strips soaked in clay and wrap them around the sealed pot until the layers of clay-soaked cloth are about one inch thick around the clay pots. Dry the clay ball created by this process in the Sun and fire it in dry cowdung cakes. It is not necessary to fire it in cowdung cakes; one can fire it in a potter's kiln. After the ball is red hot let it cool by itself inside the kiln. Then take the ball out and break the outside layer to take the clay pots out safely. Open the pots. The bhasma (oxide) is ready.

The ancient method of firing the gems and metals was called gajput—this process began with digging a round, well-like structure about twenty-six inches deep and twenty-six inches in diameter in the earth, and then lining it with bricks. This hole was filled halfway with dried cowdung, and then the samput (clay ball made by the method described above) was placed in the center and the hole filled with six inches of dried cowdung over the samput. Then the whole thing was fired. After the fire died down, the samput was allowed to cool by itself. When it was completely cool the samput was taken out. But the author has used a potter's kiln, and the oxide made by this method is also perfect. The kiln can always be used instead of the gajput, although firing in cowdung may produce a better quality of oxide.

This oxide should be as fine as ashes and white. The powder should then be stored in a red bottle in a cool, dry place. The lid used to cover the pot should be airtight.

Dosage: 1 to 2 rattikas twice a day with either sitopiladi choorna (defined below) and honey, gulkund (rose-petal jam), malai or cream with mishri (rock sugar candy).

For different diseases it is used with different mediums, as follows:

1. For dry cough: Use it with powdered raw sugar.
2. Cough with mucus: a) If the mucus needs to be expelled from the system, coral oxide should be taken with powdered brown sugar; b) If the mucus needs to be dried, it should be taken with honey.
3. Low fever: It should be taken with sitopiladi choorna with honey. Sitopiladi choorna is made of:

> 16 gms powdered rock sugar candy
> 8 gms powdered calcium bamboana
> 4 gms pipal powder
> 2 gms white cardamom powder
> 1 gm freshly powdered cinnamon

Mix and sift the above ingredients and keep the mixture in an airtight bottle. One dose is 1 teaspoon (whether it is used by itself for cough—as it is a good remedy for cough, cold, fever—or used with pearl, coral, or any other gem oxide or powder).

4. Breathlessness with low fever: Take it with honey.
5. New fever: With honey.
6. Debility caused by decay in dhatus: Use it with ripe banana.
7. General debility: With betel leaves.
8. Leukorrhea: With cow's milk (fresh, unprocessed, not boiled).
9. Disorders created by aggravated wind element: With juice of basil (basilicum) and honey.
10. Bone fracture: With honey.
11. Aggravated bile: Wth ghee, rock sugar candy, and amla jam.
12. Eye troubles (burning, irritation): Use it with ghee, rock sugar candy, and milk.
13. Headache: Use it with milk cooked with almond paste.

14. Jaundice: Use it with ghee and sugar.
15. Rakta pitta (aggravation of bile in which the patient bleeds through the anus or nose, or in the urine): Use it with amla jam or chyavan prash.
16. Mental weakness: Use it with milk cooked with almond paste.
17. General tonic: Use it with honey.
18. Cough: Use it with juice of betel leaf and honey.
19. Heart palpitations: With milk or malai (skim of milk).
20. Diseases of liver: With honey.
21. Measles: With honey.
22. Smallpox: With honey.
23. High blood pressure: With honey.
24. Ulcers: With malai or honey.
25. Piles: With malai.
26. Fistula: With malai and honey.
27. Idleness: With honey.
28. Hyperacidity: With cold milk.
29. Urinary diseases: With honey.
30. Poisoning: With honey.
31. Bleeding piles: With malai.

The other form of medical preparation is pishthi (paste), which is more powerful and better in quality than oxide. It is made by grinding purified coral reefs in a mortar made of simak, agate, or kasauti with rose water for twenty-one days or 252 hours (one day is equal to twelve hours of grinding).

Dosage: 1 to 2 rattikas twice a day.

1. To prevent miscarriage: Apply the paste (not powder—if only the powder is available make a paste by adding rose water or kewra water—a few drops to two doses) to the navel of a pregnant woman.
2. First stage of tuberculosis: Use it with honey.

When dried in the shade this paste becomes a fine powder and can be used for all of the above-mentioned diseases in place of the oxide (bhasma).

It is also useful for the childhood disease rickets and can be given to children as young as three months of age. It is also very helpful for children who are teething.

Coral powder is very good for nursing mothers who become weak during the nursing period.

Coral powder is a fantastic remedy for premature ejaculation.

It makes the seminal fluid thick and gives one power to hold it. It also cures nocturnal emissions.

Coral powder is beneficial in treating venereal diseases and any distortion or trouble in the vaginal passage. It cures the aftereffect of poisons.

Coral is sweet, alkaline, diuretic, and a destroyer of aggravated bile and mucus. It increases semen and gives radiance to the skin.

It can be safely administered to sufferers from epilepsy, low digestive fire, dysentery, swelling in the intestines, diseases caused by impurity of the blood, excessive sweating, sweating at night, skin diseases, leprosy, weakness of nerves, asthma, mental problems, diabetes, stomach pain, and troubles caused by evil vibrations, ghosts, and evil spirits. Coral also helps people suffering mentally and physically due to an afflicted Mars in their horoscope.

CHIEF SOURCES OF CORAL

The oldest source of precious coral production has been the Mediterranean Sea, which has been used for centuries. Coral of the finest quality is obtained in bulk from the coasts of Algeria and Tunisia. Other profitable sites for coral deposits are the coasts of Spain, France, Corsica, Sardinia, and Sicily, as well as the Red Sea and the Persian Gulf. Corals are also found off the northwest coast of Africa, the coasts of Australia, and the Indian Ocean. Corals found off the shore of Spain are deep in color. Corals are also found in the seas around Japan, and Japanese corals are in demand because of the skillful craftsmen of Japan, who produce finely wrought corals.

Corals are also processed in India, where they find a large and lucrative market. Italian craftsmen also produce corals of fine quality, and Torre del Greco ranks as one of the best centers for coral carving and polishing.

Coral is a delicate stone. It should be taken off when one is working with lemon, vinegar, buttermilk, or sour yoghurt; it should be spared from all acidic products. It is easily scratched, and should be kept away from metals or jewelry; putting them together can ruin the surface of this delicate gemstone.

Mercury is neutral, emotional, joyful, and evergreen. It is famous for ready wit, wisdom, and power of communication. Related to our respiratory system, nervous system, and speech, Mercury makes people flexible, skillful, clever, and delicate. He is shown riding a lion with an elephant's trunk which points toward the dual nature of Mercury, readily apparent in those with Gemini ascendant. The lion symbolizes wisdom and the elephant memory. In his hands Mercury has a bow and arrow to shoot his target, a disc of Vishnu for protection, and a conch for liberation. He is the sport-loving prince of the assembly of gods.

6

Mercury and Its Gemstone, Emerald

हरिद्वर्णो गुरुस्निग्ध,स्फुरद्रश्मिचयं शुभम् ।
मसृणं भास्वरं तार्क्ष्यं गात्रं सप्त गुणां मतम् ॥
कापिलं कर्कंशं पाण्डु कृष्णां लघुगुराम् ।
चिपटं विकटं कृष्णां,रुक्षं तार्क्ष्यं न शस्यते ॥

MERCURY IS THE PLANET of intellect and communication. In Sanskrit, intellect is called buddhi, and the Sanskrit name of Mercury is Budha, a cognate of the word *buddhi*. It is also known as Kumar (an unmarried young prince or youth). Mercury is the prince among the assembly of nine planets.

According to the *Linga Purana* (2.13.14.15.(385)) Budha, or Mercury, is the son of the Moon by his wife Rohini. Yet in the *Vishnu Purana* (4.6), *Brahma Purana* (23), *Devi Bhagvata* (1.11), *Bhagwat Purana* (9.14), *Harivansha Purana* (1.25), *Padma Purana* (12), and *Vayu Purana* (90–91) a story is told of the seduction of Brahaspati's (Jupiter's) wife Tara by the Moon—and Budha is born from her. He is called Saumya, that is, "Son of Soma [Moon]." From Budha springs the lunar race. The Moon, being his father, is friendly toward him, but he, Mercury, knows that he is son of the wife of Jupiter—and so he is in conflict with the Moon, who seduced his mother.

Mercury is sexless and neutral and is a cold and moist planet. Being a neutral planet it changes according to its placement in a sign and house, and that is why it is said to have a "mercurial" nature. Because it is nearest to the Sun it is restless, which also makes it quick-changing, fickle, and often retrograde. (*Retrograde* denotes a backward movement.) Mercury sometimes precedes the Sun and sometimes follows it. Mercury can be seen in the morning and evening as a shining star—and sometimes even during the day because of its power of radiation. Mercury is the smallest planet of our solar system. Being adaptable, it becomes malefic when conjunct with Mars and makes its natives nervous, overly excitable, and insecure.

Mercury rules education, writers, lecturers, artists, teachers, traders, businessmen, the nervous system, lungs, and intestines. It rules intelligence, speech, self-confidence, humor, wit, astrology, mathematics, and short journeys.

As a lord of Gemini Mercury has two faces; it gives a double nature and makes one detached and independent as well as an extremist.

In astrology Mercury is regarded as a benefic planet (if not conjunct with a malefic planet). Its influence makes its natives appreciate traditional beliefs, but it does not give them mystical tendencies; it makes them independent thinkers.

Mercury rules the zodiacal signs Virgo and Gemini and is the only planet that is exalted up to 15 degrees in its own sign, Virgo—the sign of uniqueness. Its color is the green of a blade of fresh grass and it is dominated by the three doshas (humors) wind, bile, and mucus, all rajasik (active) in nature. Earth is its element, it is merchant by nature, shudra (serving class) by caste, lover of humor and wit, ever green, weak in body constitution, delicate, having mixed feelings, loves the company of learned people, and is lord of the direction North.

Friends of Mercury are the Sun, Venus, Rahu, and Ketu. Mars, Jupiter, and Saturn are neutral to Mercury, and Mercury maintains enmity with the Moon.

Mercury is best placed in the first house, where it gets directional strength. It functions best in its own signs and also quite well in Taurus, Leo, and Libra, but it does not function well in Cancer, because that is a sign of its only enemy, the Moon. Pisces is its sign of fall and up to 15 degrees in Pisces it is fallen. It is also inauspicious in Sagittarius. It works well with Ashlekha, Jyeshtha, Revati, Rohini, Hast, and Shravan nakshatras and gives auspicious results. It gives inauspicious results in Adra, Svati, Pushya, Anuradha, Chitra, and Magha nakshatras. It gives benefic results when conjunct with Jupiter and the Moon and malefic results with Mars, Saturn, Rahu, and Ketu, the malefic planets. With Venus it gives mixed results. It sets when it is conjunct the Sun and then becomes fruitless.

It gives its best results when its native is between thirty-two and thirty-five years of age.

When ill-aspected, Mercury gives chronic dysentery, constipation, lack of digestive fire, lung diseases, asthma, restlessness, kidney problems, fear, neurosis, and madness.

The day related to Mercury is Wednesday, and people born on the fifth, fourteenth, and twenty-third of any month are ruled by Mercury. The gemstone related to Mercury is emerald.

THE EMERALD

Known as markat in Sanskrit and panna in Hindi, the emerald is a silicate of aluminum and beryllium. Emerald is a gemstone of green color belonging to the family of beryl gems. This gemstone is rare because it is very difficult to find a flawless emerald. Most emeralds are defective, having a feather-like crack and inclusions. To find an emerald that is of rich green color, perfectly transparent, with a velvety reflection and high specific gravity is difficult. Aquamarine, morganite, goshenite, and heliodor are also members of the beryl family and have the same chemical constituents, except for chromic oxide, which gives emerald the green color that distinguishes it from the other varieties of beryls.

QUALITIES OF A GOOD EMERALD

1. rich green homogeneous color that is deep and pleasant, like a blade of fresh grass
2. retains its color and lustre in all kinds of lights and shades
3. vitreous lustre, radiance, luminescence, brilliance
4. velvety reflection
5. compactness, which gives it high specific gravity
6. transparence, which makes it rare and costlier than diamonds

7. soothing touch and pleasant sight, which gives peaceful vibrations and captivates the heart
8. smoothness that comes when the stone has a fine finish
9. fine cut, which illuminates it from all sides.

According to the *Agastya Mat,* as mentioned in the *Ratna Prakash,* a good emerald is transparent, without dust, pure as a drop of dew on a lotus leaf, and it sheds lustre in all directions when held on the palm in sunlight.

An emerald is rich in its luminous quality and is radiant like the sun, as is Mercury itself. Its specific gravity is 2.65 to 2.75, hardness is from 7.50 to 8, and refractive index is 1.56 to 1.59.

FLAWS OF EMERALDS

1. brittleness
2. lack of water or glittering look, lustre, luminescence; gem looks dry
3. micaceous glitter due to the presence of mica; mica particles clearly visible
4. presence of a hole
5. fissure in the surface
6. dullness; devoid of inner glow
7. unevenness of color
8. graininess
9. odd form, flatness, unevenness, depression
10. black or yellow spots
11. foreign matter inside the crystalline structure
12. brown or blackish yellow color
13. harsh appearance
14. smokiness
15. emitting bluish reflection
16. low specific gravity
17. concavity or dent in surface

Such stones have no merit and should be discarded. A real emerald of a good size is rare and it is almost impossible to find an eyeglass-clear emerald. It is known for its ability to neutralize poison. Flaws in an emerald create problems and that is why one should not wear the following:

1. An emerald that is devoid of water and is dry harms one's pets, cattle, horses, and other animals.

2. An emerald that has spots of black or other colors harms one's spouse.
3. An emerald that has a smoky substance, micaceous glitter, threads, or visible lines like feathers inside destroys the clan and is harmful to progeny.
4. An emerald having a cobweb is harmful to one's physical well-being.
5. An emerald having uneven color or two colors is harmful to vitality and intelligence.
6. An emerald with a red spot destroys wealth.
7. An emerald having a drop like the honey drop is inauspicious for one's mother and father.
8. An emerald having a dent creates fear.
9. An emerald having a yellow spot is harmful for one's son.

If, however, Mercury is positioned with Rahu, Mars, Saturn, or Ketu in the first house, one can wear an emerald with flaws, and it will give benefic results.

IDENTIFICATION OF REAL EMERALDS

1. If a real emerald is placed in a glass pot with water it radiates green light, whereas the imitation does not.
2. If a real emerald is placed on a piece of white cloth in such a way that its reflected light can be seen, it reflects green light and the spot where the light falls looks like a green patch of cloth.
3. If a real emerald is placed on the eyes it gives a cool feeling, whereas an imitation becomes warm very quickly.
4. If an imitation emerald is rubbed against a piece of turmeric root it makes the turmeric red, whereas a real emerald does not.
5. A drop of water on a real gemstone retains its shape and does not spread around like water. Even moving and inverting the gemstone does not harm the drop, whereas in an imitation it does not remain a drop but spreads like water.
6. When rubbed against a piece of wood an imitation becomes shinier whereas the real emerald does not.
7. In an imitation there are white spots.
8. An imitation emerald has a bright rather than pale hue.
9. The specific gravity of an imitation is lower than that of a real emerald.
10. The refractive index of an imitation is lower than that of the real gemstone.

CLASSIFICATION OF EMERALDS

1. Brahmin: An emerald of the color of the sirish flower (Albizzia procera) is best suited for learned and spiritually inclined people.
2. Kshatriya: An emerald of deep green color like a blade of grass is best suited for rulers.
3. Vaishya: An emerald of yellowish green color like the color of a parrot is best suited for persons of the merchant class, businessmen, and traders.
4. Shudra: An emerald of dark green is best suited for people belonging to the service class.

Besides these colors, emeralds are also found in the green color that is similar to the green found in peacock feathers; this color is very good for financial gain and therefore auspicious for merchants and traders.

RITUALS FOR WEARING AN EMERALD

An emerald should be bought on a Wednesday when the Sun is in the northern quarter in an ascending cycle. The gem should be bought and given to the jeweler two hours after sunrise. The emerald in the ring should be set when Ashlekha, Jyeshtha, Revti, or Rohini nakshatra is present—on a Wednesday, Friday, or Saturday when Virgo or Gemini is rising on the horizon.

The weight of the gemstone emerald should not be less than three rattikas. It should be set in gold during the morning hours. The stone should be mounted with an open back so that the stone touches the skin.

The best time to wear the ring is two hours after sunrise.

Before wearing the ring for the first time it should be kept immersed for some time in raw cow's milk. Then it should be washed with Ganga-water, spring water, rainwater, or water kept in a copper pot. After it has been washed the ring should be kept in a green cloth on which a Mercury Yantra is drawn with red sandalwood paste, roli, or saffron. An engraved yantra of Mercury on a bronze plate or an idol of Mercury made of bronze should be placed on the green cloth on which the yantra is drawn. As an idol needs proper invocation and worship by a priest, a yantra is better, because the worship of a yantra can be done by the person who will wear the ring. The ring should be placed before the yantra engraved on a bronze plate and flowers and incense should be offered to the yantra. The engraved yantra and the gemstone in the ring should then be worshiped by reciting the mantra of Mercury:

ॐ बुं बुधाय नमः ॐ

AUM BUM BUDHAYE NAMAH AUM

The mantra should be recited either 108 or 4,000 times and then one should meditate on the gemstone as a symbol of Mercury. After meditation one should wear the ring on the little finger or the ring finger of the right hand.

Afterwards the yantra should be wrapped in the green cloth and either donated to a priest or kept in a shrine.

The yantra to be drawn on the cloth and engraved on the bronze plate is the same, as follows:

9	4	11
10	8	6
5	12	7

The worship should be done facing East, North, or Northeast. The person worshiping should use a green straw mat, a green woolen cloth, or a green blanket.

MEDICINAL UTILITY OF THE EMERALD

For purification of an emerald the nontransparent but clear pieces of emerald (without red, black, or yellow spots) should be boiled in the concentrated solution of kulthi beans (*Dolichos biflorus*). Kulthi beans are similar in shape to moong beans. They are useful for sufferers of kidney stone and are used as dal (bean soup). The soup should be strained and boiled to make it more concentrated. To make the soup the beans are boiled in plain water, without salt or spices. The concentrated soup then should be added to a pot and the pieces of emerald should be suspended in the soup,

Emerald/Mercury: Who Should Wear an Emerald

Ascendant/Ruler	Mercury is Natural Ruler of	Relationship of Mercury with the Ruler of the Ascendant	Nature of the House Ruled by Mercury	Suitability/Unsuitability of the Emerald & its Effects
Aries/Mars	3rd house 6th house	Enemy	Inauspicious Inauspicious	Not suitable. If Mercury is in 3rd or 6th house, use emerald during major & subperiods of Mercury.
Taurus/Venus	2nd house 5th house	Friend	Auspicious Auspicious	Suitable & beneficial. Gives good fortune, intelligence, and benefits to children.
Gemini/Mercury	1st house 4th house	Mercury Himself is the Ruler	Auspicious Auspicious	Suitable & beneficial. Works as a talisman, protects, gives good health, wealth, property, domestic happiness, success in education & career. Especially beneficial during major & subperiods of Mercury.
Cancer/Moon	3rd house 12th house	Enemy	Inauspicious Inauspicious	Not suitable. Mercury is natural ruler of two inauspicious houses and an enemy of the moon. But if Mercury is in 3rd or 12th house, emerald can be used during major & subperiods of Mercury.
Leo/Sun	2nd house 11th house	Friend	Auspicious Auspicious	Suitable only in the major & subperiods of Mercury to gain harmony in domestic life, good name & fame. One can also use emerald if Mercury is in the 2nd or 11th house.
Virgo/Mercury	1st house 10th house	Mercury Himself is the Ruler	Auspicious Auspicious	Suitable & beneficial. Serves as a talisman. Gives health, wealth, happiness, success, good name, and honor.

Sign/Ruler	House	Relationship	Auspicious/Inauspicious	Notes
Libra/Venus	9th house	Friend	Auspicious	Suitable & beneficial during the major & sub-periods of Mercury. Can be worn with a diamond in the same setting for lifelong benefit.
	12th house		Inauspicious	
Scorpio/Mars	8th house	Enemy	Inauspicious	Not suitable. If necessary can be worn in major & subperiods of Mercury or if Mercury is in the 2nd, 4th, 5th, 9th, 10th or 11th house.
	11th house		Auspicious	
Sagittarius/Jupiter	7th house	Neutral	Auspicious	Not suitable, especially if Mercury is in the 7th house. If Mercury is in the 2nd, 4th, 5th, 9th or 10th house, emerald can be used during major & subperiods of Mercury.
	10th house		Auspicious	
Capricorn/Saturn	6th house	Friend	Inauspicious	Suitable, especially during the major and sub-periods of Mercury.
	9th house		Auspicious	
Aquarius/Saturn	5th house	Friend	Auspicious	Suitable. Brings more benefit if it is worn in the same setting with blue sapphire.
	8th house		Inauspicious	
Pisces/Jupiter	4th house	Neutral	Auspicious	Suitable only in the major & subperiods of Mercury, or if Mercury is in the 2nd, 4th, 5th, 9th, 10th or 11th house.
	8th house		Auspicious	

The 2nd and 7th houses are both auspicious but also death-inflicting houses, especially during the major or sub-periods of the planets that rule them. If the ruling planet is benefic and a friend of the ruler of the ascendant, that aspect can be lessened.

as mentioned before. Especially fine emerald pieces should be tied in a cloth, suspended as shown in daula yantra for ruby, pearls, or corals, and boiled in kulthi soup for twelve hours. Then they should be taken out and washed with spring water or rainwater.

Emerald Oxide

Purified emerald pieces or purified dust of emeralds obtained from the factories where the gemstones are cut and polished should be ground with the juice of manphal (or emetic nut, see glossary) and ground ginger to make a thick paste. The paste should then be made into the form of a tablet and dried in the sun. The method of sarva samput explained above should be used. The dried tablet should be placed in the clay pots and covered as usual and sealed. The cloth soaked in clay should be wrapped as explained in the process described for other gemstones and fired in a gajput or potter's kiln.

Another method is to take powdered purified emeralds, sulphur, and two forms of arsenic known as mansel and hartal in equal proportions. Grind the mixture with the juice of a jackfruit in a simak mortar. After the paste is fine enough and thick, a tablet should be made and dried in the sun. The tablet should be placed in clay pots, as explained in sarva samput, and after the sarva samput is dry it should be fired in a gajput or a potter's kiln. If the gajput method is to be used, two kilograms of dried cowdung should be used for each firing. The process of firing should be repeated eight times. If a kiln is used the sarva samput should be opened after it has become cool, to determine whether the oxide is fine or not. If not, the ingredients should be ground again with jackfruit juice and the process should be repeated until a nice fine oxide of emerald is obtained.

Dosage: ½ to 1 rattika with honey and ground pipal.

This oxide increases ojas (radiance), cures fever, coma, vomiting, thirst, problems created by any kind of poisoning, aggravated bile, acidity, asthma, jaundice, constipation, hemorrhoids, and swellings of the internal organs. Because the oxide of emerald is cold in nature it is very suitable for people with hot temperament. It also cures weakness of the heart and the stomach. It is a very useful remedy for tuberculosis, diabetes, and urinary troubles. The oxide of emerald increases memory, provides longevity, and is an effective remedy for snakebite. It also cures problems caused by evil spirits and by the planet Mercury.

Emerald Paste

Purified pieces of emerald should be ground with either sandalwood water, kewra water, or rose water. If desired, the three distillates can be mixed together in equal proportions. Then the pieces of emerald should be crushed into small particles and ground in a simak, kasauti, or agate mortar. The grinding requires fifteen days of work, at twelve hours per day, for a total of 180 hours.

The ground powder should be so fine that it should not hurt the eye tissues if applied directly to the eyes. The test is when the paste is dried in the sun and the powder is made: the powder should fly like dust and its smoothness can be felt when the pestle moves around on it.

The powder thus obtained should be stored in an emerald-green bottle in a cool, dry place.

Dosage: ½ to 1 rattika twice a day with 1 tsp. honey, amla jam, rose petal jam, or chyavan prash to which a finely ground powder of pipal is added and used whenever needed for the following (please see glossary for unfamiliar terms):

1. Kidney stone—with honey and pipal
2. Kidney disorders—with chyavan prash
3. Frequent urination—with rose petals
4. Piles—with malai (skim of milk)
5. Colic pains—with honey
6. Leucoderma (disease of the skin pigment)—with chyavan prash
7. Muteness—with honey
8. Deafness—with honey
9. Impurities of the blood—with amla jam
10. Fever—with honey
11. Fistula in anus—with honey or malai (skim of milk)
12. Jaundice—with amla jam
13. Bleeding—with honey
14. Dysentery—with amla jam
15. Cough—with honey. If cough is dry, use with malai.
16. Vomiting—with honey
17. Poisoning—with honey or malai
18. Coma—with honey
19. Swelling of internal organs—with honey

20. Indigestion—with honey and triphala choorna (powder)
21. Heart troubles—with sarpgandha powder
22. Wet dreams—with triphala powder

The emerald is cool and increases the appetite. It is good for female diseases. It increases vitality and improves physical beauty, and gives radiance and a healthy glow to the skin. It cures acidity and neurosis, and it is also good for the eyesight. Special surma (eye powder) with emerald is also available. For those who are overly thin emerald paste is very valuable: it increases their body fat and makes them healthy looking.

SOURCES OF EMERALDS

India: In ancient Indian scriptures the sites quoted for the emerald are as follows: the Maha Nadi (the word *nadi* means river. Emeralds were found in the mountains near these rivers), the Son Nadi, Gandak, the Sindh Nadi, the Himalayas, and the Girnar mountains of Mount Abu.

Emeralds found nowadays in Udaipur (Rajasthan) have a dark color but are very brittle. Emeralds found in Ajmer are of a pale green color and are very attractive, but as the color is not so deeply green they are not among the most highly priced emeralds. Some of these emeralds are of very good quality, but much care is needed in carving them into first-grade gemstones.

The emeralds found in Rajgarh mines have a rich and attractive yellowish tinge and are in no way inferior to Colombian emeralds.

Pakistan: Emeralds found in Pakistan are deep green and brittle.

Colombia: These are compact and rich in color and lustre. The old mines produced more lustrous and better colored emeralds than those of the new mines. A new product of Colombian mines, known as trapiche, is found in the form of six buds and is less flawed.

Africa: African emeralds are dark in shade and have many black spots. Their color is very much like the color of green beer bottles. The emeralds found in Kenya are similar to Colombian emeralds— soft and clean. Sendewana emeralds from Africa are the finest;

they have good color and resemble the oriental gems. Emeralds from Tanzania, Zambia, and Mozambique are not good to use because they have black spots. Rhodesian emeralds are small and not lustrous.

Egypt: These are pale and often cloudy.

Brazil: These are yellowish and have many cracks. They also are brittle. The emeralds obtained from karniba mines are nice and of superior quality.

Soviet Union: Those found in the Ural Mountains are more lustrous than Rhodesian and Brazilian emeralds, but they are less attractive than Colombian emeralds and different in texture.

Afghanistan: Those found recently in Kabul forests are of good quality, transparent, and like the old oriental emeralds.

Jagat Seth emeralds: These are said to be the emeralds of finest quality. They were brought by a foreigner from an unknown location and sold to the wealthy gemologist Jagat Seth.

Cup Emeralds: These are emeralds of the finest quality and are shaped from the broken cups of the Mughal emperor Humayun.

Synthetic emeralds: These also are on the market, and Linde Hydrothermal emeralds are the best in quality and beauty but are of no other value than show value. The best synthetic gems are made with corundum.

Doublets and Soude emeralds: These are made of two pieces of real rock crystal cemented with a thin layer of gelatin. Lucknow cutters make soude emeralds that remain their original color for a longer duration than other Soude emeralds. They exhibit a good emerald-green color because of the dye used.

Jupiter is masculine, disciplined, cooperative, and priestly. Commonly known as the teacher of the gods, it is a giant, self-illuminating planet, radiating (like a teacher) more energy than it receives. Jupiter is shown riding a white elephant, the largest mammal living on earth. In one hand he holds a scroll of sacred knowledge, in another hand a disc of Vishnu to cut through illusions. In his third hand he holds a conch shell symbolizing the sacred sounds (mantra vidya), and with his fourth hand he bestows his blessing. Jupiter rules the region between the waist and the thighs and influences the bodily elements of fat and mucous.

7

Jupiter and
Its Gemstone,
Yellow Sapphire

पतिंतायां हिमाद्रौतु त्वचस्तक्य सुरद्विष:
प्रादुर्भवन्ति ताम्यस्तु पुष्वरागा महागुणा:।

JUPITER IN SANSKRIT is known as Brahaspati or Guru. In the *Taittiriya Upanishad* Jupiter is said to be the intellect and speech of the Virat Purusha, the Cosmic Body. In the *Brihat Parasara Hora* (1.26.31) he is said to be the dwarf incarnation of Vishnu. In the *Vishnu Purana* he is said to be Brahma. Sometimes he is identified with Ganapati (Ganesh), and sometimes with Angiras (the priest of the gods and lord of sacrifices). There is also a story that the wife of Angiras gave birth to Brahaspati (Jupiter), who is the presiding deity of mental powers and the teacher of gods. He is the teacher of the science of light, that is, astrology and astronomy. He is the ruler of the Sun and the Moon and controls the movement of the planets.

In the *Rig Veda* Brahaspati is said to be born in the sky with seven faces and seven rays. Brahaspati defeats his enemies and breaks their forts. No ritual sacrifice can be complete without invoking this teacher of gods. He is the seer who perceived and wrote one of the hymns of the *Rig Veda* (10.72).

In the *Skanda Purana* it is said that Brahaspati worshiped Shiva for a thousand years and as a reward Shiva made him the planet Jupiter.

The *Brahaspati Samhita*, a book of law and politics, is attributed to him. Only a fragment of this large collection of teachings of Brahaspati is available now.

Jupiter is a sattvik and benefic planet, significator of luck and fortune, and he rules religion, philosophy, spirituality, wealth, and progeny. He is noble, buoyant, dignified, fruitful, optimistic, jovial, and masculine. If favorable, this planet gives name, fame, success, honor, wealth, progeny and good relationship with progeny, and it brings benefits to whatever planets or house it is associated with.

The color of Jupiter is yellow. Thursday is his day, and northeast is his direction. He is big, old looking, and has a pot belly. He is self-illuminating (this is said also in Western astronomy). One of his names is Guru, which means "heavy" (in weight) and also "teacher."

Through the placement of Jupiter in a birth chart we know about the benefits earned by a native from the karmas of his past lives. Jupiter also affects long-distance travel, wisdom, truthfulness, morality, charity, benevolence, compassion, and meditation.

Jupiter is exalted in Cancer and the sign of its fall is Capricorn. It gives good results when placed in Sagittarius or Pisces. The best house for Jupiter is the fourth house, where it gets directional strength.

Sun, Mars, and the Moon are its friends. Mercury and Venus are its enemies. Rahu, Ketu, and Saturn are neutral in friendship. Its signs of detriment are Gemini and Virgo. In the Uttra Phalguni, Uttrakshad, Punarvasu, Purva Bhadrapad, and Vishakha nakshatras it gives benefic effects.

Jupiter is very important for a female, because it determines her marriage and her relationship with her husband.

Jupiter rules over the liver, thighs, circulation of blood in arteries, and fat in the human organism. It rules over gold and bronze in metals, wheat and barley in grains, yellow flowers, fruits of yellow color, onions, and garlic.

Jupiter influences people during the fifteenth, sixteenth, twenty-second, and fortieth year of age, and it is said that if Jupiter is posited in the first, fourth, seventh, or tenth house in a positive (unafflicted) manner, it can save the native from the evil effects of all planets.

All people with high ambitions, calm persons, priests, religious teachers, politicians, ministers, foreigners, and persons in the legal profession are influenced by Jupiter.

Diseases connected with an afflicted or wrongly posited Jupiter are liver ailments, jaundice, arthritis, dropsy, dyspepsia, disorders of the pancreas, catarrh, abcesses, and carbuncles. It can give diseases of phlegm, swelling, and tuberculosis when afflicted.

THE YELLOW SAPPHIRE

The yellow sapphire is known as pushparaga in Sanskrit and pukhraj in Hindi. A gem of the corundum family, yellow sapphire is a twin of ruby and blue sapphire. It is found in yellow, golden, and orange colors, as well as in a colorless variety known as white sapphire. The best gem is said to be of lemon-yellow color. The color in yellow sapphire is due to the presence of iron and titanium.

For gaining the favor of the planet Jupiter, scriptures recommend that one select a pukhraj that is transparent, even, smooth, yellow like the color of the Cascaria ovata flower, and with a tenuous lustre that sparkles.

QUALITIES OF A GOOD YELLOW SAPPHIRE

1. heaviness or high specific gravity that can be felt when placed on the palm
2. rich velvety lustre that can be seen with the naked eye
3. transparency, which makes it clean and pure
4. evenness in surface, without any variation in thickness
5. uniformity of color, without any layers
6. solidity, hardness
7. self-luminous quality: it should emit light all over its surface
8. smooth feel
9. regular shape
10. pleasant appearance

FLAWS OF A YELLOW SAPPHIRE

1. dullness—harmful for health
2. crack inside the gem—creates fear of thieves
3. milky appearance inside—harmful for progeny
4. flimsy inside the substance of the gem—brings injuries
5. dents or pits—bring bad luck and poverty
6. visible stains or black spots—gives sorrow
7. asymmetrical shape—brings bad luck
8. a hole, slit, or cavity inside the gem—brings poverty and bad luck
9. fibers in the texture—create problems in the family
10. roughness in touch—brings ill luck
11. dry-looking, because of the lack of fire and water—brings disease
12. mixed color, brownish color, or dark yellow—brings suffering
13. grainy surface—brings bad luck
14. red spots—bring poverty and destroy wealth
15. black spots—bring sorrow and destroy pets and cattle
16. white spots—shorten life span

IDENTIFICATION OF A REAL YELLOW SAPPHIRE

1. When placed on a white cloth and exposed to sunlight, it gives yellow hue to the spot where the light is reflected.
2. If kept in milk for twenty-four hours it does not change color.
3. It cures poisonous insect bites immediately if rubbed on the afflicted area.
4. All other gems of the same color and appearance have lower specific gravity, are less hard, and have a different refractive index than the yellow sapphire.
5. It increases in brilliance when rubbed on a touchstone.
6. The lustre of a synthetic gem resembles the lustre of glass.
7. A synthetic gem becomes warm soon when placed on the eyelids.
8. The milky spots in a synthetic gem are dry and without brilliance, whereas in a real gem these milky spots are rich in flicker and lustre and have the gleam of fresh cow's milk.

CLASSIFICATION OF YELLOW SAPPHIRES

1. Brahmin: White-colored—best suited for spiritually inclined and learned people
2. Kshatriya: Rose-colored and pink-tinted gems—best suited for rulers

3. Vaishya: Yellow- or golden-colored gems—best suited for merchant class
4. Shudra: Dark green variety—best suited for serving class

RITUALS FOR WEARING A YELLOW SAPPHIRE

A yellow sapphire should be bought on a Thursday, in an ascending cycle of the Moon and when Pushya Nakshatra is present. If the nakshatra is not Pushya, then Punarvasu, Vishakha, or Purva Bhadrapad are also auspicious for buying a yellow sapphire. The gem should be given to the jeweler on the same day, between sunrise and 11:00 A.M.

The weight of the gem should not be less than three rattikas. The ring should be set in gold and polished and finished the same day as mentioned above. One should not wear a pukhraj (yellow sapphire) of six, eleven, or fifteen rattikas. A pukhraj of five, seven, eight, ten, twelve, or fourteen rattikas is considered auspicious.

The best time to wear a pukhraj ring is in the early morning.

Before wearing the ring for the first time it should be immersed in cow's milk for a few minutes and then it should be washed in rainwater, spring water, or water kept in a copper pot over night. After it has been washed, the ring should be placed on a yellow cloth upon which a Jupiter Yantra has been drawn with roli and a yantra (or idol of Jupiter in gold) engraved on a silver plate should be placed on the same cloth. As described above, because an idol needs special worship it is advised that one use a yantra engraved on a silver plate. One should offer flowers and incense to the engraved yantra and to the stone that has been set in the ring and then recite the mantra of Jupiter:

$$\text{ॐ बृं बृहस्पतये नमः ॐ}$$

AUM BRIM BRAHASPATAYE NAMAH AUM

The mantra should be recited either 108 or 19,000 times, as prescribed, and then the wearer should meditate on the gemstone as a symbol of Lord Jupiter. After meditation the ring should be worn on the first finger, which is the Jupiter finger, otherwise on the ring finger of the right hand.

In the case of an idol the Homa with the same mantra repeated

Yellow Sapphire/Jupiter: Who Should Wear a Yellow Sapphire

Ascendant/Ruler	Jupiter is Natural Ruler of	Relationship of Jupiter with the Ruler of the Ascendant	Nature of the House Ruled by Jupiter	Suitability/Unsuitability of the Yellow Sapphire & its Effects
Aries/Mars	9th house 12th house	Friend	Auspicious Inauspicious	Suitable. Gives religious tendency, good fortune, wealth, honor, intelligence, good name, fame, and charitable nature. Good for progress.
Taurus/Venus	8th house 11th house	Enemy	Inauspicious Auspicious	Not suitable. Wear only during the major & sub-periods of Jupiter for financial gain.
Gemini/Mercury	7th house 10th house	Enemy	Auspicious Auspicious	Not suitable, except when Jupiter is in the 7th or 10th house. Beneficial during major & subperiods of Jupiter. If yellow sapphire is not suitable, it should be given away or donated to one's teacher.
Cancer/Moon	6th house 9th house	Friend	Inauspicious Auspicious	Suitable & beneficial. Brings good fortune, good name, fame, good progeny, religious attitude. Especially good during the major & subperiods of Jupiter.
Leo/Sun	5th house 8th house	Friend	Auspicious Inauspicious	Suitable & beneficial. Wear especially during major & subperiods of Jupiter. If possible, wear in the same setting with ruby.
Virgo/Mercury	4th house 7th house	Enemy	Auspicious Auspicious	Suitable only in major & subperiods of Jupiter. Especially beneficial if Jupiter is in 4th house. Elderly people of this ascendant should avoid use of yellow sapphire.

Sign/Ruler	House	Relationship	Auspicious/Inauspicious	Description
Libra/Venus	3rd house 6th house	Enemy	Inauspicious Auspicious	Not suitable, except when Jupiter is in his own 3rd or 6th house. Wear only during the major & subperiods of Jupiter.
Scorpio/Mars	2nd house 5th house	Friend	Auspicious Auspicious	Suitable & beneficial. Especially beneficial in the major & subperiods of Jupiter. Elderly people should see if the yellow sapphire suits or not.
Sagittarius/Jupiter	1st house Ascendant 4th house	Jupiter Himself is the Ruler	Auspicious Auspicious	Suitable & beneficial. Wear it throughout life. Meditate on the gem after waking up in the morning before starting the day. Yellow sapphire brings good fortune.
Capricorn/Saturn	3rd house 12th house	Enemy Neutral	Inauspicious Inauspicious	Not suitable. Wear only during the major & subperiods of Jupiter if Jupiter is in the 3rd or 12th house.
Aquarius/Saturn	2nd house 11th house	Enemy Neutral	Auspicious Auspicious	Not suitable. Wear only during the major & subperiods of Jupiter when Jupiter is in his sign in 5th house.
Pisces/Jupiter	1st house Ascendant 10th house	Jupiter Himself is the Ruler	Auspicious Auspicious	Suitable & beneficial, especially when Jupiter is in the 10th house. Wearing yellow sapphire is a must during the major & subperiods of Jupiter. Wear throughout life.

The 2nd and 7th houses are both auspicious but also death-inflicting houses, especially during the major or sub-periods of the planets that rule them. If the ruling planet is benefic and a friend of the ruler of the ascendant, that aspect can be lessened.

1,900 times is necessary. After worship is completed the idol and its asana should be donated to the priest. In the case of an engraved yantra no Homa is required and the yantra can either be donated to a priest or kept in one's personal shrine.

The yantra that needs to be drawn on the cloth and on the silver plate is the same numerical yantra and is as follows:

10	5	12
11	9	7
6	13	8

The worship should be done facing northeast, sitting on a yellow asana made of wool. First, the engraved yantra should be washed and dried with a clean yellow cloth. Then it should be honored by a tilak of yellow sandalwood ground with saffron and camphor or with roli. Then flowers and incense should be offered and the ring placed on the cloth on which the yantra is drawn before it is put on the engraved yantra. The gemstone set in the ring should also be honored with a tilak. Then the mantra recitation should be done, followed by meditation on the engraved yantra and the gemstone; then the ring should be worn.

A ring worn in this manner brings good luck, peace, and prosperity. Pukhraj (yellow sapphire) bestows vigor, vitality, wisdom, longevity, name, and fame. If someone is having problems in finding a good mate for their daughter that problem will also be solved.

One who wears yellow sapphire progresses in the spiritual field and becomes free of all fears of evil vibrations, ghosts, and genii. Disease and madness caused by afflicted planets also are cured. As long as the ring is on one's hand one will never die an accidental death.

MEDICINAL UTILITY OF THE YELLOW SAPPHIRE

For preparation of the medicinal bhasma (oxides) and pishthi (paste/ powder), nontransparent but clean, unspotted pieces of pukhraj should be selected. One can also use the small pieces and dust of the gem, which are of no use to jewelers. This can be obtained from the factories where the gems are cut and polished. These pieces then should be tied in a cloth and boiled in kulthi extract (as described in the chapter on emeralds) in a daula yantra for three days and three nights.

Another method is to prepare kanji by boiling 1 kilogram of rice in 16 kilograms of water. The water should be strained after the rice is boiled and cooked. The rice should be discarded (it can be fed to birds or cattle) and the strained water should be again boiled to evaporate one-quarter of the water. Three-quarters of the water remaining after evaporation should be kept in a clay or porcelain pot and about one tablespoon of rock salt should be added to it. Then this water should be allowed to ferment for three days. After it starts smelling sour (not too sour) it should be used for purifying the pukhraj. The rice water should be mixed with an equal amount of fresh water and placed in a daula yantra, and the gems tied in a cloth should be suspended in the mixture and boiled for three days and three nights.

Pukhraj Oxide

After the pieces of yellow sapphire are purified they should be ground to make a powder from them. This can be done in an iron mortar, because if it is ground in a simak or any other stone mortar it will ruin the mortar. Then take powdered sulphur, hartal, and mansel in equal proportions and mix the powdered yellow sapphire equal in weight to the sulphur or one-third of the total weight of the mixture of sulphur, hartal, and mansel. Grind the entire mixture in the juice of a fully ripe jackfruit in a simak or any other stone mortar, such as kasauti or agate. Grind the mixture for twelve days, at eight hours a day for a total of ninety-six hours. Make a tablet from the paste and dry it in the sun. Then use the gajput method of firing and seal the tablet in a sarva samput, as described in the section on emerald oxide. Five kilograms of dried cowdung cakes should be used for firing the pukhraj. Repeat the process of firing eight times. A potter's kiln can also be used for firing the pukhraj. Each time the sarva samput has to be made fresh and fired either in a gajput or a kiln until a nice white oxide is obtained.

Dosage: 1/2 to 1 rattika in 1 tsp. honey.

This oxide is a vermicide; it also increases bile and gives strength. It is good for problems created by poisons. It cures vomiting and problems created by aggravated wind and mucus. It cures burning sensations, problems of the blood, hemorrhoids, and leprosy, and it strengthens gastric fire; it cures jaundice, gastritis, constipation, flatulence, cough, colds, asthma, nosebleed, apoplexy, tumors, tuberculosis, general debility, and ailments caused by loss of seminal fluid. It also cures problems created by an afflicted Jupiter.

Pukhraj Pishthi (Paste or Powder)

Powder the purified pukhraj with rose water or kewra water or with the extracts of sandalwood, rose water, and kewra water mixed in equal proportions. Grind it in any of the three mortars used for grinding ruby for 15 days, at 8 hours per day for a total of 120 hours.

Some Unani hakims make a mixture of rose water, kewra water, and sandalwood extract and heat the pieces of pukhraj. They dip them in this mixture ten to twenty times and then pulverize them in the same mixture of rose, kewra, and sandalwood.

When the paste is so fine that it can be used in the eyes without hurting them, it is ready. The pishthi is then dried in the shade and powdered. Pukhraj pishthi is much milder than its oxide and does not increase or aggravate bile.

Dosage: 1/2 to 1 rattika with 1 tsp. honey or other suitable adjuncts as necessary, twice a day.

For mucus that is dry and needs to be expelled from the system, the pishthi mixed with malai (skim of milk) is best. A pinch of ground red cardamom can be added to increase the effect. For mucus that needs to be dried, a pinch of freshly ground black pepper should be added to the honey. For mucus that creates congestion in the lungs and causes difficulty in breathing, about ten to fifteen drops of juice of fresh ginger could be added. For patients suffering from asthma it should be given with honey and sitopiladi (see the chapter on coral for description of sitopiladi).

For colds, mix with honey and a pinch of fine-ground fresh black pepper. For general debility it should be used with honey, and after the medicine the patient should drink cow's milk that is as fresh and warm as possible (warm from the body temperature of the cow, not from heating).

For weakness caused by a loss of semen, the pishthi should be used with honey, and then the patient should drink milk boiled with dates with a pinch of fine-ground saffron added to the milk before drinking. Adding almond paste to the milk would also provide additional help, if the patient has a good digestive system.

For vomiting the paste can be given with honey and a pinch of fine-ground red cardamom seeds. For poisons it should be administered with sweet cow's butter or ghee and rock sugar candy.

In tuberculosis where the lungs are infected it should be given with honey to which a pinch of freshly ground black pepper is added. In leprosy, pukhraj pishthi should be administered with ghee and fine-ground rock sugar candy. In hemorrhoids it should be given with malai.

In all other diseases mentioned before under pukhraj, oxide pishthi should be given with honey.

CHIEF SOURCES OF YELLOW SAPPHIRES

Like other members of the corundum family, pukhraj is also found as crystals in rocks of limestone and schists and in riverbeds and streams.

The primary sources in India, as mentioned in its ancient scriptures, are the Mahanadi and Brahmputra rivers, the Himalayas, the Vindhyachal Mountains, Orissa, Bengal, and Kashmir.

The best yellow sapphires, famous for their lustre, smoothness, brilliance, and transparence, come from Mogok, situated in the upper region of Burma. It is a pity that the stone is not found in sufficient quantities in these mines.

Sri Lanka produces sapphires in yellow, light green, and colorless varieties in sufficient quantities. These sapphires are of somewhat inferior quality to the Burmese pukhraj, because of lack of water and fire, that is, lustre and brilliance. In the Western world they are renowned as "oriental topaz."

Yellow and white varieties are also found in Indochina, in New South Wales and Queensland in Australia, and in Zimbabwe.

Yellow, smoky yellow, blackish, and colorless white sapphires are also found in Thailand. They are hard and lustrous and are sold at a very high price when flawless.

Light blue and light green varieties of sapphires are also obtained from the granite caves of the Ural mountains in the U.S.S.R.

Good quality sapphires in shades of yellow, green, pink, red, blue, violet, and white (colorless) are found in abundance in Brazil.

Venus is feminine, hedonistic, beautiful, and attracting. It rules over the sensuous side of human nature. Venus is shown riding a horse, like a romantic hero. He is famous as the teacher of demons (anti-gods). In one hand he holds scrolls, because he is a writer of scriptures, and in another hand a sword to overcome obstacles. In his third hand he holds a lotus of purity, and in his fourth hand the reins of the horse of heroic desires.

8
Venus and
Its Gemstone,
Diamond

तस्यास्थिलेशों निपपातयेषु भुवः प्रदेशेषु कथंचिदेव,
वज्राणि वज्रायुध निर्जिगीषोर्भवन्ति नानाकृति मन्तितेषु ॥

VENUS, known as Shukra in Hindu mythology, is the son of
the great seer Bhrigu. Bhrigu was an astrologer and taught
his son all of the spiritual sciences and scriptures. Because
of Shukra's enmity toward Brahaspati (Jupiter), he (Shukra) agreed
to be the teacher of the asuras (antigods). As mentioned above,
Jupiter is the teacher of the gods. When Shukra (Venus) became
the preceptor of the antigods, in order to protect them against the
gods and subgods he worshiped Shiva and learned from him the
method by which he could bring them back to life even after they
were killed in battle: the great science of reviving the dead, called
mrityu sanjivini vidya.

Shukra in Sanskrit means "semen," and Venus is the presiding
deity of semen. In the visible world his form is the planet Venus.

The planet Venus is feminine, watery, and gentle. Rajasik in nature, it belongs to the brahmin caste, and is described as a youth
of fair complexion, with curly hair, attractive eyes, radiant body,
and a sensual nature. An embodiment of love, he is a benefic planet

and governs the refined attributes, romance, beauty, sensuality, passion, sexual pleasure, marriage, love matters, comforts, luxuries, jewelry, wealth, prosperity, art, music, dance, theater, actors, poets, musicians, the season of spring, rains, aquatic creatures, and bedroom. In the body he rules over the reproductive system, eyes, throat, chin, cheeks, and kidneys.

As a benefic planet Venus enhances the house in which it is posited and is a good influence on planets it aspects and on the planets that are associated with it.

Venus is also important because of its association with the science of mantras and medicine, Tantra, the casting of spells, hypnotism, mesmerism, and alchemy.

It rules the second and seventh houses of every native's horoscope—the houses of wealth and of conjugal relationship, respectively—the two very important houses of worldly life. Like its opponent Jupiter it is also a wealth-giving planet.

Mercury and Saturn are its friends and the Sun and Moon are its enemies. Mars and Jupiter are neutral in friendship to Venus even though Venus considers Jupiter its enemy. Taurus and Libra are the zodiacal signs whom Venus rules, and Venus gives good results when placed in these signs. It is exalted in Pisces and fallen in Virgo.

When rightly aspected Venus is strong, and it brings wealth, comfort, attraction to the opposite sex in the early part of life, a well-proportioned body, and the attractive features necessary for a sensuous nature. It makes its natives tender, gentle, and considerate; lovers of jewelry, sour (pungent) taste, white dress, decoration, perfume, tasty food, and the fine arts. It inspires them to be poets, musicians, and seekers of truth and knowledge (secret sciences). The native loves the company of the members of the opposite sex, artists, and musicians.

When afflicted or ill-aspected, Venus creates problems in marriage. It causes diseases of the eyes, ovaries, and mucous membranes. The native may suffer from gout, Bright's disease, cysts, swelling of the internal organs, anemia, complications caused by overindulgence in sex, amusement, eating and drinking, venereal disease, seminal diseases like spermatorrhoea (in which semen gets into the urine or feces), nocturnal emission, sterility, and discharge of semen with urine.

The nakshatras connected with Venus are Bharni, Purva, Phalguni, and Purva-shada.

Sagittarius and Capricorn are its friendly signs and Cancer and
Leo its enemy signs.

Venus becomes fruitless when posited in the fifth house and inauspicious in the seventh house. It is best placed in the fourth
house, where it receives directional strength. Its greatest influence
on an individual extends from the ages of twenty-five to twenty-
seven.

Venus rules over queens, persons employed in the hotel business,
sweet-makers, white flowers and fruits, white horses and elephants,
silk, jewelry, rock sugar candy, rice, and cotton.

Venus gives a mucus-dominated body chemistry.

Its metal is silver, day is Friday, and direction is southeast. Those
born on the sixth, fifteenth, or twenty-fourth day of any month
are influenced by Venus.

THE DIAMOND

The gemstone of Venus is the diamond, which is known as vajra
in Sanskrit and heera in Hindi.

The diamond is pure carbon, having the most compact arrangement of carbon atoms found in nature. It occurs as isometric crystals or crystalline masses, both colorless and with tints of pink,
brown, black, yellow, and blue.

Most attractive to the eyes, the diamond is famous for its play
of colors. It emits a very delicate bluish, reddish, or a mixture of
blue and red radiance of glittering lustre when exposed to light.
The gem is luminous and dazzling, and emits sparks of light.

It is a common myth that diamonds shine in the dark, but although they do shine and radiate light in the dark, some source
of light is necessary. They do sparkle and shine and catch the eye
if a very feeble source of light is in the vicinity, and when one
observes them, one feels dazzling light with glittering lustre coming from the gem.

A fine diamond is effulgent, radiant, and delightful. It is as soothing to the eyes as the Moon; it is lovely and magnificent and has
the self-luminous quality of a clear crystal. It is brilliant and radiates

rainbows of light all around. When immersed in water a diamond appears to be floating. It gives a cool feeling when placed on the eyelids without being affected by the body temperature. When a drop of water is placed on the gem it remains a drop and does not spread like water, even if the gem is inverted. The corners of the gem appear to sparkle with a white gleam of light, like a star in a dark night.

Ancient Hindu scriptures mention eight types of diamonds. These divisions are based primarily on their color and are as follows:

1. *Hanspati:*   This diamond is of transparent white color like a conch, milk, yoghurt, or the feathers of a swan. It is the favorite of the creator, Brahma, who rides on a swan.
2. *Kamlapati:*   This diamond is of transparent pinkish white, like the color of a lotus petal. It emits a delicate reddish tint and is the favorite of the preserver, Vishnu, who is known by the name Kamlapati.
3. *Vasanti:*   This diamond is of transparent yellow-white, emitting a lemon-yellow tint like a yellow sapphire or a marigold flower or a canary flower. It is the favorite of Lord Shiva.
4. *Vajraneel:*   This diamond is of transparent blue-white, like the color of the neck of a bluejay, and emits a very delicate blue radiance. It is a favorite of Indra, the king of subgods and of heaven.
5. *Vanaspati:*   This diamond is of transparent green-white, like the color of a fresh blade of grass, or of sea-green aquamarine. It emits a very fine bluish green tint. It is a favorite of Varuna, the lord of the causal waters that surround the world.
6. *Shyamvajra:*   This diamond is of transparent smoky-grey color and has a dark shimmer. It is a favorite of Dharmaraj, also known as Yama, the lord of death and cosmic law.
7. *Telia:*   This diamond is of oily, dark color. It is very smooth, like oil, and also has a dark shimmer like the shyamvajra mentioned above. It is also a favorite of Yama.
8. *Sanloyi:*   This diamond is of yellow-green or pale green color, and it also has a dark shimmer or a red and brown tint, dazzling with glittering lustre.

According to the *Garuda Purana,* diamonds also have three genders, as follows:

1. *Masculine:*   The diamond that has eight faces (octahedron) or six angles and that displays rainbow colors when reflected on water; is light in weight but large, has a round shape but shows clearly

its eight facets; and is free from inclusions or line is a "nara," or male, diamond.

2. *Feminine:* The diamond that has twelve lozenge-shaped faces (a rhombic dodecahedron); is round and long, has dots and lines, but possesses other qualities of color display and explicitly exhibits all of its facets is termed "nari," or female, diamond.

3. *Neutral:* The diamond having only three angles (which are turned), is round, large, and heavy in weight, is termed "napunsak diamond" or "eunuch diamond."

Diamonds are also found in cubic form and hexoctahedron form, that is, having fourteen faces.

In their natural state, diamonds are covered with a black membrane. This black coating is made of the same substance as the diamond and keeps the crystal hidden inside.

Being the hardest of all gems, diamonds were not modeled into jewels in ancient times. Up to the thirteenth century Indian jewelers gave less importance to diamonds than to rubies, emeralds, and pearls. In the thirteenth century Indian jewelers invented the art of cutting facets by grinding a diamond with another piece of diamond on a grinding wheel, which enhanced its brilliance and the play of colors known as "fire." Its adamantine lustre is now well known, and its perfect cleavage makes it easy and simple to cut and polish. Its specific gravity is quite constant, and it has the highest refractive index of all gemstones. When it is properly cut it reflects light and becomes more lustrous. It refracts and bends light and turns it back to the eyes of the observer, which makes it effulgent and gives it superiority over all other gems.

When the diamond obtained from mines is not of gem quality, it has an important use in industry, where it is used as an abrasive.

QUALITIES OF A GOOD DIAMOND

1. hardness
2. lustre
3. transparence
4. smoothness
5. luminosity
6. pleasant appearance
7. play of colors—spraying blue, red, and rainbow-colored rays
8. good color: The finest diamonds are colorless

FLAWS IN A DIAMOND

1. *Dullness—a gem that is earthy and devoid of lustre:* Such a diamond brings numbness in the organs of the body and destroys wealth.
2. *Filth in the edges, corners, or middle of the diamond:* Such a diamond is injurious to health, wealth, and comfort.
3. *"Feathers of a crow":* A diamond having a blemish like the black feather of a crow is very inauspicious and is supposed to bring death to the one who wears it.
4. *Red spots:* A diamond having a red spot in its body is supposed to be the most inauspicious and should be discarded altogether as it destroys the wealth and prosperity of the one who wears it.
5. *Black spots:* A diamond having black spots is also inauspicious; it brings financial crisis and destroys mental peace.
6. *Greasy:* A diamond that is greasy is inauspicious and brings misfortune.
7. *Fissure in the body:* A diamond having a fissure brings diseases.
8. *Pale or brown in color:* A diamond pale or brown in color is destructive.
9. *Hole:* A hole in the diamond makes it inauspicious and brings death or severe affliction.
10. *White spot:* A white spot is tolerable, although it is a flaw; it neither harms nor benefits the wearer much.
11. *Ridges on the surface:* Not beneficial, not harmful: it is powerless.
12. *Ridges inside the diamond:*
    a) Left to right—destroy peace and comfort
    b) Like a tangent—inauspicious for one's spouse
    c) Straight ridges—fatal
13. *Inclusion resembling a barleycorn:* Inauspicious except when the dot or spot having the shape of barleycorn is white.
14. *Brittleness:* When the diamond is extremely hard, cutting and polishing becomes difficult; it is also considered unlucky.

Other than these flaws, if a diamond has the appearance of a drop of water, it is defective and inauspicious.

IDENTIFICATION OF A REAL DIAMOND

1. A real diamond when placed in warm milk cools the milk.
2. A real diamond when placed in liquid butter or ghee (clarified butter) at room temperature solidifies the butter or ghee.

3. A real diamond sprays rainbow-colored lights when placed in sunlight.

4. A real diamond when placed in the mouth of one who stammers stops the stammering.

5. A real diamond makes the one who wears it attract members of the opposite sex.

6. Inclusions or ridges of a real diamond are on the facets, whereas in an imitation they are not.

7. A real diamond cannot be scratched by any other stone except a diamond. An imitation sapphire can be rubbed by a diamond under observation. If the imitation gem is easily scratched the diamond is real.

8. A real diamond is cool to the touch and when placed on the eyelids it does not become warm, whereas an imitation would soon get warm.

9. An imitation can be rubbed with a file (or on a grinding wheel), whereas a real gem cannot.

10. A real gem is heavier than an imitation.

11. A real diamond does not lose its lustre by wearing—perspiration does not affect it.

12. A real diamond is a poor conductor of electricity, and becomes positively charged when rubbed.

13. A real diamond is transparent in x-rays, whereas imitations are not.

CLASSIFICATION OF DIAMONDS:

1. *Brahmin:* A diamond bright as a conch shell and colorless but having a blue tinge and emitting light, a delicate blue radiance, and red rays, a diamond with a brilliant lustre, that is delightful, magnificent, effulgent, radiant, and free from inclusions or dots of red, black, or white is termed "brahmin." It develops and refines mental power, purity of thoughts and actions, it enhances spirituality and is best suited for intellectuals and spiritually inclined people.

2. *Kshatriya:* A diamond that is transparent white and emits bright red light, has a fine mixture of yellow and white or red, or pink like the eyes of a rabbit, that is effulgent, smooth, and free from inclusions is termed "kshatriya." It gives inspiration and courage. It is best suited for rulers and is said to make them unconquerable.

3. *Vaishya:* A diamond that is yellowish white, transparent, smooth, delightful, and radiant, that emits a lemon-yellow hue

and is free from inclusions or dots is termed "vaishya." It is best suited for people belonging to the merchant class.

4. *Shudra:* A diamond that is white in color with a dark shimmer or blackish tinge, or smoky in appearance, though transparent, is called a "shudra" diamond. It is best suited for people of the service class and generates a spirit of service.

RITUALS FOR WEARING A DIAMOND

A diamond should be bought on a Friday when Bharni, Purva Phalguni, or Purvakshad nakshatra is present—or when Venus is in Taurus, Libra, or Pisces. It should be bought in the morning between sunrise and 11:00 A.M.

As the diamond is a costly gemstone it should be at least 1 rattika (.59 metric carat) in weight. The setting should be silver, white gold, or platinum, and the gem should be flawless. If one can afford it, the gem should be one and one-half carats in weight.

The gemstone should be given to the jeweler on the same day, and the ring should be made and the gemstone set on a Friday under the lunar mansions (nakshatras) mentioned above. The mounting should be open-backed. The gem should touch the skin of the one who wears it.

The best time to wear a diamond is morning, during Pushya Nakshatra.

Before wearing the ring for the first time it should be immersed in raw (cow's) milk. After some time it should be cleaned with Ganga-water, spring water, rainwater, or water kept in a copper pot overnight. After it has been washed the ring should be placed on a white cloth on which the yantra of Venus is drawn with rice-paste to which a pinch of saffron is added. An engraved yantra of Venus on a silver plate of about 7 grams of weight should then be placed on the same white cloth. An idol of Venus in silver can also be used, but as the idol needs a special priest to do the rituals, yantra is better. Perfume, incense, flowers, and a ghee lamp should be offered and then one should do japa of the mantra for Venus, as follows:

ॐ शुं शुक्राय नमः ॐ

AUM SHUM SHUKRAYE NAMAH AUM

The mantra should be recited either 108 or 16,000 times. Then one should meditate on the gemstone as a symbol of Venus. After meditation the ring should be worn on the ring finger of either the right or left hand. Wearing it on the little finger is also beneficial.

After the rituals are finished the engraved yantra should be wrapped in the white cloth on which the yantra is written with rice-paste and either donated to a priest or kept in a shrine.

The yantra of Venus to be written and engraved is as follows:

11	6	13
12	10	8
7	14	9

The worship should be performed facing east or southeast. One should use a white asana made of wool. First the yantra should be offered a bath, then it should be dried with a white cloth, and then honored with a tilak of white sandalwood paste. Next, the flowers should be offered and the perfume applied to the yantra and to the stone in the ring. The ring should also be honored with a tilak. Then the lamp should be lit and the incense offered. After this, recite the mantra for the prescribed number of recitations, and meditate on the yantra and the gemstone. Then the ring should be worn.

A ring worn in this manner removes the evil effects of an ill-aspected Venus, brings wealth, health, prosperity, removes fear of evil spirits, cures diseases, makes one invincible, removes enmity, and saves one from electric shocks, poisonous insects and animals, and accidental death.

Diamond/Venus: Who Should Wear a Diamond

Ascendant/Ruler	Venus is Natural Ruler of	Relationship of Venus with the Ruler of the Ascendant	Nature of the House Ruled by Venus	Suitability/Unsuitability of the Diamond & its Effects
Aries/Mars	2nd house 7th house	Enemy	Auspicious Auspicious	Not suitable. Wear only in the major & subperiods of Venus or when Venus is exalted in 12th house.
Taurus/Venus	1st house 6th house	Venus Himself is the Ruler	Auspicious Inauspicious	Suitable & beneficial. Brings good luck & success. Especially beneficial in major & subperiods of Venus.
Gemini/Mercury	5th house 12th house	Friend	Auspicious Inauspicious	Suitable & beneficial. Brings good fortune, good name, fame, progeny, happiness, and prosperity. Especially beneficial in major & subperiods of Venus.
Cancer/Moon	4th house 11th house	Enemy	Auspicious Auspicious	Not suitable generally, but can be beneficial during major & subperiods of Venus.
Leo/Sun	3rd house 10th house	Enemy	Inauspicious Auspicious	Not suitable, except when Venus is exalted in 8th house or in his own 3rd or 10th houses. Beneficial in major & subperiods of Venus.
Virgo/Mercury	2nd house 9th house	Friend	Auspicious Auspicious	Suitable & beneficial. Brings good luck, good name, fame, honor, success in career, financial gain, and good progeny.
Libra/Venus	1st house 8th house	Venus Himself is the Ruler	Auspicious Inauspicious	Suitable & beneficial. Brings good health, success, and longevity. Especially beneficial during major & subperiods of Venus.
Scorpio/Mars	7th house 12th house	Enemy	Auspicious Inauspicious	Not suitable. Avoid wearing diamond.

Sagittarius/Jupiter	6th house	Enemy	Inauspicious	Not suitable. Wear only if Venus is in the 10th house or, if necessary, during major & subperiods of Venus.
	11th house		Inauspicious	
Capricorn/Saturn	5th house	Friend	Auspicious	Suitable & beneficial. Brings good luck and is especially beneficial in major & subperiods of Venus.
	10th house		Auspicious	
Aquarius/Saturn	4th house	Friend	Auspicious	Suitable & beneficial. Brings good luck and inheritance of property. Especially beneficial during major & subperiods of Venus.
	9th house		Auspicious	
Pisces/Jupiter	3rd house	Enemy	Inauspicious	Not suitable. Avoid wearing diamond.
	8th house		Inauspicious	

The 2nd and 7th houses are both auspicious but also death-inflicting houses, especially during the major or sub-periods of the planets that rule them. If the ruling planet is benefic and a friend of the ruler of the ascendant, that aspect can be lessened.

MEDICINAL UTILITY OF THE DIAMOND

Diamond is the hardest of all gemstones, and it should never be used orally in the form of a pishthi (paste). Only its bhasma (oxide) is used in Ayurveda. If a diamond particle gets into the stomach it can be fatal. Therefore it is purified very carefully when its oxide is prepared.

Diamond Oxide

To purify a diamond the powdered gemstone is sealed in the root of kateli (a yellow-flowered cactus) by making a hole in the root and placing the pieces of diamond inside. The part of the root that is taken out is put back as a seal, and the entire thing is tied with a thread to ensure that the pieces remain inside the root. Then kulthi beans are boiled in water. After the beans become soft the water is drained from the beans. This water is used for purifying the diamonds that have been sealed in the kateli root. The root is then suspended in a daula yantra; the water obtained from boiled kulthi beans is used in the daula yantra for boiling the gemstone. The boiling is done for three days, so a sufficient amount of water from the kulthi beans is required. After seventy-two hours of boiling, the root is taken out of the kulthi bean water and allowed to cool, and the purified gempowder is then taken out.

Another way of purifying diamonds if kateli root is not available is the following: Heat the pieces of diamond in a crucible and when it becomes red-hot dip the pieces of diamond in liquid mercury, kept in a porcelain pot. Repeat the process one hundred times. Strain the diamond pieces through a fine cloth, and separate it from the diamond pieces. The diamond oxide can now be made.

There are three methods given in *Rasa Tantra Sar* for making diamond oxide, as follows:

1. Mix purified diamond with purified hartal, purified sulphur, purified hingul (lead oxide), and purified swarn makshika (marcasite, pyrite) in equal proportions. Grind the mixture in a simak mortar in the juice of the bark of the gooseberry plant. Make a tablet from the

paste, dry it in the sun, and fire it in a sarva samput in a gajput. Repeat the process seven times. Then grind the same mixture in the juice of the bark of a pippli plant, and dry it in the sun after making a tablet from the paste. Place it in a sarva samput and fire it in a gajput. Repeat the process seven times. After fourteen firings, a nice, smooth diamond oxide for medicinal use is ready.

2. Purified pieces of diamond or diamond dust should be heated on a piece of mica and dipped in the urine of a frog. Repeat the process twenty-five times. The diamond should not be touched by hand, for one may develop white spots. Then take two crucibles of the same size, place a neem leaf on each crucible, and put the pieces of diamond on the leaf—not directly on the crucible. Cover the diamond with neem leaves and cover one crucible with the other. Then seal them with clay and wrap them with a strip of cloth soaked in clay. Add sufficient layers of clay-soaked cloth, and make a ball. Dry this clay ball in the sun and fire it in a gajput or a potter's kiln. Let it cool by itself. Break the cloth layers, and carefully take out the crucibles. Open and take the oxide out of the crucibles. Grind the oxide with rock salt and concentrated water in which kulthi beans have been boiled. Make a paste, and make a tablet from the paste. Dry the tablet in the sun and place it in the crucible. Wrap it with cloth soaked in clay. Then make a clay ball, dry it, and fire it again. Repeat this process seven times. Each time the oxide should be ground with kulthi bean water and rock salt, and a tablet should be made and fired in the same way. After seven firings the oxide is ready for medicinal purposes.

3. Heat the purified pieces of diamond in an iron cup, and when the entire thing is red-hot dip it in twelve grams of rose water. Repeat the process 108 times. Then powder the pieces of diamond in rose water in a simak mortar, make a tablet of the paste and dry it in the sun. Enclose it in the crucibles (sarva samput). Wrap it with the clay-soaked cloth, make a ball, dry it, and fire it in a gajput or kiln. Repeat the firing process fourteen times, each time grinding it in rose water and sealing it in crucibles (sarva samput). After fourteen firings take the oxide (which will be in the form of a tablet) and grind it in the juice of ghee kunwar (aloe vera) and seal it again as mentioned before in a sarva samput, and fire it. Repeat the process twenty-eight times. If the oxide does not become soft, red ashes, repeat the process; otherwise the bhasma (oxide) is ready for medicinal purposes. Generally, it takes from twenty-eight to thirty-five firings.

Dosage: 1/64 to 1/32 rattika (1 rattika = .59 metric carat) with gold oxide, mica oxide, or poorna chandrodaya rasa. Oxide of diamond is useful in all kinds of disorders created by aggravated wind, bile, or mucus, and in tuberculosis, disorders created by fat, obesity, cholesterol, chronic diarrhea, stomach disorders, chronic dysentery, impotence, and viral infections.

Diamond oxide provides prana (life force). It is useful for epilepsy, paralysis, insanity, hernia, premature old age, sterility, and uterine diseases. It is useful for general debility, weakness of mind, diabetes, and jaundice. It makes the body strong and provides longevity. It is used in angina pectoris, poor circulation, anemia, weakness of nerves, poor vision, blindness, menstrual disorders, leukorrhea, and burning sensations within the body.

SOURCES OF DIAMONDS

India: Golconda in Andhra Pradesh (in South India) was famous for its high-quality diamonds, such as the kohinoor.

Diamonds have also been found as water-worn pebbles in the Mahanadi and Godavari rivers.

The Panna mines are located in Vindhya Pradesh in Bundelkhand. Panna diamonds are of a very complex form of the cubic system bounded by forty-eight similar faces. The crystals are brilliant white or blue-white—rich in fire and water, lustrous, and very seldom clouded or flawed. Their main defect is spots and opaque inclusions of a jagged outline. Diamond production in India is now insignificant, although before the discovery of the Brazil mines in 1725, India was the only major site of diamonds.

Brazil: The mines of Minas Gerais and Bahia in Brazil are important sites for diamond production. Most of the product is of industrial use, but a few gem-quality stones—rich in fire, water, and lustre—are also obtained. Previously they were brought to India for cutting and polishing. Brazilian mines produced good gem-quality diamonds up to 1834.

Africa: African mines produce over 95 percent of the world's diamonds. These mines were discovered in 1867 on the south shore of the Orange River near Hopetown in South Africa. The Congo basin, where diamonds are found in abundance, was the more important site up to 1970.

U.S.S.R.: Russian mines also produce good-quality diamonds in the Ural Mountains. Russian mines produce twice as many diamonds as Indian mines.

The United States, Canada, Guyana, and Australia also have diamond mines, but none of these sites is of any commercial value.

The most famous diamonds in ancient times came from India, which now is mostly a site for cutting and polishing diamonds; there are thousands of diamond cutters engaged in the gem industry in Gujarat. Antwerp and Amsterdam are also famous for diamond cutting.

Saturn is neutral, slow-moving, inert, and malefic. The planet of darkness and confinement, it governs the skeleton, skin, nervous system, and old age. It makes its natives reserved, reflective, rebellious, and patient. Saturn rides a vulture, the bird that lives on dead bodies. In one hand he holds a sword of lawlessness and terrorism, and in another hand a trident of Shiva (the trident of destruction). In his third hand he holds a mace of strength and material power, and in his fourth hand the reins of the vulture of old age that lives on the memory of past days.

9
Saturn and Its Gemstone, Blue Sapphire

तत्रैव सिंहल वधू कर पल्लवाग्र,
विस्तारिणी जलनिधेरूपकच्छ भूमिः।
सान्द्रेन्द्र नीलमणि रत्नवती विभाति'

S ATURN (Sanskrit, Shani) is darkness, the enemy of light. In the *Linga Purana* it is said that Shani was born from the solar deity Rudra. The *Markandeya Purana* states that Shani is the son of the Sun god by his wife Chaya (shadow, shade). In Sanskrit he is called Shani or Shanaishchara (the slow mover), because he takes about two and a half years (or thirty months) to pass through each constellation of the sidereal zodiac.

Saturn is cold and dry, tamasik (lethargic), and is an elderly planet. His sight is bad, and he is said to be "malefic amongst the malefics." Saturn destroys the house it occupies (except if posited in the seventh house, where it receives directional strength) and any houses it aspects, or any planet it conjoins or aspects. The third, sixth, and eleventh houses are good houses for Saturn, because as a general rule all malefic planets become benefic when they are posited in either of the three above-mentioned houses. When it is posited in these three houses, or is well placed in the seventh house, or well aspected, it gives its natives integrity, wisdom, spirituality, fame, patience, ability to lead, authority, long life, organizational abilities, sincerity, honesty, love of justice, awareness of right and wrong (because it rules the inner conscience), nonattachment, and asceticism. When it is ill-posited or ill-aspected it brings miseries, sorrow, delay, obstruction, disappointment, disharmony, disputes, dejection, difficulties, despondency, and destruction (death). It makes its natives undisciplined, irresponsible, dishonest, dull, addicted to drugs, sadistic, greedy, lonely, and afraid. Accidents, humiliation, prison, lawsuits, suicidal tendencies, fear of theft, thefts, blame, bad karma, enmity, pessimism, and premature aging are also attributed to an ill-aspected or ill-posited Saturn.

Saturnine natives are defensive, nervous, and secretive.

Saturn rules over longevity, transport, prisons, machinery, construction workers, carpenters, miners, masons, real estate agents, mechanics, laborers, vendors, ascetics, monks, hermits, social servants, old age, psychosomatic troubles, wood, coal, iron, steel, lead, sesame seeds, salt, black beans, water buffalo, and all black objects.

In the body Saturn rules the nails, hair, teeth, bones, and nervous system (nervous system because the activity of nerves is related to the air element, and Saturn gives a wind-dominated body chemistry). Paralysis, rheumatism, and neurosis are all related to disturbance of the body gases. Diseases of the ears, black jaundice, gout, deafness, muteness, depression, anxiety, colic pains, insanity, and asthma are also connected with a Saturn that is ill-aspected or badly placed in the birth chart.

Saturn rules over the zodiacal signs Capricorn and Aquarius. It is exalted in Libra and fallen in Aries. Mercury, Venus, Rahu, and Ketu are its friends and the Sun, the Moon, and Mars are its enemies. Jupiter is neutral in friendship. Its friendship with Mercury is sattvik and with Venus is rajasik. Pushya, Anuradha, and Uttra Bhadrapad are the nakshatras that it rules. Its friendly zodiacal signs are Taurus and Gemini and it works well and gives good results in Sagittarius and Pisces. Enemy signs are Cancer, Leo, and Scorpio. Saturn is powerful in the descending moon cycle and gives its best results—or worst results—between thirty-six and forty-two years of age. It rules the direction west, Saturday is its day, and black is its color.

Those born on the eighth, seventeenth, or twenty-sixth of any month are influenced by Saturn.

Blue sapphire is the gemstone of Saturn.

THE BLUE SAPPHIRE

Known as indra neel and neel mani in Sanskrit and neelam in Hindi, the blue sapphire is a gem of the corundum family. Sometimes white sapphires, rubies, and blue sapphires are found in the same mine, and that is why there is a mixture of colors in the crystals of these gems. Ruby is harder than white sapphire (known as pukhraj), and blue sapphire is harder than ruby. Sometimes a single specimen from the corundum family may contain all three colors, or a pukhraj may contain a pink shade, a ruby may have a blue shade, and a neelam (blue sapphire) may have a red shade, but what distinguishes them from each other is their hardness. Each gem possesses its distinct hardness, and as stated before, blue sapphire is hardest. Ruby crystals are generally six-sided prisms and blue sapphire crystals are found as twelve-sided prisms.

QUALITIES OF A GOOD BLUE SAPPHIRE

1. smoothness
2. transparence
3. uniformity in color
4. high specific gravity
5. brilliance, exhibiting a star-like effect from inside when viewed in reflected light, emitting rays of light from inside
6. solid and compact body
7. color similar to that of the neck of a peacock, or a velvety cornflower-blue
8. good cut and nice shape

FLAWS OF A BLUE SAPPHIRE

1. milky—brings poverty
2. dull (without lustre or devoid of brilliance)—harms friends, brothers, and near relations

3. film like a cobweb—brings disease
4. fissure or cracks in its structure—causes accidents, injuries caused by weapons, and financial crisis
5. depressions, cavity—causes boils and ulcers and increases poisonous material in the body
6. white lines, capillary, hair-like or thread-like inclusions—bad for the eyes; gives pain in the body
7. double colored—harmful for progeny and one's spouse; creates fear of enemies
8. having white, red, black, or honey-colored spots—makes one leave one's house and is injurious for one's personal health and progeny (especially sons)
9. opaque—powerless; harmful for the body
10. multicolored—increases anxiety and mental problems
11. greenish in shade—causes financial loss

IDENTIFICATION OF REAL BLUE SAPPHIRES

1. A real blue sapphire emits blue light and, if placed in a glass of cow's milk, the milk appears to have a bluish tinge.
2. A real blue sapphire emits blue light in sunlight, and if placed on a white piece of cloth, it makes the cloth appear blue on the spot where the reflected light falls.
3. A real blue sapphire emits blue sparks when placed in a glass of water.
4. A real blue sapphire picks up bits of straw because of its electrical property; that is why it is called "tringrahi" in Sanskrit (*trin* means a small piece of straw and *grahi* means that which accepts or holds).

All tests mentioned under the section "Identification of Real Rubies" are also applicable to blue sapphire, because ruby and sapphire belong to the same corundum family and, as mentioned above, are sometimes found at the same site.

One test prescribed by the scriptures is to have a woman of fair complexion hold a bowl of milk on a moonlit night with one hand, and let her hold in her other hand the piece of blue sapphire being tested. She should allow the moonlight to reflect to the bowl of milk: the milk, the bowl, and the part where the reflected light falls on the woman will all appear to have a blue tinge.

CLASSIFICATION OF BLUE SAPPHIRES

1. Brahmin: A blue sapphire that is white or light blue in color and has a blue lustre is suitable for learned or spiritually inclined people.
2. Kshatriya: A blue sapphire having a reddish tinge is best suited for rulers and those in administrative jobs.
3. Vaishya: A white-colored blue sapphire having a deep blue tinge is best suited for merchants and businesspeople.
4. Shudra: A blue sapphire having a dark tinge is best for people who belong to the service class.

RITUALS FOR WEARING A BLUE SAPPHIRE

A blue sapphire should be bought on a Saturday when Saturn is posited in Capricorn, Aquarius, or Libra, or when on a Saturday there is Shravan, Dhanishtha, Kshat Bhikha, Purva Bhadrapad, Uttrakshad, Chitra, Svati, or Vishakha.

The weight of the gemstone should not be less than 4 rattikas. A blue sapphire weighing 5 or 7 rattikas (2.59 or 4.13 metric carats) or one weighing 5 carats is supposed to be auspicious. The gemstone should be flawless.

The gemstone should be bought in the evening hours and given to the jeweler on the same day, who should prepare a ring from a mixture of gold, iron, and silver. Tantriks claim that for Saturn the following mixture of five metals is best: 1 part gold, 2 parts silver, 3 parts lead, 4 parts iron, and 1 part copper. Instead of copper, zinc can be used. The ring also should be made in the evening hours of a Saturday when either Saturn is in the zodiacal signs mentioned above or the nakshatras mentioned above are present. The weight of the combination of metals should not be less than 9 rattikas. The ring should be taken from the jeweler on a Saturday evening, and the best time to wear the ring is evening.

Saturn is a friend of Mercury and Venus. To add additional power to the ring, emerald and diamond could also be embedded in it. The back should be open to allow the gemstone to touch the skin of the finger.

When the ring is ready one should—on a Saturday when the

Blue Sapphire/Saturn: Who Should Wear a Blue Sapphire

Ascendant/Ruler	Saturn is Natural Ruler of	Relationship of Saturn with the Ruler of the Ascendant	Nature of the House Ruled by Saturn	Suitability/Unsuitability of the Blue Sapphire & its Effects
Aries/Mars	10th house 11th house	Enemy	Auspicious Auspicious	Suitable only when Saturn is in the 2nd, 9th, or 10th house or exalted in 7th house. Wear only during the major or subperiods of Saturn. Beneficial for those having Saturn in the 10th house.
Taurus/Venus	9th house 10th house	Friend	Auspicious Auspicious	Suitable & beneficial. Blue sapphire gives success, good name, fame, prosperity, and favor from authorities. Wear it with a diamond in major & subperiods of Saturn.
Gemini/Mercury	8th house 9th house	Friend	Inauspicious Auspicious	Suitable & beneficial. Wearing with emerald will bring lifelong benefit. Blue sapphire alone is beneficial during the major & subperiods of Saturn.
Cancer/Moon	7th house 8th house	Enemy	Auspicious Inauspicious	Not suitable. Avoid wearing blue sapphire.
Leo/Sun	6th house 7th house	Enemy	Inauspicious Auspicious	Not suitable. Avoid wearing, possessing, or owning blue sapphire.
Virgo/Mercury	5th house 6th house	Friend	Auspicious Inauspicious	Suitable & beneficial only during the major and subperiods of Saturn.
Libra/Venus	4th house 5th house	Friend	Auspicious Auspicious	Suitable & beneficial. Blue sapphire set with a diamond during the major & subperiods of Saturn brings beneficial results.

Sign/Ruler	House		Relationship	Status		Notes
Scorpio/Mars	3rd house	4th house	Enemy	Auspicious	Auspicious	Suitable only during the major & subperiods of Saturn. Especially good if Saturn is in the 4th house.
Sagittarius/Jupiter	2nd house	3rd house	Enemy	Auspicious	Auspicious	Not suitable. Wear only if Saturn is in the 1st house.
Capricorn/Saturn	1st house Ascendant	2nd house	Saturn Himself is the Ruler	Auspicious	Auspicious	Suitable & beneficial. Wear throughout life.
Aquarius/Saturn	1st house	12th house	Saturn Himself is the Ruler	Auspicious	Inauspicious	Suitable & beneficial. Wear in the same setting with a diamond.
Pisces/Jupiter	11th house	12th house	Enemy	Auspicious	Inauspicious	Not suitable, except if Saturn is in the 11th house. Wear only during the major & subperiods of Saturn.

The 2nd and 7th houses are both auspicious but also death-inflicting houses, especially during the major or sub-periods of the planets that rule them. If the ruling planet is benefic and a friend of the ruler of the ascendant, that aspect can be lessened.

above-mentioned zodiacal signs or nakshatras are present—first immerse the ring in cow's or water buffalo's milk, then wash it with Ganga-water, spring water, rainwater, or water kept overnight in a copper pot.

Then one should write a Shani (Saturn) Yantra on a black cloth with red sandalwood paste, rice-paste, or roli. Then an engraved yantra or idol of Saturn made in iron or steel should be placed on the black cloth upon which the yantra of Saturn is drawn. Before placing the idol or Saturn Yantra engraved on the iron or steel plate it should be given a bath and dried with a clean black, green, or white cloth. Then a tilak of roli or white sandalwood paste with a pinch of saffron and organic camphor should be given to the engraved yantra and the ring to honor both, and the engraved yantra and the ring should be placed on a black cloth on which the yantra has already been drawn. Then one should light a lamp. The asana for sitting should be made of black wool and one should face the west while worshiping the yantra. Then one should light a lamp and offer flowers and incense to the engraved yantra and the gemstone embedded in the ring. Both should be regarded as symbols of Lord Saturn, and then the mantra of Saturn should be recited, as follows:

ॐ शं शॉनेश्चराय नमः ॐ

AUM SHAM SHANAISHCHARAYE NAMAH AUM

The mantra should be recited either 108 or 23,000 times. The worship should start two hours before sunset. After recitation of the mantra one should meditate on Saturn, whose color is black and who is seated on a vulture.

After meditation one should wear the ring on the middle finger of the right hand, which is the Saturn finger. One should pray to Saturn for bestowing the best results and providing help in over-coming difficulties.

The yantra to be written on the black cloth is the same as that to be engraved on the steel or iron plate, as follows:

4	9	2
3	5	7
8	1	6

A ring worn this way brings good luck, relieves poverty and suffering, provides vitality, vigor, life force, longevity, happiness, peace, and prosperity. It also cures problems caused by an afflicted, ill-aspected, or wrongly posited Saturn.

The steel yantra should be wrapped in the black cloth on which the yantra is drawn and donated to a shrine of Saturn or kept in one's personal shrine. It should be worshiped during the major period or subperiod of Saturn. Blue sapphire is the most powerful of all gemstones and shows its effect within a few hours. One should not use it if one does not need it.

MEDICINAL UTILITY OF THE BLUE SAPPHIRE

To purify a blue sapphire one should boil it in grass from which neel (the blueing used for whitening clothes) has been extracted. In ancient times blueing was extracted from neel grass. This grass can be obtained from Indian herb shops. A concentrated solution of it should be made by boiling it in sixteen times more water than the weight—or its juice should be extracted and then the uice should be boiled. When one quarter of the water or juice emains it should be placed in a daula yantra and pieces of blue apphire should be tied in a cloth, suspended in the concentrated solution, and boiled for three days. Then it will be ready for making an oxide or pishthi (paste).

Blue Sapphire Oxide

Take purified blue sapphire and powder it with sulphur, hartal, and mansel in equal proportions, with the juice of a ripe jackfruit in a simak mortar for twelve hours. Then make a tablet from the paste and dry it in the sun. Place the tablet in a clay pot and cover it with a pot of the same size, seal the pot with clay and wrap it with cloth strips soaked in clay. Make a small clay ball as prescribed in the sarva samput. Dry it in the shade and fire it in the heat of 5 kilograms of cowdung in a gajput or in a potter's kiln. Repeat the process eight times. Each time the tablet should be ground with jackfruit juice, and the tablet should be made fresh, then dried, and then placed in the sarva samput and fired in a gajput or kiln. After each firing it should be allowed to cool. Now the oxide is ready for medicinal purposes.

Dosage: 1 to ½ rattika twice a day with 1 tsp. honey, sweet butter, or powdered rock sugar candy.

Blue Sapphire Paste

Blue sapphire that has been purified should be finely powdered and sieved through a piece of fine, thin cloth. Then in a simak, agate, or kasauti mortar it should be ground in rose water or bedmusk water (a distillate of cane) for fifteen days. When the paste becomes so fine that it does not hurt the eyes when applied as surma, it should be dried in the shade and ground into an even finer powder.

Dosage: 1 to ½ rattika twice a day with honey, malai, cream, ginger juice, and powdered rock sugar candy, or betel juice and powdered rock sugar candy.

Blue sapphire oxide or powder (pishthi) is bitter and is a powerful remedy for chronic fever, asthma, mucus, hemorrhoids, epilepsy, hysteria, neuritis, pain in the joints, insanity, weakness of mind and brain, loss of memory, and confusion.

It increases the digestive fire and strengthens the eight dhatus. It increases ojas (radiance) and pranic power. It cures ailments caused by the aggravation of wind, bile, and mucus. It gives lightness and is very good for the heart. It is prescribed for patients of heart disease, tuberculosis, and diseases of the urinary tract.

Blue sapphire pishthi can also be made into small pills and dried in the shade and given for any of the diseases mentioned above as well as for baldness, skin diseases, migraine, heartburn, nervous disorders, gout, rheumatism, stiffness of the joints, colic pains, lack of appetite, and bloating of the stomach.

For mucus problems it should be taken with freshly ground juice of ginger and rock sugar candy.

For breathing problems (e.g., asthma), it should be taken with the juice of betel leaf or with malai.

For disorders of bile it should be taken with honey.

For disorders of wind it should be taken with cream, honey, or malai.

For weakness of the mind and brain, it should be taken with almond kheer (a paste made from unroasted almonds that are soaked overnight in water, peeled, finely ground, and cooked with dates and milk with a pinch of saffron).

For pains it should be taken with water.

A mixture with honey can be used in any of the above-mentioned diseases.

SOURCES OF BLUE SAPPHIRES

Kashmir: As mentioned in the ancient scriptures, blue sapphire was found in the area of the Mahanadi and Brahmaputra rivers, the Himalayan region, and the area of Mount Abu in Rajasthan. But the finest variety of neelam came from Kashmir. Today, Kashmir blue sapphires come from an area near a village called Khan Sumzam. The variety is known as mayur neelam, because the color of these sapphires resembles the beautiful hue of the peacock's neck (*mayur* means peacock). Even a small amount of that fine color gives the whole gemstone a beautiful color. Kashmir sapphires do not change their color in the presence of electric light, while sapphires obtained from other mines show a navy blue hue under an electric light.

The sapphires of the old mine in the Zanskar Range of Kashmir, which were rich in lustre, large in size, and without many flaws are no longer available. They were also not suitable for medicinal preparations because they contained other minerals, and much foreign material adhered in their layers. The sapphire that is mined now in Kashmir often has cavities, holes (small, circular dents), and windows (deep holes or cavities), and sometimes an ambiguity of colors. It needs special skill to cut the jewels out of those crystals that are covered with a hard crust of earth. The flawless specimens, however, exhibit fine gem qualities and are shaped into excellent-quality gems.

Salem: A new mine of sapphires is now operating in Salem, Tamil Nadu state, in southern India. These sapphires are similar in color to the sapphires found in the mines of Bangkok, Thailand, but they have a deeper greenish tinge that comes from the fusion of blue and yellow colors.

Burma: Sapphires from Mogok, Burma, are fine in color and lustre and are found in all sizes. They are free of foreign matter and are good for preparing medicines. Their color has very little tinge of green, and they are of high gem quality. They exhibit a fine six-pointed star when observed in the light. Burma neelam are easy to cut and polish—better than Kashmir neelam, which remain thick after cutting and exhibit no stars.

Thailand: The sapphires found in Thailand are darker than others and have a mixture of greenish hues. They are the hardest and toughest sapphires, and smooth as silk. Black sapphires, which are in fact very deep blue, are also found in Thailand, but star sapphires are not found there.

Sri Lanka (Ceylon): Sapphires produced in Sri Lanka are inferior in quality to Kashmir and Burma sapphires. They are rich in water and comparatively large in size, but they have a mixture of reddish tinge in their blue color, and little fire. They have a dark tinge and are not attractive. Six-lined stars are found in Ceylon sapphires, but the crystals show steep pyramidical faces with a blue base, where the rest of the crystal is colorless; and this can be seen by turning them sideways. The color spots of these sapphires differ from those in Kashmir sapphires, and they are not as powerfully radiant as the Kashmir sapphire, a gem that is entirely radiant.

Queensland, Australia: The blue sapphires produced here are similar to the sapphires of Thailand, but the difference is in their color and fire. Queensland sapphires are darker in hue and poor in fire.

Cambodia: Beautiful and lovely-colored gems are also found in Cambodia.

United States: Blue sapphires are found in Montana, from river gravel near Helena. Except for a few finely colored, hard, lustrous stones, most of the stones are small and poor in quality. Cawes County in North Carolina may also be mentioned for producing a few gems, among them star sapphires.

U.S.S.R.: Blue sapphires of inferior quality are also found here, near Troitsk Miesk in the Ural Mountains.

Zimbabwe, South Africa: This also is a site for blue sapphires, but they do not exhibit gem qualities; they are too dark and unattractive.

Rahu is neutral, active, and disruptive. It creates confusion and affects the psychological makeup of its natives. Rahu is shown as a disembodied head riding a chariot and shouting obscenities. The chariot is pulled by a tiger, representing the mind roaming in the forest of desires. Rahu works on the mental level, making its natives rebellious, destructive, impulsive, and secretive.

10

Rahu and
Its Gemstone,
Hessonite

हिमवत्युत्तरढेशे वीर्य पतितं सुराद्धृषस्तस्य संप्राप्तं
भीष्मरत्नानाम्

IN THE MOST ANCIENT SCRIPTURES on astrology we do not find the names of Rahu and its counterpart, Ketu; instead, only seven planets are mentioned: the Sun, the Moon, Mars, Mercury, Jupiter, Venus, and Saturn.

The name of Rahu first appears in the *Mahabharata,* when we read the story of the churning of the Ocean of Milk in the search for ambrosia—the elixir of immortality known as amrita in Sanskrit. Rahu was the son of Danava Vipracitti by his wife Simhika, and a brother of Maya Danava, the great magician and architect.

According to legend the gods and antigods (danavas) were both sons of the sage Kashyapa, by different wives. The gods were rich in spiritual powers, and the antigods were rich in material wealth and physical strength and were more involved in the gratification of the senses. Sometimes the danavas performed great austerities and received powerful boons from Lord Brahma or Shiva—and then they waged a war with their stepbrothers, the gods and subgods, and drove them out of their abode, heaven. The gods found themselves weak and wanted to obtain the ambrosia to become immortal. But ambrosia was in the depths of the Ocean of Milk and could not be obtained without churning the ocean. The gods needed the help of the danavas. The danavas too were interested in becoming immortal. They agreed to join in this venture, on the condition that they too would get a share of the elixir of immortality. The ocean was churned and amrita was secured. Vishnu, the lord of preservation, assumed the form of a beautiful maiden Mohini and started distributing amrita. Rahu observed that Vishnu was tricking the danavas and giving them varuni (liquor) instead of amrita—and was giving gods the nectar.

The danavas were enchanted by the beautiful maiden Mohini and were drinking liquor without noticing the trick. Rahu decided to trick the gods—he disguised himself as a god and drank the amrita. Surya (Sun) and Chandra (Moon) discovered the disguised Rahu when nectar had only reached his throat. They informed the gods and Vishnu. Vishnu instantaneously cut the head of Rahu with his discus and threw it into the sky. The head began to cry for justice and help, and the trunk fell upon the earth and rolled around shaking the earth, trembling the mountains, felling trees, and shaking the islands, making them clash against each other. The headless trunk (Ketu) also had its share of ambrosia and was immortal. In the end the two parts of Danava Rahu, which had attained immortality, were placed in the planetary orbit 180° apart from each other, so that they could never unite. Because Sun and Moon were the two luminaries who discovered Rahu in disguise, Rahu and his counterpart, known as Ketu, became the enemies of Sun and Moon. This enmity continues, and whenever Sun and Moon come close to Rahu or Ketu they try to swallow them. Because Rahu has only a head they escape through his neck, and since Ketu is headless they also get out of his body through his neck, and because they have drunk the nectar they are all immortal, and so the fight continues. Whenever Rahu and Ketu get a chance to attack Sun and Moon, they attack—and cause a solar or lunar eclipse (*Bhagvat Purana* 10.8.9).

Rahu and Ketu are two parts of the same danava and are 180° apart from each other. Whenever either Sun or Moon are conjunct with Rahu or Ketu, a solar or lunar eclipse takes place. In astronomy Rahu is considered the dragon's head and is also known as the north node of Moon, the point where the Moon's orbit crosses the ecliptic. Ketu is known as the dragon's tail, which gives birth to comets and meteors and is known as the descending or the south node of the Moon. When Sun, Moon, and Rahu or Ketu fall in the same zodiacal longitude, a solar eclipse takes place. Rahu is responsible for solar, Ketu for lunar eclipse. Because Sun, Moon, and the nodes move at a particular speed, it is possible to calculate solar and lunar eclipses centuries ahead of time. This makes them significant for astronomers and astrologers both. Though they are included in planets, Rahu and Ketu are not real luminaries and are regarded as shadow planets. They do not have ability to cast aspects, as other planets do, they do not rule any zodiacal signs and are not characterized as male or female. Because they are related to Moon as its north and south nodes, they reflect the basic bipolarity of energy within the cosmos (the macrocosm) and the individual (the microcosm). They are both regarded as malefic half-planets and they bisect the natal chart of every individual.

Rahu is regarded as similar to Saturn in its effect. Smoky blue is its color, instinctual and animalistic its nature. Because of its disguising nature it is supposed to fulfill its desires recklessly. Because it could not enjoy its life as a whole being, it is eternally dissatisfied. Rahu is interested only in achieving all that gives pleasure, and even if it achieves all it wants, it is never satisfied (which is true of our animalistic nature).

Although Rahu rules no sign of the zodiac, the zodiacal sign Virgo is its sign. Virgo is in fact assigned to Mercury, but Rahu being akin to Saturn and Mercury being a friend of Saturn, Rahu thus has authority over Virgo. Rahu is exalted in Taurus (according to some astrologers it is Gemini) and its sign of debilitation is Scorpio (or Sagittarius according to some scriptures). Friendly signs are Gemini, Virgo, Libra, Sagittarius, and Pisces. Cancer and Leo are its enemy signs. Mercury, Venus, and Saturn are friendly planets. Rahu is an enemy of Sun, Moon, and Mars. Venus, Moon, and Mars feel enmity with Rahu and Jupiter is neutral. Rahu gives auspicious results in Taurus and Libra. In eighth and ninth houses it is supposed to be strong and powerful. According to some scholars of astrology Rahu is also powerful in the first house. Third, sixth, tenth, and eleventh houses are thought to be the best houses for malefic planets.

Rahu is supposed to be dark blue or of smoky blue color, malicious-looking, evil-natured, related to the wind element, old, Shudra by caste, destructive, intelligent but lazy, having big plans that require time, tamasik—a danava-nature planet (half planet).

Rahu is the head of the danava and so is generally supposed to rule the head, but in fact it affects the feet, represents physical or muscular strength, hard labor, bad karma, and hedonism. It brings difficulties, suffering, anxiety, enmity, insatiable worldly desires, ignorance, and love of worldly benefits and sensual gratification.

Rahu is capable of giving power when rightly posited or exalted, and it gives fame, success in politics, money, and physical beauty (i.e., attraction). If Rahu is seen by Jupiter or Venus it gives one access to secret knowledge and tantra as well as skill in painting, printing, and publishing.

Rahu gives the effect of the planet in whose house it is placed and according to the house in which it is placed.

Rahu gives its effects between forty-two and forty-eight years of age.

The most detrimental effects of Rahu occur when Rahu is conjunct with any other planet. It destroys the house in which it is posited, except the third, sixth, ninth, and eleventh houses.

Rahu destroys one's ability to judge, makes one dull and devoid of reasoning and logic, and everything becomes out of control. It works by inducing lethargy, insensitivity, and selfishness. Although it gives beneficial results while posited in the above-mentioned signs and houses, the gains obtained during its major period do not last long, and one always feels anxious and dissatisfied, even if one gets everything one desires.

Rahu creates physical and mental illnesses that cannot be diagnosed and cured easily. It gives suicidal tendencies, fears, phobias, poisonous bites, murder, theft, imprisonment, and diseases like cholera, dysentery, rheumatism, windy colic, piles, skin diseases, rheumatic tumors, swelling of the uterus, and constipation.

Rahu rules over mustard seeds, black sesame seeds, woolen rugs, iron, mirrors, swords, and objects of blue color. In the body it rules over bones, fat, and skin.

Rahu also influences those who work with machines, photography, printing and publishing, painting, hunting and those who are violent and aggressive. Rahu also rules over navigators and travelers and is called a planet of traveling. It makes people go underground and lose contact with other people. It also rules over detectives and spies, criminals, revolutionaries, anarchists, and terrorists.

In numerology we assign Rahu the numeral four and observe its influence on people born on the fourth, thirteenth, twenty-second, and thirty-first day of any month. Number thirteen is regarded as an ominous and unlucky number. Number twenty-two is known as a mystic number, and the influence of Rahu makes those born on the 22nd face difficulties.

The gemstone related to Rahu is gomed, known as hessonite or cinnamon stone.

HESSONITE (CINNAMON STONE, OR ZIRCON)

Its Sanskrit name is gomedak or gomed-medak, and its Hindi name is gomed.

A good-quality gomed or hessonite, the gemstone of Rahu, is one that reflects the color of the urine of a cow, that is, having a nice honey color. It is a silicate of zirconium and is commonly found in igneous rocks but is fairly rare as a gemstone. Zircon has a considerable range of colors and is found in red, blue, green, yellow, orange, and brown shades. Blue and green hessonite or the white colorless variety of hessonite are not associated with Rahu. White or colorless hessonite is used as a substitute for diamond and is associated with Venus. Because of its transparency, brilliance, waxy adamantine finish, and rich lustre (fire and water), it is sometimes mistaken for a diamond. Its softness and the ease with which it can be scratched, however, help to distinguish it from a diamond. Its clear brown crystals turn blue when heated and so make better gems, but it is mostly found in opaque form. Hessonite is found as alluvium in gem sands and gravels, in metamorphosed limestone, granite, and pagmatite in association with diamond, ruby, sapphire, garnet, and tourmaline. Like rutile and cassiterite it has two axes of equal length and the third unequal. All the three axes are at right angles to one another, which makes it easy for gem cutters to give it a fine shape. Its use is very popular in jewelry.

A pure and transparent hessonite having a delicate hue, brilliance, lustre, and uniform color neutralizes the evil effects of Rahu, and if Rahu is well posited it gives beneficial results during its major period and subperiods, removes fear, creates clarity of mind, and helps spiritual growth.

QUALITIES OF A GOOD HESSONITE

1. color similar to the clear urine of a cow
2. transparency
3. high specific gravity
4. tender and smooth feel
5. freedom from layers
6. brilliance
7. uniform color
8. evenness of surface and waxy adamantine finish
9. attractive shape and size

FLAWS OF A HESSONITE

1. dullness—bad for one's spouse and faculty of reasoning
2. fibrous—it is not powerful though not harmful (If the native has Rahu conjunct the Sun or Moon and Mars, a defective hessonite also gives beneficial results.)
3. micaceous—creates fear of evil spirits
4. rough—destroys one's reputation in society
5. unattractive—creates disease
6. fissures—opposition from society and diseases of the blood
7. spotty—makes one leave his place of birth, country, state, village, town
8. having a hole or dents—destroys wealth
9. blood-red in color—destroys skin color and produces stains on skin and body
10. double color—troublesome for father
11. blisters—brings mental problems
12. flat—brings humiliation
13. having white spots—gives fear, phobia, and sickness
14. having a black spot—bad for one's spouse
15. having a red spot—injurious for progeny
16. ambiguity of color—brings confusion and mental illness
17. layers—brings misfortune
18. having many defects—harms one's marital life

IDENTIFICATION OF REAL HESSONITE

1. If a real hessonite is left in cow's urine for twenty-four hours the color of the urine changes.

2. Real hessonite shines more if rubbed with sawdust, whereas the imitation will lose its lustre.
3. Real hessonite retains its lustre if rubbed on a touchstone.
4. Real hessonite, when immersed in a glass of cow's milk and held against sunlight, changes the color of the milk and the milk appears more yellowish.
5. Real hessonite is devoid of concentric rings of air bubbles.

CLASSIFICATION OF HESSONITE

1. *Brahmin:*   Clear transparent hessonite of cinnamon-brown color, light yellow color, or yellowish brown with a reddish hue is of Brahmin varna and is good for scholars and spiritually inclined persons.
2. *Kshatriya:*   Hessonite of deep yellow or crimson color with dominance of red color is best suited for rulers, officers, and ministers of states.
3. *Vaishya:*   Reddish brown hessonite with a yellow hue is best suited for merchants and businesspeople.
4. *Shudra:*   Reddish yellow hessonite with a cinnamon-brown shade is best suited for people belonging to the service class.

RITUALS FOR WEARING A HESSONITE

A hessonite should be bought on a Saturday when Adra Nakshatra or Kshat Bhikha Nakshatra is present. It should be bought in an ascending moon cycle, in the morning before 10 A.M. and given to the jeweler the same day. The jeweler should set it the same day or on a Saturday when the above-mentioned nakshatras are present.

The weight of a hessonite should not be less than 4 rattikas. The gem should not be 7, 10, or 16 rattikas in weight, nor should it weigh 6, 11, or 13 carats.

The hessonite should be set in a ring made of the five metals recommended for blue sapphire (see chapter 9) or in a ring made of iron or steel. The mounting should have an open back to allow the gemstone to touch the finger.

The best time to wear a hessonite is two hours after sunset.

Before wearing it for the first time, wash the ring first with cow's milk and then with water kept in a copper pot, Ganga-water, rainwater, or spring water.

After washing, the ring should be placed on a blue cloth on which the yantra of Rahu is drawn with roli or white sandalwood paste.

An engraved yantra of Rahu on an iron or steel plate should then be washed the same way as the ring and placed on the cloth on which the yantra of Rahu is drawn.

Then one should honor the engraved yantra and the hessonite ring as symbols of Rahu, offering light (ghee lamp), flowers, and incense to both. Then one should worship Rahu reciting the mantra for Rahu:

ॐ रा राहुवे नमः ॐ

AUM RAM RAHUVE NAMAH AUM

The mantra should be recited at least 108 times or 18,000 times. After mantra reciting (which should be done silently or mentally), one should meditate and pray for favorable results, then wear the ring on the middle finger or little finger of the left hand.

The yantra to be drawn is as follows:

13	8	15
14	12	10
9	16	11

MEDICINAL UTILITY OF HESSONITE

Good-quality hessonite that may have inclusions, fiber, cracks, fissures, or other flaws making them useless for jewelry may be used for medical purposes. Dust and other particles also may be used. These should be purified first in a daula yantra with juice of jasmine for three days.

After this the hessonite fragments should be heated on a piece of mica until they become red-hot. The heated pieces should then be dropped in the juice of amla fruit. This process should be repeated twenty-one times.

The hessonite is now purified, and either oxide or paste can be made for oral administration.

Hessonite Oxide

Mix mansel, hartal, and gandhak (sulphur) in equal proportions and add to it an equal weight of purified pieces of hessonite. Powder this mixture in the juice of jackfruit in a mortar made of simak, agate, or kasauti for twelve hours. When the paste is ready make a tablet and dry it in the sun. After the tablet is dry put it in a sarva samput and fire it in a gajput or potter's kiln. Repeat the process eight times.

The writer of *Rasa Choodamani*—another Ayurvedic scripture on preparation of rasayanas (elixirs)—recommends that:

> Gomed should be heated on a piece of mica. After it is red-hot it should be dropped in jackfruit juice. The process should be repeated seven times—and then sulphur equal in weight to gomed should be mixed and powdered in jackfruit juice in a mortar and then fired ten times in gajput.

Dosage: ½ to 1 rattika with malai or honey twice a day.

Hessonite Pishthi or Paste

Take sandalwood dust, kewra flower (a variety of cactus flower), and rose flowers and distill each of them. This distillate is known as arq, a Persian word meaning essence or juice. Or take kewra water and rose water in equal proportion and distill sandalwood dust, make its arq, and add it to the kewra and rose water mixture. The three distillates that make up the arq should be equal in proportion.

Now take purified hessonite pieces and powder them in this mixture mentioned above in a simak mortar for fifteen days. When the paste is fine enough to be used as surma directly in the eyes, allow it to dry and powder it. Instead of this mixture, purified hessonite may also be powdered in bedmusk (distillate of cane) arq.

Dosage: ½ to 1 rattika with malai, cream, or honey.

Pishthi or oxide is prescribed for acute gastritis; ailments caused by aggravated mucus (kapha) and bile (pitta); tuberculosis, jaundice, ailments caused by low digestive fire, and loss of taste. Disorders created by aggravated wind, rheumatism, piles, fever with cough, foul breath, rheumatic tumors, swelling of the uterus, lack of ojas (glaze) on the skin, constipation, and windy colic may also be treated with hessonite pishthi.

Hessonite pishthi or oxide gives lustre to the skin, improves the faculty of reasoning and thinking, gives strength to dhatus (body and semen), and gives longevity.

It also cures disorders created by Rahu.

SOURCES OF HESSONITE (CINNAMON STONE OR ZIRCON)

India: Hessonite is found in the gem gravels of Kashmir, Kulu, Simla, Sindhu (Indus River), Nadi, Bihar, and the Mahanadi River. They are of beautiful blue and bluish green shade. Sometimes one specimen has two shades. Yellow and violet shades are more prominent in some. The gem-quality stones, as we have mentioned before, are rare, but some that are of that quality are highly priced. Mostly dull, dark brown with blackish crystals are available in Bihar area as water-worn pebbles.

Burma: Supposed to be the producer of best hessonite gems. They are found in the Mogok area, which is also famous for rubies, sapphires, and other gemstones. As we have already mentioned, hessonite stones are found in association with diamonds, rubies, sapphires, quartz, garnet, and tourmaline. Burmese hessonite or zircon is rich in lustre and brilliance because of the abundance of water and fire (this is found in Sri Lankan zircons to a lesser degree, making them inferior to Burmese in quality and effect). Burmese hessonite is rare because the mines do not produce much.

Sri Lanka (Ceylon): Produces hessonites in abundance, though the quality is inferior to those of Mogok. Sri Lanka is famous for producing the finest transparent, colorless zircons. These are rich in lustre and brilliance, and even jewelers mistake them for diamonds from a distance. They are known as Matara diamonds. On close examination one can see the difference and distinguish them. Matara zircons are used as a substitute for diamonds. The cinnamon-color stones found in Sri Lanka are lighter in color, and the dark ones have a blackish hue not found in Burmese hessonite. In clarity and transparence, they equal the Burmese gems but are poor in water and fire. They are found as four-sided prisms ending in four-sided pyramids.

Zircons are also found in Australia (New South Wales), France, the Soviet Union, South Africa, and Brazil. Australian zircons are beautiful red gems. African hessonite is yellowish brown and is found in association with diamonds. They also used to be found in Switzerland, but they are not produced today.

The United States also produces zircon. The North Carolina gems are the best quality in the U.S., but these have no commercial value. St. Lawrence County, New York, produces hessonite of very inferior quality. Pikes Peak in Colorado produces zircon, but it discolors on heating. In Pennsylvania zircons are found in small quantity, because the gem-quality stones are rare.

Ketu is neutral, hybrid, inert, distorting, and disruptive. It creates disturbances in the physical bodies of its natives, causing them to lose interest in life. Ketu is shown as a headless torso with a fish body, called the dragon's tail. He holds a flag of self-glory in his hand. Ketu is less destructive than Rahu and leads its natives toward liberation from the bondage of life and death by making them passive.

11
Ketu and
Its Gemstone,
Cat's-eye

निर्हाद कल्पाद्द्रितिजस्य नादात् वैदूर्य मुत्पन्नमनेक वर्णम्

KETU IS THE REST of the body of Rahu. It also got its share of ambrosia, became immortal, and was placed 180° away from Rahu. Ketu is a headless half-planet, shadowy as Rahu and malefic—though not as malefic as Rahu—and is therefore considered a moksha-karak (cause of liberation from the cycle of birth and death, or indicator of enlightenment, which frees one from the bondage of birth and death). It bestows spiritual tendencies, asceticism, and nonattachment to worldly desires and ambitions. Ketu is also a half-planet that bestows wisdom, powers of discrimination, and *gyana*—spiritual knowledge, the knowledge of the self. It gives psychic abilities to its natives and makes them masters of the healing arts, natural healing, healing herbs, spices, foods, tantric healing, healing of persons possessed by evil spirits, ghosts, and astral forces. Ketu natives also have the ability to go unnoticed or merge into the crowd of common folk.

Ketu's effects are similar to those of Mars, but this is only one way of describing the malefic effect and power of Ketu.

Ketu can be more destructive if it is inauspiciously posited or closely conjunct another planet. Ketu destroys the potency of the planet with which it is conjunct or the house in which it is posited, making the planet behave in an uncontrollable manner.

Ketu's sign is Pisces—as Rahu's is Virgo. The sign Pisces belongs to the guru, Jupiter, and Ketu also has dominion over it. Ketu is exalted in Scorpio, and Taurus is its sign of fall (according to some scholars, Ketu is exalted in Sagittarius and its sign of fall is Gemini).

Ketu's body is supposed to be composed of a man's torso in its upper half and a fish body as its lower half. It is tamasik, of hybrid generation, malefic, awful, and devious in nature. It is neither feminine nor masculine (although some scholars consider it feminine), wind-dominated, aged, powerful at night, animalistic, obsessive, compulsive, and unconscious in behavior.

Rahu and Ketu both are considered elemental and instinctual forces. But Rahu is hedonistic and Ketu is unattached to worldly desires. If Rahu is beneficial to somebody, Ketu is inauspicious and destructive to the same individual.

Ashvini, Mul, and Magha nakshatras are Ketu's nakshatras. Gemini, Virgo, Sagittarius, Capricorn, and Pisces are its friendly signs. Cancer and Leo are enemy signs. Ketu is a friend of Mercury, Venus, and Saturn. Jupiter is neutral in friendship. Sun, Moon, and Mars are Ketu's enemies. It is powerful in Taurus, Sagittarius, and Pisces. According to some scholars, Rahu and Ketu have similar effects—they both destroy the ability to reason and make one animalistic and compulsive. But as a general rule one should remember that if Rahu is favorable to somebody Ketu will be unfavorable. Exalted Ketu (i.e., in Scorpio) gives benefic results, as it does when rightly posited in the third, sixth, or eleventh houses. Rahu affects mind and Ketu body.

Ketu rules the soles of the feet and is the regent of the northwest quarter. By seeing the position of Ketu in a native's horoscope we know about hands and feet, skin diseases, leprosy, and accidents. Ketu also rules over maternal relations. It gives its best and worst results from the ages of 48 to 54. Ketu rules over sesame seeds, black or dark green cloth, flags, oil, gold, iron, weapons, and handicapped people.

When afflicted or ill-posited, Ketu gives imprisonment, accidents, fear, anxiety, leprosy, skin diseases, starvation, and death by starvation. Ketu makes people conspirators and gives nightmares. It gives pain in joints, diseases of joints and nerves, and excessive heat in the body.

Ketu destroys in an awful and devious way. It is associated with smoky-grey clothes.

Ketu in numerology is associated with the numeral 7. Anybody born on the seventh, sixteenth, or twenty-fifth day of any month is influenced by Ketu.

Ketu's gemstone is cat's-eye.

THE CAT'S-EYE

Known as vaidurya mani in Sanskrit and lahsunia in Hindi, cat's-eye is a gemstone that comes from the gem mineral chrysoberyl. It is an aluminate of beryllium—a mixture of aluminum and beryllium—having traces of oxide of iron and chromium, which serve as coloring agents and give it brownish and greenish tinges. The chrysoberyl mineral produces three types of gems, as follows:

1. *Alexandrite*: dark green in color and red by transmitted light. Its clarity, hardness, and red-green color make it a valuable gem of good quality.

2. *Cat's-eye*: with a chatoyant glowing from inside like the eye of a cat and having white fibers. The brighter the fiber, the higher the quality of the gem. Cat's-eye has a silky streak of light that moves with the turning of the stone like a gleam in a straight line across the stone. Cat's-eye also is found in three varieties:

1) Cat's-eye with a golden hue with a bright white and silky lustre exactly like the eye of a cat. This is supposed to be finest in the gem family of cat's-eye and is known as kanak-khet (*kanak* means gold and *khet* means field).
2) Cat's-eye with a smoky hue with bright white and silky lustre is not as fine as the cat's-eye of golden color, but the stone is very attractive. It is called vaidurya of dhum-khet (*dhum* means smoke).
3) Cat's-eye having a dark color. It is brown in shade with chatoyant of white, silky lustre, very attractive and shining. It is known as cat's-eye of krishna khet (*krishna* means dark).

These three varieties are high in gem quality but different in effect. Golden cat's-eye is more powerful and finer in gem quality than the other two varieties. A similar streak of light is found in Indian moonstone, which is a cheaper variety stone of the quartz family.

3. *Chrysolite*: this is devoid of the white fiber that is responsible for the chatoyance. This variety is also known as cat's-eye because it has similar shades, hardness, shine, and lustre to other varieties, but no streak of light.

The gemstone alexandrite is cut in gem form, but the two other members of the chrysoberyl family mentioned above (cat's-eye with chatoyances and chrysolite without white fibers) are cut in a cabochon form and not with facets. Gem cutters who cut these forms of cat's-eye have to cut the rounded surface parallel to the hollow internal channels to allow reflected light to move across the stone and the line of light to become perfectly visible to the eye of the viewer.

QUALITIES OF A GOOD CAT'S-EYE

1. smoothness
2. brilliance of chatoyance
3. high specific gravity—heavier than average stone of the same size
4. having three streaks of light, similar to the sacred thread worn by brahmins in India
5. quality of mineral
6. straightness of the chatoyance

Cat's eye is found in many colors: yellow, black, dark or smoky-green, and white. The only thing common to all shades is the band of light moving across the stone, the chatoyance. The light reflected by the inside of the gem sometimes glows with varying colors and lustre, but a gem having a white band of light is supposed to be best. Some gemologists believe that cat's-eye is found in six colors: yellow, black, deep or smoky-green, golden, smoky-grey or greyish green, and white.

Cat's-eye shines like the eye of a cat in darkness, but it does not shine in total darkness.

In ancient scriptures cat's-eye is divided into three categories: gems with the color of the leaves of palash—shining, dark green, ones with the hue of the neck of a peacock, and ones with the golden hue of a cat's-eye.

The special feature of a cat's-eye is to reflect bands of light in milky white, greenish white, golden, and yellow colors. When the stone is turned and seen from the back the bands of light appear to be threads of silver. Threads are known as sutra in Sanskrit—and another name for cat's-eye is sutramani—a gem with threads. The gem without these threads is called karketak (chrysolite).

FLAWS OF A CAT'S-EYE

1. dullness—the cat's-eye that is not brilliant and is shining and flimsy is injurious for physical health and personal wealth
2. micaceous—injurious for progeny (sons) and family
3. crack inside the gemstone—brings injuries from sharp-edged weapons
4. cobweb inside the gemstone—brings imprisonment and is harmful for the wearer
5. having five streaks or bands of light—brings misfortune
6. stains of red color—bring quarrels in family and are harmful for progeny (sons)
7. spots of any color but the color of the stone—bring disease and increase opposition and enemies or fear of foes
8. holes or dents—bring diseases of the stomach
9. black spots—deadly and bring death
10. having curved or shimmering threads—brings diseases of the eyes
11. having honey-brown spots—bad for one's spouse
12. having white spots—bad for elder brothers
13. rough in texture—powerless and unlucky
14. flat—devoid of effect and therefore not suitable for wearing
15. red streaks of light—injurious for eyes
16. watery and dull—unhealthy for wearing
17. uneven in shape—unlucky
18. layers or inclusion of ashes—brings misfortune

IDENTIFICATION OF REAL CAT'S-EYE

1. If a real gem is placed on a bone directly for more than twenty-four hours, it makes a hole in the bone.
2. If a real gem is put in a dark place, it shines like the eyes of a cat.
3. If a real gem is placed in a dark place, beams of light seem to be coming out of the gem.
4. If a real gem is rubbed against a cloth, its brilliance increases.
5. Real cat's-eye has two and a half or three streaks or threads of light, which move across the middle of the round surface of a cabochon-cut gemstone.

CLASSIFICATION OF CAT'S EYE

1. *Brahmin:* Cat's-eye of a yellowish radiance with a white fiber, silky lustre, and pale chatoyance. It is best suited for scholars and people with a spiritual turn of mind.
2. *Kshatriya:* Cat's-eye of cream color with a golden hue and silky lustre. It is best suited for individuals belonging to the ruling class, such as magistrates, ministers, executives, and officers.
3. *Vaishya:* Cat's-eye of yellowish green color with white fiber, silky lustre, and chatoyance. It is best suited for people of the merchant class, traders, and businesspeople.
4. *Shudra:* Cat's-eye of smoky, dark color or black color. It is best suited for people belonging to the service class.

Wearing a cat's-eye increases physical strength, radiance, stamina, happiness, wealth, and the joy of having progeny. One obtains victory over foes and is saved from injuries caused by weapons and accidents. Cat's-eye removes poverty and cures illnesses caused by inauspicious Ketu. One who is favored by a cat's-eye is never punished by the government, and his secret enemies cannot conspire against him.

It is believed that, like coral, cat's-eye shows a change in its radiance and color before the wearer actually notices the symptoms of diseases in his own body. Before a fever is noticed the cat's-eye will look dry, and before one catches cold the cat's-eye looks wet. This happens because cat's-eye has microscopic holes and can be influenced by body temperature if it is tied around the arm.

RITUALS FOR WEARING A CAT'S-EYE

A cat's-eye should be bought on a Wednesday, Thursday, or Friday when Moon is in Aries, Sagittarius, or Pisces or when Moon is in Ashvini, Magha, or Mul nakshatras, in the morning hours of an ascending moon cycle. The gemstone should be given to the jeweler the same day, and the jeweler should set it in a mixture of five metals: iron, silver, copper, gold, and zinc, as prescribed for hessonite or blue sapphire, or in iron.

The weight of cat's-eye should not be less than 5 rattikas (2.95 metric carats). Cat's-eye of 2, 4, or 11 rattikas should never be worn. It should be mounted with an open back to allow the gemstone to touch the skin.

The time to wear a cat's-eye ring for the first time is two hours after sunset, or in the evening.

Before wearing the ring for the first time, wash it with cow's milk first and then with Ganga-water, spring water, rainwater, or water kept in a copper pot overnight.

After washing, the ring should be placed on a smoky-grey or smoky-green cloth on which a yantra of Ketu has already been drawn with roli or with sandalwood paste.

An engraved yantra of Ketu on an iron plate or silver plate should be washed the same way as the ring and placed on the same cloth behind the ring.

The one who is going to wear the ring should honor the engraved yantra and the gemstone mounted in the ring as a symbolic representation of Ketu, offering tilak, light (ghee lamp), flowers, and incense to them. One should worship Ketu, reciting the mantra of Ketu:

ॐ कें केतवे नमः ॐ

AUM KAIM KETAVE NAMAH AUM

The mantra should be recited 108 times or 17,000 times as prescribed, and then one should meditate on the engraved yantra. After meditation one should wear the ring on the little finger of the left hand.

The yantra to be drawn on the cloth and engraved on the iron or silver plate is as follows:

14	9	16
15	13	11
10	17	12

After the ring is worn once, the engraved yantra should be wrapped in the cloth and either donated to a shrine or kept in one's personal shrine.

SOURCES OF CAT'S-EYE

India: In India, cat's-eye is found in the Himalayas, Vindhyachal Mountains, Trivandrum, Atak-Katak, Shripur, and Sundervan areas as water-worn pebbles and in layers of metamorphic rocks of pegmatite and micaceous sheaths. Indian cat's-eyes are of fine quality. The best cat's-eye is found in Trivandrum in southern India.

Burma: Cat's-eye found in alluvial deposits of Mogok is considered to be the best in quality. It is better than Trivandrum cat's-eye.

Sri Lanka (Ceylon):   Good varieties of gem-quality cat's-eye are found in abundance in Sri Lanka. The biggest and heaviest cat's-eyes have been found in Sri Lanka.

Brazil: Also produces good gem-quality cat's-eye in lesser quantity.

Soviet Union: Ural Mountains.

United States: Does not produce good gem-quality cat's-eye, but alexandrite and chrysolite are found there.

China, Madagascar, and Rhodesia also produce good-quality cat's-eye in small quantities.

12
Semiprecious Gemstones and Gems of Medicinal Value

INDIAN TEXTS on gems mention eighty-four kinds of gems. Nine of these—known as nav-ratnas—have been discussed in the preceding pages in brief. Some of the other seventy-five ratnas, or gems, are used by astrologers, gem therapists, tantriks, and medicine men of the Ayurvedic tradition.

Many of these gems are rarely used, but they do exist. Some of them (e.g., paras mani) do not exist now, but their names are mentioned in the list of eighty-four gems. Many more exist but are not mentioned in scriptures and are only mentioned in books on rocks and minerals. Most of these are semiprecious gemstones. Some are transparent, brilliant, lustrous, and attractive, some are opaque but lustrous and attractive. Some are only of medicinal use, and some are only used to make idols, floors, pots, decorative items, and so forth.

These gems—used by gem therapists, astrologers, and medicine men—are the ones we will discuss now.

1. **Amber**, known as kaharua in Hindi. It is not a gemstone but a fossil resin. Saints in India wear one big bead of amber around

their necks and believe that amber saves them from being un-balanced. This may be true because amber possesses a magnetic property: It attracts straw and produces negative electricity when rubbed. It has a very fine odor, which is extracted and made into perfumes of high price. When rubbed on cloth amber produces a very nice and sweet smell. Its magnetic quality works on the electromagnetic field of the body and enables the wearer to achieve more self-control and better physical health. Because of its power to attract pieces of straw it is known as trinkant mani, which means a gem that holds pieces of trin (straw). Amber is found in many shades and varieties, of which green and blue amber are the rarest. It is found in forms both transparent and opaque. Some transparent beads reflect light and are fluorescent, but most of the raw material is opaque, discolored, and full of cracks and hairs of calcite. Amber is found on the shores of the Baltic Sea, in Sicily, sometimes on the east coast of England, and in China, Thailand, and Burma.

Burmese amber, known as burmite, is harder and heavier than that of the Baltic Sea or German amber succinite.

The amber smell is very healthy for the body and pleasant for the mind. Raw, good-quality amber is used in the gem remedy *jawahar mohra* as a special gem tonic and also in many aphrodisiacs.

2. *Agate,* like amber, is not a real stone. It belongs to the family of cryptocrystalline quartz grouped under chalcedony. Chalcedony is a group term used for a waxy, smooth form of quartz with hidden or microscopic crystals lining the cavities, filling cracks and forming crusts; it is sometimes transparent, usually translucent. Agate is chalcedony with a banded or irregular, variegated appearance. Bands are mostly found in parallel waves resulting from the difference in the deposition of layers of cryptocrystalline silica and amorphous hydrated silica. Petrified wood is usually an agatized wood. Agate is tough and hard and often contains foreign matter when recovered from the mines. It is also found as water-worn pebbles in the river beds in the Vindhyachal and Satpura ranges, the Himalayas, and in many other places in India. Agate found in the Narmada River is known as rudhiraksh and is used for worship as the symbol of Lord Shiva. It is known as narmadeshwar or narvadeshwar.

These narvadeshwars are found in the form of a lingam, or

phallus, which is a symbol of Lord Shiva. They become shiny and smooth when polished. Agate is also used in jewelry, decorative items, and the handles of knives, cups, and idols of deities.

The use of agate beads for rosaries and necklaces is very popular among Sufi saints and Hindu sadhus in India and Persia. They are supposed to bring calmness and good luck. As a member of the family of quartz it has magnetic properties and helps the electromagnetic field of the body, removes anxiety, absorbs excessive body heat, and gives calmness. Calmness leads to good luck. It is also used for making mortars and grinding pearls and other precious gems for medicinal preparations.

Agate is very popular among Ayurvedic doctors (vaidyas) and is used in many medicinal preparations, especially in an eye remedy known as surma and in jawahar mohra, a special gem tonic.

Agate is first purified by heating it to red-hot and then dropping it into rose water or cow's milk. The process is repeated twenty-one times and then it is used in surma or other medicinal preparations. Instead of rose water, distillate of bedmusk (a cane distillate) may be used.

Agate pishthi is made by grinding fine powder of purified agate in rose water for seven days.

Dosage: 1 to 3 rattikas twice a day with honey.

Agate is prescribed for heart troubles, weak heart, general debility, eye troubles, bleeding leukorrhea, blood in sputum, and anxiety. Pishthi of agate calms the mind.

As a member of the quartz family it is associated with the planet Moon.

3. *Amethyst* is known as kataila or jamunia in Hindi, because of its purple color like that of the jamun or jambufruit. It is of the crystalline variety of quartz. The color in the gemstone is caused by traces of iron and manganese. The more deeply colored specimens are cut as gems. Long ago, amethyst was highly prized, but it lost much of its value after great deposits of amethyst were found in Brazil.

Amethyst is a favorite semiprecious gemstone of gem therapists and astrologers. It is prescribed during the phase (major period and subperiod) of Saturn and is supposed to be a stone belonging to Saturn because of its purple color. Otherwise it should be associated with Moon as a member of the family of quartz.

Qualities of a Good Amethyst

1. lustre
2. transparence
3. evenness of color
4. hardness
5. smoothness
6. attractive shape and size

Flaws of an Amethyst

1. dullness
2. opaqueness
3. unevenness of color
4. patchy, striated, zoned
5. inclusions
6. air bubbles

When a crystal of amethyst is cut at a certain angle to its axis, pressure on it generates a minute electrical charge, and it transmits short light waves of ultraviolet color that work on the skin and help the body. Its electrical or magnetic property brings electrochemical balance in the body and helps the body's electromagnetic field.

Amethyst provides good understanding, enhances the faculty of judgment, and brings detachment from worldly things. It also helps one to maintain good temper, avoid errors, and achieve self-discipline and high standards in life. It helps one to gain stability of mind and removes anger and anxiety by transmitting light waves and absorbing excessive body heat.

Before wearing it for the first time one should perform the rituals prescribed for blue sapphire, but the engraved yantra and the yantra drawn on the cloth is not necessary. The ring should be purified and honored the same way and japa (recitation of the mantra of Saturn 108 times) definitely would help the amethyst work better.

Good varieties of amethysts are also found in Mogok, Burma, and Thailand. Amethysts of red and cinnamon color are also found, but they are not associated with Saturn.

4. *Aquamarine*, known as beruj in Hindi, is a light sea-green (blue-green) variety of transparent beryl gem—hard and transparent. Aquamarine is a silicate of aluminum and beryllium in which traces of chromium are found. The chromium acts as a coloring agent and gives the stone a delicate blue hue. It also occurs as yellowish golden beryl. It belongs to the family of emeralds and contains the same minerals that become emerald when they have the intense green color similar to the color of a fresh blade of grass. Aquamarine is cheaper than emerald and more transparent but light in color.

Like emerald, aquamarine is associated with the planet Mercury and provides safety to sailors. It is used as a substitute for emerald.

It is rich in lustre and brilliance and, according to the Greek geographer Strabo, it was used in the ornamentation of Indian drinking cups around 45 B.C. to 21 A.D. It was produced in India before 400 B.C., according to S. Ball, a British astronomer, and India was its chief source, according to Pliny, the Roman writer, 23 A.D. to 79 A.D.

It is also soothing for the heart, pleasant to the eyes, and helpful in maintaining electrochemical balance. Because of its electrical property it helps the electromagnetic field of the body and is used by gemologists, gem therapists, and Indian astrologers. It helps in overcoming the anxiety and restlessness typical of the mercurial temperament of ill-posited Mercury natives.

It can be safely used by all. It is especially calming if used as a necklace, armlet, amulet, or pendant. In females it increases feminine qualities.

Aquamarines are mainly greenish blue or yellowish blue. The yellow variety is also found in South India, but these differ in color from yellow topaz.

5. *Achroite*, known as dantala in Hindi, is an important stone in a special medicinal preparation for teeth and is given to patients having dental troubles.

Achroite is a transparent, smooth, brilliant stone belonging to the family of tourmaline. Because the mineral is very soft it is not used in jewelry as much as tourmaline; even then, fine crystals are shaped in gem form and used as a gem.

Because it is colorless it is associated with Moon.

It is also a silicate of aluminum and boron and several other minerals like tourmaline.

Crystals and gems can be used for healing in the same way as agate, citrine, and amethyst.

6. *Antimony* is known as surma in Hindi. In one form it is found as stibnite with pyrite, galena, and arsenic minerals. It is found as a crystal. Native antimony is also found as a mineral but is rare. As a crystal in its ore form, it is found as an iron-black or lead-black stone, slightly grey and shining. It is used for making a special eye remedy—an eye salve or eyewash. This preparation is commonly known as surma, most probably after the name of the stone.

To make surma, antimony crystals are rubbed on a flat stone to a fine powder (by rubbing for a fair amount of time, which takes many days). The powder thus obtained is greyish black. Many gems ground fine in a mortar are also added. (We have already mentioned the word surma as a special eye remedy made from precious and semiprecious gems when discussing those gems.) The gems are sometimes used alone, sometimes with antimony powder and herbs. One of the most famous medicinal plants—neem—is also used in the preparation of surma. Sometimes pieces of antimony are allowed to stay at the root of a neem tree (*Azadirachta indica*), and then they are reduced to a fine powder, which is directly applied to the eyelids. This makes a very fine surma excellent for preserving eyesight.

Surma made of gems and antimony, known as kahl-ul-jawahar, is available in the markets of India and is used by millions of Indians for eye health.

7. *Basri* is dull in lustre, yellowish grey in color. It is a valuable stone and is used only for preparing the eye remedy known as surma. Because of its dullness, it cannot be used as a gemstone and is therefore not used by astrologers and gem therapists.

8. *Bloodstone (heliotrope),* known as pitonia in Hindi, is found as a bright or dark green stone with small, blood-like spots of red color from which it derives its name. It belongs to the waxy, smooth form of quartz.

Bloodstone is supposed to be a healing gem for disorders created by aggravated bile, which is known as pitta in Sanskrit, from which it derives its Hindi name, pitonia. Its pishthi is prescribed for disorders of the bile.

The color green in bloodstone is due to the presence of iron and chlorite and the red color due to hematite. Bloodstone is a mixture of quartz with uncrystallized opal quartz.

Bloodstone is rich in oxygen, which composes 53.3 percent of the stone, and silica, which accounts for 46.7 percent. This composition makes it good for curing bile diseases.

Because of its electrical property it is good to wear as a necklace. It will help maintain the body's electromagnetic field and electrochemical balance. Bloodstone does not lose its lustre, because it is not affected by body acids.

Bloodstone is also used for certain eye remedies, or surmas. Bile is found in the eyes and is responsible for good vision. By using a fine powder (surma) of bloodstone, the bile that helps in vision is balanced, and problems of vision caused by disorders of this bile can be cured.

Bloodstone is also prescribed for anemic people, who benefit by wearing a necklace of it. It also helps women during menstruation and in excessive bleeding. To cure *pitti*—a kind of rash in which the skin develops red spots and itching—wear beads of bloodstone in an amulet or necklace.

9. **Braunite**, known as dar-e-chana and yellowdite, is hard and opaque purplish brown with yellow, smoky spots or brown and grey spots. It is important because it is used for making mortars and pestles for grinding Ayurvedic medicines, though it is not hard enough to grind pearls and other precious and semiprecious gemstones. The color spots are due to the presence of iron, barium, cobalt, and zinc.

Braunite is found in India, New South Wales (Australia), and Europe as the cubic crystal ore of manganese.

10. **Basanite,** known as kasauti in Hindi, is a velvet-black variety of quartz. It is a bright black stone used by jewelers as a touchstone or "gold tester," for testing the purity of gold alloys. When rubbed across it, gold leaves a streak, which is then moistened with a solution of nitric and hydrochloric acid. This reveals the nature of the gold under test. In fact, the stone helps jewelers

find the truth, that is, the quality. Medicine men use mortars and pestles made of this stone. Because of its hardness it is used for grinding oxides of metals and gems and also for grinding small pieces of gems for making their pishthi or paste.

Hindus worship this stone as a symbol of Lord Vishnu, the god of preservation, and they know it as shaligram. For devotees of Vishnu it is more precious than gems.

Because of its association with the quartz family, basanite is of therapeutic value. If a round stone is immersed in water that has been stored in a gold, silver, or copper pot, it magnetizes the water. When drunk, this water helps the body in maintaining electrochemical balance and calms down the system instantaneously. To accelerate the process one may add one or two fresh leaves of basilicum (basil), known as tulsi in Hindi. This water is used as holy water in Hindu temples, where shaligram is given a bath and the water is called charanamrita, or nectar from the holy feet of the Lord.

11. **Carnelian,** known as raat ratuva in Hindi, is a member of the cryptocrystalline quartz family. It is a colored, gem-quality variety of jasper, found in bright brown, ocher, and orange-red shades. Red carnelians are used in ornaments, and yellowish and brownish varieties are called *sard*. Carnelian is a clear chalcedony and has electrical properties that provide a healing quality. Sometimes very beautiful and lustrous specimens are seen embedded in decorative items and rings.

Carnelian is a special remedy for night fevers. In such cases, one gets fever only during the night. Ratuva (carnelian) is rubbed on the soles of the patient's foot from heel to toe; it absorbs excessive body heat and heals the patient. That's why it has the name ratjari mohara (rat = night, jari = fever, mohara = gem). Carnelian gives patience and self-confidence and removes the evil influence of the evil eye.

Carnelian and sard are found throughout the globe.

12. **Citrine,** known as sunehla in Hindi, is a variety of crystalline quartz belonging to the family of amethyst. Citrine and amethyst have almost the same chemical composition, but the color in citrine is caused by the presence of iron, whereas in amethyst the color is due to the presence of manganese. Citrine is also called false topaz and golden topaz, but it is lighter in weight

than topaz. It is transparent and lustrous and is used as a substitute for yellow sapphire, the gemstone of the planet Jupiter, by gem therapists and Indian astrologers. Brazil produces good crystals of gem quality and is a center for commercial supply of the natural gemstone citrine.

Like amethyst, citrine also is useful for the body. Because of its electrical properties, it can help the electromagnetic field of the body if worn in a necklace or ring. It brings undisturbed sleep and removes fear at night.

13. *Cairngorm,* or smoky topaz, known as dhunaila in Hindi, belongs to the same group of crystalline quartz as citrine, amethyst, rose quartz, and gold quartz. It also is transparent, has a fine lustre, and is used for manufacturing sunglasses and cheap jewelry—as are other members of the transparent, gem-quality quartz family. Cairngorm is assigned to the planet Jupiter. Gem therapists and Indian astrologers prescribe it as a substitute for yellow sapphire.

It is useful for the body's electrochemical balance and electromagnetic field, if worn like a necklace or ring, because of its electrical properties.

14. *Epidote,* known as dur in Hindi, belongs to the group of complex silicates of calcium, aluminum, and water. It forms as crystals or as thin green-colored crusts in nearly every type of metamorphic rock (rock that has been altered by heat, pressure, or chemical action) and in cracks and seams. It is a common mineral wherever igneous rock (rock formed at a high temperature or from molten lava) has come in contact with limestone. It is found in Italy, France, and Germany in colors ranging from green to brown and black and is hard and nontransparent. Epidote is used for making toys and figures of deities.

If it is shaped like an egg it can cure anxiety and help the body by absorbing excessive heat when held in the hand; and it can be used in gem therapy.

15. *Flint,* known as chakmak in Hindi, is a type of quartz with hidden or microscopic crystals, that is, cryptocrystalline quartz. It is found as grey, brown, or black nodules in chalk, with which it is covered. It is duller, more opaque, and rougher than chalcedony and breaks with conchoidal (shell-like) fractures, producing sharp

edges. Because of this quality, it was used for making arrowheads and tools in the beginning of civilization. When struck with iron pyrites, flint was used for making fire.

Because it can be easily powdered, it is useful for making pottery and flint glass. It is also used for lining the grinding balls used in manufacturing paint mixtures. It is found in abundance in Bihar, Orissa, Madhya Pradesh, Uttar Pradesh, Vindhya Pradesh, Bombay, and Andhra Pradesh in India. It is also found in Pakistan, Baluchistan, Europe, and in Arizona in the United States.

It was an important stone of ancient man—a real gem—for providing humans with fire and weapons.

Its chemical formula is the same as amethyst's, but there is no similarity between the two gems except that both of them belong to the quartz family. Flint belongs to a group in which quartz is microscopic and hidden, along with chert, jasper, carnelian, onyx, and agate. Flint is the dullest of them all.

16. *Garnet* is known as tamda in Hindi. Garnets are more popular as gems than as rock-forming minerals. They belong to a close-knit family of silicate minerals with many common characteristics, and many gems belong to the garnet group of gemstones. Their crystals are isometric, usually having twelve or twenty-four sides, but sometimes combined forms with thirty-six or forty-eight faces are also found.

Garnets are a combination of calcium, magnesium, iron, aluminum, silicon, and oxygen. Sometimes chromium and titanium are also found in garnets.

Fresh crystals have a glossy lustre and are found in red, brown, yellow, green, and black colors. White or colorless garnets are rare. Garnets having a light color are transparent to translucent; dark-colored varieties are translucent to opaque.

Garnets of red color resemble ruby and spinel, but spinel is softer than garnet and ruby is much harder than garnet. These garnets are used as a substitute for ruby and are assigned to the Sun. Garnet is used as a gemstone in rings, necklaces, pendants, and other forms of jewelry. Transparent, clear, lustrous garnets are supposed to be good for obtaining favor from the planet to which they are assigned.

Six varieties of garnets are categorized as gem-quality garnets. They all differ in chemical composition, but they belong to the group of silicate minerals. Almandite, pyrope, and green demantoid are well known for their gem quality.

1. *Almandite:* also known as carbuncle, is the commonly available garnet found in many metamorphic rocks. It is basically an iron-aluminum compound. Whenever some of the iron is replaced by magnesium, the stone becomes red, like pyrope. A clear, transparent, lustrous specimen of such a mixture becomes precious garnet, as it is cut as a gem. Its pale violet variety is known as rhodolite.
2. *Andradite:* is composed primarily of calcium and iron. Like almandite, it is also very common. When found in yellow or green, it is called topazolite; when red, it is known as andradite; when black, melanite; when green, it is demantoid, a gem-quality garnet.
3. *Grossularite:* is a calcium-aluminum garnet normally colorless to white, but colored when it contains iron as an impurity. Iron makes it assume various shades of yellow, cinnamon brown, rosy red, and green. The name comes from its resemblance in color to the Siberian "gooseberry green" variety of grossularite garnet.
4. *Pyrope:* known as precious garnet, is mined in large quantities for garnet paper. It is found at its best, clear and perfect, in South African "blue earth" with diamonds. It is a magnesium-aluminum garnet with a little trace of calcium and iron impurity. It is found in a deep red color that appears black from a distance.
5. *Spessartite:* is quite a rare member of the group of aluminum garnets. It contains magnesium and aluminum, which gives it a violet tint that makes it gem-quality and valuable. Gem-quality stones are found in Virginia granites.
6. *Uvarovite:* is a less common variety of garnet found in serpentine rock and in limestone associated with the ore of chromium. The rich green color is due to the presence of chromium, which makes it a highly prized garnet.

Garnet is used in ornaments and other decorative items because it is a semiprecious stone, and therefore inexpensive. It is also used as a pishthi in Ayurveda and acts like ruby. Garnet oxide and pishthi are made the same way as those of ruby. It stops bleeding and cures diseases caused by formation of stones in the body, promotes vigor and vitality, and acts as a sexual stimulant.

17. **Gauri** is a variety of agate, semiprecious chalcedony. It is found in many colors and contains bands of milky color; it is used

for making mortars and pestles. Because it is comparatively hard, jewelers use it for measuring weight.

18. *Gold stone* is also known as star stone, and sang-e-sitara or taramandal in Hindi. It is often found with realgar or stibnite, usually in massive forms though sometimes as sheets, but never in the form of crystals. Gold stone can be reddish brown, brownish orange, or ocher brown, with golden stains that glitter like gold. It is a very weak and soft stone and is used for rings and pendants. The genuine stone, which has an olive-green shade, is hard to find.

19. *Green quartz* is also known as bamboo stone. Its Hindi name is bansi (*bans* means bamboo). It is a soft stone of the color of bamboo, opaque and translucent. When polished it becomes shiny and smooth and it is used for making toys and floors. Oval forms can be used for absorbing heat and temporarily curing anxiety.

20. *Green zade,* also known as aventurine and in Hindi, margaz, is an opaque, green stone. It is found in South India and is used for making toys and beads for rosaries and necklaces. The color resembles the color of emeralds. Some specimens are opaque and also translucent. It is also used as a gemstone of Mercury; people who cannot afford emerald necklaces wear it as a necklace for befriending Mercury. Its blue variety has been discovered recently and is known as blue margaz, or sodalite in English.

21. *Hazrat ber*—its English name is not known to the author, but it resembles a plum in shape and is a hard stone with a rough, granular surface. It is considered a gem because of its medicinal value. Purified by boiling in a daula yantra with cow's milk and ground by rubbing on a flat stone with rose water, hazrat ber is reduced to a fine paste and given in very small amounts with honey for urinary troubles and nausea or vomiting.

22. *Jade* (known as yashav in Hindi) is the name given to a group of opaque, waxy, or pearly minerals. It is mostly found in green, but yellow, white, and pink shades of jade are available. There are two kinds of "true jade": jadite—a gem form of pyroxene, and nephrite—a form of amphibole.

Light, translucent, emerald-green jade is considered a precious stone.

Jade is a very hard stone and is used to make mortars for the making of paste from hard stones such as rubies.

Chinese jade is softer than jade found in India and Afghanistan and is therefore good for carving. Jade becomes lustrous when polished and is used in decorative items, plates, cups, idols, and sculptures of gods and subgods. Carved jade has been used in palaces and temples and was used for centuries before Christ.

Pink jade is also considered fine, but the emerald-green variety is highly prized, especially when sold as carved figures, cups, or plates.

Jade is a member of the family of quartz gems, to which many other semiprecious stones like moonstone, malachite, lapis lazuli, turquoise, jet, and rodonite belong. The main source of supply are the Kochin Hills in Burma, though it is also found in Tibet, Mexico, South America, New Zealand, eastern Turkestan, Siberia, and British Columbia.

Like margaz, jade is also used as a substitute for emerald, and is associated with the planet Mercury.

As a member of the quartz family, it helps the body and is of therapeutic importance. Like kidney stone, it is also supposed to be a cure for kidney ailments.

Jade is connected with many qualities. It is believed to be a remedy for all kinds of internal disorders and can be taken orally as a fine powder mixed with water. According to the Chinese it is the most precious stone. They believe that it prevents fatigue, prolongs life, and prevents decomposition of the body after death.

23. *Kansla,* a variety of tourmaline, is found in a cloudy, greenish shade of white, although blue and green varieties are also found. It is hard, tough, and transparent, and is good for stone carving and making idols of deities. Heated tourmaline develops an electric charge.

24. *Lodestone,* known as chumbak in Hindi, is a magnetic iron ore (magnetite)—a natural magnet. It is opaque, dull in lustre, and either deep red or black. It is strongly magnetic and so of great therapeutic importance. Magnetite from Magnet Cove, Arkansas, is more powerful in magnetism.

25. **Lapis lazuli,** known as lajwart in Hindi and as rajwart in Sanskrit belongs to the family of quartz gems. It is a rock mineral rich in lazurite, which is highly valued for ornaments. Lapis lazuli is a combination of sodium silicate, calcium, and aluminum with traces of sulphur and chlorine. It is completely opaque with a waxy lustre that increases when the gem is polished. Its color is similar to the color of the neck of a peacock—with spots of a gold color, known as "golden fly," shining brightly and clearly visible. This metallic lustre of golden yellow color is due to the presence of iron pyrites.

Lapis lazuli has been popular for its ornamental value since ancient times. It is probably the oldest stone of India, and is well known for its systematic mining in the Oxus Valley of Afghanistan about seven thousand years ago. These mines still produce a substantial amount of gemstone even now.

The best quality lapis lazuli is found in a deep blue or ultramarine color with golden specks. It is used by gem therapists and Indian astrologers as a substitute for blue sapphire—the gemstone of the planet Saturn—and it is also used by Ayurvedic doctors in preparing medicines. As a medicinal gem lapis lazuli is of great value. It is also used for making the special eye remedy, surma.

Rasa Tantra Sar recommends lapis lazuli with gold spots for the making of medicinal preparations. It should be boiled with a mixture of cow's urine, lemon juice, jawakhar, and papadkhar (salts obtained from herbs) for six hours in a daula yantra. It is then purified and suitable for making medicines.

To make lapis lazuli oxide, take powdered purified pieces of lapis lazuli and add an equal amount of sulphur, then add lemon juice, and grind the mixture in a mortar made of agate, simak, jade, or any stone suitable for grinding gems, for twelve hours. Make a tablet of this and dry it in the sun. Then make a sarva samput as described in previous chapters and fire it either in a gajput or a potter's kiln. Repeat the process seven times. The oxide will be ready for oral use and will be of a dirty red color.

Dosage: 1 to 2 rattikas three times a day with malai, rock sugar candy, or sweet butter and rock sugar candy powdered fine.

Usage: Lapis oxide is cool, heavy, digestive, and a complete medicine, having all the six rasas (tastes). It increases digestive fire, cures aggravated bile, hemorrhoids, tuberculosis, jaundice, coughing, and illnesses created by humors of mucus and wind. It is specially prescribed in urinary diseases experienced in old age.

To make lapis lazuli pishthi, take powdered purified pieces of lapis lazuli and grind them with fresh apple juice in a mortar used for gems for fourteen days. After fourteen days of grinding fill the mortar up to about an inch above the surface of the lapis paste. Stir it for three hours each day for three days. Afterwards, when the paste settles down, drain off as much apple juice as possible. Allow the juice to dry—a fine paste will remain. This paste should be ground again to make the paste finer. Dry the paste. Now it can be given for oral use.

Dosage: 1 to 2 rattikas two or three times a day as necessary with 1 tsp. of honey, rose petal jam (gulkand), or murabba of amla.

Usage: Beneficial for urinary troubles of old age, tuberculosis, cough, burning sensation, hemorrhoids, jaundice, diabetes, general debility, insomnia, red eyes, restlessness, and neurosis.

26. *Malachite,* also known as kidney stone and as dane fireng in Hindi, belongs to the quartz family of gems. The stone is greyish green, sometimes transparent, and lustrous, displaying a streak of light that moves when the stone is turned. It is often found with azurite, but it is more common than azurite. Both occur in smooth, irregular masses in the upper levels of mines. Compact, deeply colored specimens are cut for gems or ornaments. Jewelers in India prescribe a test for finding out the essence of malachite: rub a knife blade soaked in lemon juice on the malachite. The blade turns the color of copper if the essence is copper, white if the essence is silver, and yellow if the essence is gold. The variety with gold as its essence is rare.

It is prescribed by gem therapists, Ayurvedic doctors, and Indian astrologers to clients suffering from kidney stones and other disorders of the kidney. It is used both orally—as a fine paste—and externally, when it is applied on kidneys. The paste is made by rubbing the stone on a flat stone. For oral use, the stone should be ground with rose water; for external use plain water may be used.

When worn as a necklace or ring, it relieves kidney pain. Other members of the quartz family are jade, moonstone, amazonite, lapis lazuli, rhodonite, rhodochrosite, hematite, jet, obsidian, and turquoise. But only malachite has the property of healing kidney disorders, especially expelling or dissolving kidney stones. It works through the electromagnetic field of the body, and when used orally helps the body's electrochemical balance.

27. **Moonstone,** known as chandrakanta mani or godanti in Hindi, is an albite with a bluish sheen. Albite is one of the plagio-clase feldspars. (Feldspars form the most abundant group of minerals found in nearly all igneous rocks and in the rocks formed from them. All are aluminum silicates combined with one or two metals. They are five times as common as quartz. Their crystals are very similar in form and the crystal angles are all close to 60° and 120°. Feldspars show two good cleavage faces at right angles and they usually have a smooth, glassy, or pearly lustre. From the chemical point of view they belong to two groups: (1) potash feldspars and (2) sodium feldspars and calcium feldspars. Moonstones are found in both groups of feldspars.)

Moonstone is a sodium feldspar with a rather low specific gravity, frequently containing potassium. A common feldspar is orthoclase feldspar. It is white, yellow, or pink and known as potash feldspar. A variety called adularia is used for making moonstone. This moonstone is soft and smooth, sometimes cloudy, translucent, and colorless. Another variety of moonstone is transparent and belongs to the quartz family, but it is not classified as godanti, which is a lemon-colored, translucent, and opaque gemstone with the color of a cow's tooth, from which it derives its name (*go* = cow, *dant* = tooth).

Moonstone resembles cat's-eye only in its opalescence and bands or streaks of light, but its specific gravity is lower than cat's-eye, and it is less hard. Green moonstones are sold as cat's-eye as are yellow and brown moonstones. These are not cat's-eye, however, because cat's-eye has asbestos as an impurity, which gives it a chatoyance not found in moonstone.

Moonstones also influence the body's magnetic field and are of much therapeutic importance. They are very cheap and very popular in jewelry. They are also used for making a round egglike shape and are worshipped as lingam (phallus)—a symbol of Lord Shiva.

Godanti is really moonstone. Quartz is sphatik mani—also associated with moon. Godanti is assigned to Moon, which is why it is called chandrakant mani (*Chandra* being one of the names of the Moon and *kant* meaning light). Godanti, or Chandrakant Mani, is commonly used by gem therapists to provide lunar energy, to cure anxiety, and to strengthen the will. It is used by Indian astrologers for befriending the Moon. Ayurvedic doctors use it in medicinal preparations, first purifying it for oral use as an oxide or paste.

To make moonstone oxide, first boil it in lemon juice in a daula yantra for three hours.

Take 40 grams of purified godanti and grind it with aloe vera juice in a simak or other mortar. Then a tablet should be made and dried in the sun. After it is dry it should be placed in a sarva samput and fired in a gajput or potter's kiln.

Dosage: 2 rattikas to 8 rattikas with sudarshan choorna (a formula available in Ayurvedic pharmacies), powdered rock sugar candy, or 1 tsp. honey.

Usage: This oxide contains sulphur and is used for fevers of all kinds and headache. For women it is prescribed for leukorrhea and excessive bleeding. It is also an excellent remedy for dry cough, burning sensation, thirst, high blood pressure, headache caused by stress, insomnia, restlessness. It calms the mind, strengthens the heart, and cures stress.

It is very useful for children—in fevers, coughs, colds, breathing problems, weakness of bones, weakness of digestive fire, constipation, and indigestion. It can be given without any fear of after-effects, but it should be given in small doses—in heavy doses it can damage the liver.

For making an oxide, use godanti of the finest quality and see that it is free of all kinds of impurities.

28. *Marcasite,* known as swarnmakshika in Sanskrit and sona or sohan makkhi in Hindi, belongs to the group of metallic minerals. It is found in radiating coxcomb form in clays, peat, and coal as crystals that are soft and that crumble and break easily. Marcasite is also known as white pyrite, though it is lighter and more brittle than its cousin pyrite, which is known as fool's gold. Pyrite and marcasite are both swarnmakshika. Pyrite is used to obtain sulphur and sometimes iron. They are usually found as crystals—but sometimes as grains and masses—in light, brassy yellow color. Marcasite may also be white; in that case it is known as rupa makkhi. Rupa makkhi is lighter in weight and more brittle than light, brassy yellow pyrite. It is mainly used for preparing medicines and has no other importance in the gem world.

For medicinal preparations, sona makkhi is first purified. The method of purification is different from the usual method: mix 3 parts powdered swarnmakshika, with 1 part powdered rock salt and 5 parts fresh lemon juice. Take an iron pan (Chinese wok) with a heavy bottom and place the mixture in it over a flame. Stir the mixture constantly after it starts boiling. The lemon juice should be vaporized by boiling. After all the juice evaporates the powder should be heated and stirred constantly until the wok becomes red-hot. Then take the wok off the fire and allow the powder to cool. After it cools, the powder should be washed with water four to six times. This process of washing dissolves the salt in the mixture. After this the powder should be dried in the sun. It is now purified and can be used for preparing medicines.

The best shiny and pure swarnmakshika should be selected for making a medicine.

To make swarnmakshika bhasma, or oxide, pulverize purified swarnmakshika for twelve hours in concentrated water of kulthi. After it becomes a fine powder, it should be made into a tablet and dried in the Sun. When it is dry place it in a sarva samput (two clay bowls of the same diameter) and fire it in gajput or a potter's kiln. When it is cool, it should be carefully opened and the oxide taken out.

Another method for making the oxide is to powder swarnmakshika (already purified) in castor oil first, then in buttermilk, and then in the urine of a male goat. After it becomes a fine powder it should be dried and shaped into a tablet and fired in a sarva samput. This process should be repeated three times. After the first two firings the sarva samput should be allowed to cool naturally, the oxide should be taken out and ground with goat's urine and then reshaped into a tablet and fired again. The three firings make the oxide more effective.

Dosage: 1 to 3 rattikas with 1 tsp. honey or with malai or cream. The medicine is for oral use only.

Usage: This oxide is used for jaundice, diabetes, leprosy, heat in a hot climate, disorders of bile, burning in the eyes, red eyes, vomiting, boils, bilious diabetes, leukorrhea, urinary troubles, headache, poisoning, hemorrhoids, worms, and so forth.

The oxide tastes bitter. It subdues bile, increases blood, and may be used as an aphrodisiac. It strengthens the white and red blood corpuscles and is a good way to administer iron. It may be used in many ways by tender babies, old women, and old people. In diseases of bile and aggravated mucus it works as an excellent remedy.

For headaches that tend to subside after vomiting, accompanied by a bitter taste in the mouth and distaste for food that one generally likes, the oxide is very useful.

For those with wet dreams, it should be given with rock sugar candy or honey.

For insomnia sufferers it should be given with powdered ginger and amla murabha.

For debility caused by old age it should be given with cow's milk.

For vomiting caused by indigestion it should be given with 1 tsp. of honey.

Swarnmakshika oxide is also used as a tonic for general weaknesses caused by a sudden shock and fantasizing.

It cures vomiting caused by excessive drinking.

In diseases of bladder where the patient cannot hold the urine and urine passes out drop by drop all the time, the oxide of swarnmakshika should be given with shilajit.

For palpitation of heart, trembling of the limbs, tonsil problems, irritation of the salivary glands, enlargement of the liver, swelling of the limbs, skin irritation, loss of radiance of the body, small boils, and dry skin, swarnmakshika oxide is a very useful remedy. It also cures problems created by excessive smoking, diseases of the endocrine glands, and enlargement of the testicles.

29. *Mysore Star,* known as seengli in Hindi and star ruby, belongs to the corundum family of gems. It is found in a variety of deep crimson and scarlet colors, both opaque and translucent. It is not lustrous when recovered from mines, but acquires lustre when polished. There are white streaks in its texture. When the stone is given a cabochon cut, a six-pointed star, good lustre, and no bubbles, inclusions, cobwebs, cracks, dents, or ambiguities of color, is supposed to be a fine-quality gem suitable for use as a substitute for ruby. Gem therapists and Indian astrologers prescribe it as a remedy for an afflicted, ill-posited Sun. It is used in rings and pendants. Because of its association with corundum gems, Mysore star is an effective and useful stone for gem therapy. It is found in Mysore and is therefore known as Mysore ruby, though

it is much softer than ruby and is blackish red rather brilliant ruby-red.

30. **Moss agate,** known as sijari in Hindi, is a wonderful stone found in riverbeds with figures of sunrise, sunset, birds, animals, and trees printed on the stone. The figures cannot be seen as long as the stone is not cut, but when the stone is cut into layers, the slices show the pictures clearly.

These figures are not simply inclusions of some minerals or impurities, nor are they fossils—they are formed by the reflections of trees, birds, and animals when the substance is being formed. Something like a photographic process seems to register these impressions on the stone—as images are registered on film through a camera lens. These stones are found in all sizes. They are mostly found in Vindhyachal and Madhya Pradesh areas. The author has seen these stones in the Ken River in Banda district, Uttar Pradesh.

The moss agate belongs to the family of chalcedony. It is found in many shades of yellow to brown. The pictures are not colorful but are all in one tone, for example, in brown stones the images are in sepia. They can be lighter or darker in color than the rest of the stone, but not multicolored as in color photography. Mass agate is a stone worth collecting—it is pleasant to look at and to touch.

31. **Onyx,** a cryptocrystalline quartz, is agate with even and parallel bands. Usually it is found in black and white or brown and white shades and is smooth, waxy, and translucent. Because of its straight bands of black color alternating with milky white layers or bands it is beautiful. It is used for making inexpensive jewelry, necklaces, amulets, talismans, lamps, bowls, and decorative work in temples, particularly in the capitals of pillars. Like agate, it is supposed to bring good feelings, good health and good luck.

Onyx is one of the earliest known gems in the West. The first reference to it is found in Genesis, and it was one of the twelve stones high priests wore on their breastplates. Moses was asked by God to make an offering of the onyx. It is said that David collected onyx for setting in his temple with other glistering stones.

32. **Opal,** known as upal (which means a precious stone) in Sanskrit, is a noncrystalline form of quartz. It is a silica gem containing varying amounts of water (3 to 9 percent) that is deposited in

layers at low temperatures, filling cavities in volcanic rocks or veins around hot springs. It makes up the skeleton of diatoms and silicate sponges. It is usually colorless, milky white, or green-yellow to brick-red. In gem-variety opal there is a fantastic play of colors due to inclusions of material having a different refractive index than the original substance. Light is refracted on the inner layers and fissures of the opal.

Opal has a greasy and glassy lustre, and it is pearly and resinous and therefore translucent. It is softer than many other members of the quartz family. Opaque opals are also found; these sometimes show luminescence when they are immersed in water. Some opaque opals show opalescence, especially when they are wet.

The main varieties of opals have different names according to their color.

1. *Common opal:* This stone is mainly translucent to opaque and is found in varying shades. When it is milky white, yellowish, bluish, or greenish with a play of colors, it is called a milk opal. Petrified wood with an opaline coating is called wood opal. Red, brown, or yellowish brown opal resembles jasper and is called jasper opal.
2. *Fire opal:* Semitransparent or transparent opal of orange-yellow or flaming red color with a play of colors is termed fire opal.
3. *Precious opals:* These opals are found in light colors, dark grey, blue, and black and are known by different names. The light-colored variety of opal is called white opal, and the dark ones are called black opals. Both varieties have an excellent play of colors.

Good, gem-quality opals have brilliance, play of colors, glassy and greasy lustre, and no visible cracks.

Only fire opals can take a brilliant cut. Other varieties of precious and gem-quality opal are given a cabochon cut, which helps in exhibiting the sheen, play of colors, opalescence, and asterism. They are most often given a domed cabochon cut, where the upper portions much higher and more convex than the underside. The amount of water in precious opal varies from 3 to 21 percent; in other varieties it is usually 3 to 9 percent.

Opal was once regarded as a very precious stone—second to the emerald—but somehow it lost its popularity and became an outcast. Some people regarded opals as ominous, but this belief is not common anymore, and gem-quality opals are becoming popular again.

Opal is a very soft stone. Cracks may form in it after it is used for some time from its reaction to chemicals found in sweat. People love opal for its play of colors, but also may be helpful to the body's electromagnetic field because it belongs to the quartz family. It does not have many medicinal properties and has not yet become a favorite stone of gem therapists, although it is known to give its wearer a spiritual bent of mind and faith in God.

33. *Peridot,* also called chrysolite or olivine, is the most common member of a group of silicates. It is known as ghritmani in Sanskrit and as zaberjad in Urdu and Persian (because for centuries it was obtained by jewelers from the Island of Zeberged, or St. John, in the Red Sea). It is found in different shades of green, yellow, brown, and grey and also in a transparent, colorless variety. Transparent specimens of green, yellow, brown, grey, and colorless varieties are used for gem purposes. Peridot is different from emerald and topaz in color, because it has a pale olive-green or bottle-green shade due to the presence of iron and magnesium. It has a glassy lustre. Crystals of peridot are relatively rare, though occasionally some have been found up to several inches long. Peridot is found in igneous rocks that are rich in magnesium and low in quartz—such as basalt, gabbro, and metamorphosed dolomites. Clear varieties are cut as the gem peridot, and nontransparent varieties are made into beads for necklaces, but transparent and nontransparent varieties have a velvetiness that make them a favorite of gem cutters.

Peridot is supposed to influence the psyche and is regarded as a good stone for promoting a better marital relationship. It is prescribed by gem therapists to women having troubled relationships or problems with their husbands, or to husbands who want to have better relationships with their wives. It increases tolerance and feelings of love.

Peridot is found in Egypt, Burma, Norway, Canada, Brazil, and in the American states of Arizona, Vermont, New Hampshire, Virginia, Pennsylvania, North Carolina, Oregon, and New Mexico. The best variety is supposed to occur in the Bernardmyo Valley ten miles north of Mogok in Burma. It varies in shade from yellowish green to olive green. Large gems are cut from these peridots for pendants and necklaces.

Peridot is also used in Ayurveda as pishthi (powder) and is prescribed for hiccups, dysmenorrhea, metroragia, and other female diseases (that is why it is often prescribed for women). To males it gives strength and vigor when given with suitable accompaniments—malai or honey.

Peridot gives good health, wealth, children, and happiness to the one who wears it and to his family, which is why it is prescribed for those who have bad marital relationships. It cures epilepsy, protects from poisonous insects, and heals bites. It keeps one young and delays old age if one drinks wine (asava) from a cup made of peridot. It is also believed that it keeps the breasts firm and in good shape if it is worn by women as a necklace.

34. *Porphyry,* known as sange simak in Persian and simak in Hindi, is a member of the family of igneous rocks. It is a very hard stone, and completely opaque. It is found in a dull red color with white spots in its matrix. It is used to make mortars for crushing hard stones like ruby and sapphire.

35. *Quartz* is known as sphatik in Sanskrit, billor in Persian, and rock crystal in English. It is one of the most common minerals in the earth's crust. It is found in crystalline masses, and when conditions are suitable it forms hexagonal crystals. Most of the semiprecious stones belong to the quartz family. Quartz is sometimes colorless but is more commonly white. It is sometimes found in yellow, brown, pink, green, blue, and black shades. In crystalline form, quartz has a glassy lustre.

The use of the colorless variety of crystalline quartz was very popular in ancient days in India for making ornaments, necklaces, rosaries and Shiva lingams. From 323–185 B.C., when India was ruled by the Maurya kings, quartz urns, caskets, vases, and pitchers became a part of the royal treasure. It is said that rock crystal (sphatik) cups and bowls were used to detect poison in food. If poison is poured in a cup made of rock crystal, the color of the crystal pot changes from transparent white to smoky grey.

Using a rosary made from rock crystal aids concentration, cools the body, and calms the mind. It is beneficial for gaining knowledge of the past, present, and future when used for concentration. Wearing a rock crystal necklace or pendant ensures sound, undisturbed sleep.

Nowadays, rock crystal has become very important because of its piezoelectric property. When crystal quartz is cut in an exact angle to its axis and subjected to mechanical pressure, it generates minute electrical charges at the end of the axes, and the crystal expands and contracts, which sets it into constant mechanical vibration. This constant rate of vibration makes quartz useful for radio and television transmission, telephone and cable equipment, radar work, depth-sounding apparatus, acoustic antisubmarine devices, clocks, resonators, range finders, and instruments used for measuring pressure, making lenses, prisms, and optical instruments. But only the finest and purest variety of quartz can be used in electronics and optical instruments; the other varieties are valuable as semiprecious gemstones.

Quartz gems are popular among gem therapists because they produce electrochemical balance in the body chemistry of the wearer, remove anxiety, and make one calm and centered.

36. **Serpentine,** known as zahar mohra in Hindi, is a magnesium silicate with water. It may include small amounts of nickel or iron and is regarded as a decomposition product of igneous rocks rich in ferromagnesian silicates. The fibrous form of serpentine known as chrysolite asbestos is very useful in fireproofing and insulation. The fibers spin well, conduct heat very slowly, and do not burn. Common or massive serpentine varies in shade from cream white to all shades of green to black. Streak is translucent white to opaque. It has a greasy or waxy lustre.

There are micaceous and mottled varieties of serpentine other than the fibrous asbestos, and some of them are fluorescent. It is used in firebrick and for making cups, mortars, and carvings. It is also used by Ayurvedic doctors in many medicines and is indicated for stomach troubles. It is supposed to be an efficacious remedy for typhoid fever, high blood pressure, eye troubles (redness of the eye), nervousness, vomiting, and loose bowel movements of children (yellow and green bowel movements). It cures intestinal ulcers and strengthens the body. It is said that if poison is put in a pot made of serpentine the poison loses its deadly effect.

Polished massive serpentine is used for ornamental and decorative purposes. Translucent, yellowish serpentine is cut and polished for gems. A mortar made of serpentine turns red when yellow turmeric is ground in it.

Serpentine found in Khatoon, Persia is considered to be the best and is used for making medicinal preparations in Unani and Ayurvedic medicines, in which it is known as zaharmohrakhataii.

37. *Spinel,* known as naram in Hindi, is an oxide of aluminum and magnesium. It is found in many shades from red to brown, green, blue, and purple. Spinel is striking for its lustre, brilliance, and color—only it is soft, mild, and delicate. Gentle and easy to cut, spinel is believed to be a softer counterpart of precious gemstones. Sapphire has sapphirine (blue spinel), golden sapphire has rubicelle (yellow or orange spinel), tourmaline has almandine (purple and violet spinel), and emerald has chlorospinel (grass-green spinel). Ruby has its softer counterpart, spinel ruby, also known as balas ruby (paler type of red spinel).

Ruby spinel has a fine, crimson-red color. It is beautiful, brilliant, lustrous, and attractive. Rose and pink spinel is termed balas ruby. Gem-quality red spinel is found in Sri Lanka, Burma, Thailand, and Madagascar. Badakshan, Persia was the best source of supply of spinel of good quality. They were rich in lustre, and they can still be found, but they are rare.

When the term spinel is used without any adjective it means the red ruby spinel or spinel ruby, also known as suryamani, or gemstone of the Sun. It is rich in water and devoid of any dark shades. It is blood-red in color and perfectly transparent. It is also known as lalri in Hindi and is prescribed as a substitute for ruby.

Prescribed by Ayurvedic doctors as a powder (pishthi) and used orally with honey or malai, it is supposed to be a very efficacious medicine for general weakness, stomach ailments, and problems created by imbalance of the wind, bile, and mucus. It is a good remedy for seminal diseases when taken with suitable medicines. It provides longevity.

38. *Tiger's-eye,* also known as tiger stone, is a member of the quartz family that has inclusions. Like cat's-eye, it contains fibers of asbestos, but it is very different from cat's-eye, although it is also known as marine cat's-eye. A white band of light moves across the surface with the movement of the stone—as in cat's-eye—but it is opaque, whereas cat's-eye is not. It is found in golden brown and yellow shades, with clear bands of white. Although inexpen-

sive it is an attractive stone with a glassy lustre. Beads, cabochons, and toys are manufactured from this stone.

39. *Topaz,* known as topas in Hindi, is an alumino-fluoro-silicate. It is a rare and fine stone, but the gem sold as topaz in the market is actually false topaz and belongs to the quartz family. Real topaz is a precious stone and is striking for its lustre, brilliance, hardness, and color. It belongs to the same group of gems to which emerald, ruby, and sapphire belong. Topaz has been also mistaken for pukhraj (yellow sapphire) by many Western gemologists. It is one of the twelve gems worn on the breastplate by high priests in ancient days, but that topaz was most probably a citrine or peridot. It was believed that topaz brought friendship and fidelity to its wearer. Romans praised topaz as a stone that preserves one from ailments of the chest and lower abdominal tract. Topaz was believed to be a good stone for travelers because it saved them from accidents and depression. Topaz was very popular in India, and in the West it was known by the name oriental topaz.

Because it is quite hard, topaz takes a fine polish and can be given a brilliant cut or the step cut. Topaz is found in crevices and cavities of highly acid igneous rocks, such as granite, rhyolite, gneiss, and schist. It is found in Sri Lanka, Germany, Sweden, Japan, the Ural Mountains in Siberia, Mexico, California, and New Hampshire. Its characteristic color is yellow, orange, and brown, which accounts for its association with Jupiter and its substitution for yellow sapphire, but it is also found in white, green, and blue. Fired or heated topaz assumes a red color and is sometimes mistaken for spinel ruby. Precious topaz is a perfectly transparent, light, dazzling gold color with a touch of red. The stone is prone to inclusions, and one who is interested in buying a real gold topaz should carefully select a flawless piece that is eyeglass clear.

Golden topaz, smoky topaz, and many other cheap stones that are sold as topaz, actually belong to the quartz family and not to the family of crystals called orthorhombic crystals. These have three axes all at right angles, but all of different length; they are in prismatic form with a pyramidlike termination. Brazilian topaz is supposed to be the finest.

40. *Tourmaline* is a stone that contains a greater variety of elements than any other stone. Its chemical composition varies

from stone to stone. Being a very complex silicate, tourmaline appears in multicolored forms, depending upon the varying amounts of lithium, potassium, sodium, iron, manganese, magnesium, calcium, and intrusions of granite.

Because of its electrical properties, it is used for frequency control in shortwave radio apparatus and pressure gauges. As a gemstone this quality helps the body's electrochemical balance and is therefore a favorite stone of gem therapists and tantriks. An octagonal gemstone tourmaline—whether white, red, yellow, blue, or pitch-black—that is transparent, clear, with a lovely hue, and rich in water and fire is highly appreciated. The stone has high specific gravity and is found in various colors with a dark lustre and tough texture. Brilliant, deep, and clear colors are found only in good pieces of tourmaline.

Tourmaline also is famous for its light-absorbing power and is used for the production of polarized light. When it is worn as a gem, it absorbs light and transmits it to the skin and helps the electrochemical system.

Colorless tourmaline is known as achorite, blue tourmaline as indicolite or Brazilian sapphire or Brazilian tourmaline. Green tourmaline is known as Brazilian emerald. Yellowish green tourmaline is known as Brazilian peridot. Pink and red tourmaline is known as rubellite, which is a lithium tourmaline. Black Norwegian tourmaline is known as schorl.

Tourmaline can be used by everybody without any fear. This stone is never inauspicious and always benefits its wearers. It helps in many ways:

- by conduction of lightwaves.
- by balancing the electrochemical system.
- by calming the system and enabling its wearer to concentrate on any subject and remain engaged mentally for a longer time than is usually possible.
- by absorbing evil vibrations and protecting the wearer from evil or negative vibrations.
- by increasing the ability to discriminate and make decisions.
- by informing its wearer through dreams about forthcoming accidents. According to tantriks, tourmaline gives information about future accidents and bad events by showing them to the wearer in dreams.

Tourmaline is given to clients who are going to appear in an interview or an examination, because it quiets the nerves, removes nervousness, and makes one single-minded and centered. It saves one from unnecessary discussions and, as stated before, one's ability to discriminate and decide increases.

Tourmaline absorbs light and transmits electrical charges when worn as a gem. It helps the intellect, wit, and sharpness of the brain, which is why it is given to the children who are weak in learning or who suffer from some kinds of mental illnesses.

It is said that one who wears tourmaline will never suffer humiliation.

Like turquoise, this stone protects travelers. It saves them from storms, lightning, and accidents. It also warns its wearer of forthcoming accidents by changing color.

Tourmaline should be mounted in silver and worn after it has been worshiped like an emerald, because this stone is also connected with the planet Mercury.

Medicinal utility: According to the author of *Rasa Ratna Sammuchchaya,* tourmaline has eight varieties, of which the best for medicinal purposes is the black one (schorl).

Tourmaline is also found in diamond mines. After purification, this tourmaline is converted into bhasma (oxide) and it works the same way as diamond oxide does.

The purification process of tourmaline is the same as that for diamond. Pieces of tourmaline are set in the tube-root of kateli and then purified. Another method is to heat pieces of tourmaline on a mica sheet until it becomes red-hot and then the hot, glowing tourmaline should be dropped in the urine of a horse and the process should be repeated twenty-one times. Both methods may also be used together one after the other (that is, first it should be purified by heating and cooled by the urine of a horse and then in the kateli root).

The purified tourmaline is powdered in an agate mortar and an equal amount of powdered sulphur is added to it. After this the tourmaline powder and sulphur mixture is ground in lemon juice and then it is fired in gajput the same way as lapis lazuli. The process of firing is repeated eight times, until a dirty red oxide is obtained. If the oxide is still hard it should be fired twice in gajput.

Dosage: 1/8 to 1/2 rattika with honey, cream, or malai.

Usage: Its oxide is beneficial for all problems created by the aggravation of wind, bile, or mucus.

Tourmaline oxide is known as rasayan because it contains all the six rasas, or tastes (sweet, sour, saline, pungent, bitter, astringent). It cures weakness of dhatus (raj, rasa, rakta, mans, asthi, meda, majja, and shukra). It cures sterility, syphilis, diabetes, gonorrhea, jaundice, fever, asthma, cough, seminal and uterine diseases, tuberculosis, and it provides longevity.

Tourmaline oxide is frequently used as a substitute for diamond oxide because it is costly and difficult to make diamond oxide.

41. *Turquoise* is known as firoza in Persian and peroz in Hindi. Though it is a pebble—not a stone—and it is opaque, its beautiful greenish blue or sky blue color and healing qualities have made it a favorite stone of gem lovers especially Muslim gem therapists and American Indians. Turquoise is a phosphate of aluminum and copper, contains a small amount of water, and becomes lustrous when polished. The gem turquoise is very soft and is easily destroyed by heat and water, but when it is pure sky blue in color it looks very attractive and is prized by Indians, American Indians, and people of the Middle East. It is found in various shades of blue and green, but blue is supposed to be better than green turquoise. Big pieces of turquoise are rare, but the stone is found in abundance in Afghanistan, Persia (Iran), Egypt, Arabia, Australia, and some parts of the United States and Mexico. Persian turquoise is supposed to be the best.

The gemstone turquoise is associated with the planet Ketu. The stone is famous for changing color, and its color fades away in time, but one can maintain its color if one protects it from heat and water.

Turquoise is used as a pishthi (powder) by Ayurvedic doctors and Unani hakims in many medicinal remedies. It is supposed to be a cure for poison and a blood purifier.

Turquoise saves the body from poisons; it removes toxins and poisonous matter from the body. It is believed that one who wears turquoise will not die from poisoned food. It changes color to warn its wearer about conspiracies against him.

This stone also serves as a protective charm for travelers who go into difficult passages and dangerous spots. It saves its wearer from accidents and the evil eye. It cures headache and is therefore prescribed by tantriks and gem therapists to their clients who suffer from regular headaches. If the eyes are touched by turquoise, it helps eyesight and cures eye ailments.

The stone also changes color with the change of season, and serves as an indicator of weather changes.

Turquoise brings success and respect.

The stone also is a true friend: It protects its wearers by every possible means and takes all evil vibrations on itself to save the wearer. It absorbs all negative energy and does not let it disturb the wearer.

The stone is also a good stone for lovers. *for sun people*

The stone only works as a protector when it is given as a gift of love to the wearer.

This stone is favorable for Taurus, Libra, Gemini, Virgo, Sagittarius and Pisces ascendants, and for those whose moon is in these signs.

This stone can be worn by everybody, but if it becomes dull, less lustrous, or it loses color or appears dry, the wearer should immediately take it off and not use it.

42. **Zircon,** known as tursava in Urdu, is a silicate of the mineral zirconium. It is commonly found in igneous rocks. Gem-quality zircons are fairly rare. Zircon crystals have two axes of equal length and one unequal. All the three axes are at right angles to one another (tetragonal). These crystals are commonly brown, but red, yellow, blue, and colorless varieties are also found. Clear, transparent, white zircons are prized as gems, and are used as a substitute for diamonds, which are associated with the planet Venus. Clear brown crystals turn blue when they are heated and make a better gem.

Zircon is usually found as well-developed crystals in sand gravels and as water-worn pebbles. Clear, transparent, yellow, orange-red, and brown varieties are known as hyacinth and jacinth. Gomed or hessonite—the gemstone of Rahu—is also a zircon but it is a special variety, which reflects the color of the urine of a cow or the color of honey.

Zircon is found in the alluvial soils of the Ranchi and Hazaribagh districts of Bihar and also in parts of Uttar Pradesh, Kashmir, Himachal Pradesh, and other places in India, but the ones found in Sri Lanka are supposed to be the best in quality. They are also found in Australia (New South Wales), Madagascar, the Ural Mountains, France, west Africa, Oklahoma, and in Litchfield, Maine, North Carolina, and Florida.

Zircon, like topaz and onyx, was one of the twelve stones which high priests wore on their breastplates in ancient times.

Zircon is supposed to bring good luck, wealth, and happiness to its wearer. It makes one prosperous and bestows honor, wisdom, and nobility of heart.

Like diamond, white zircon has its play of colors, it keeps one joyful and calms the mind.

Zircon cures nervousness, stimulates appetite, gives wisdom, saves its wearer from enemies and fear of getting struck by lightning and poisoning. It is also used as a medicine by Ayurvedic doctors and its pishthi (powder) is used orally in acute gastritis, piles, fever, cough, rheumatism, and constipation. It is supposed to cure suicidal tendencies.

Cubic Zirconia = Poor man's diamond /
Each ~~cost~~ stone cost only $ 5.00/100 a piece

Part **III**

Gem Therapy

13
Healing With Gemstones

THE HEALING POWER of gems is not purely a superstition; if it were, oral administration of gems as oxides and powder would not be so widely practiced and so effective. Ayurvedic medicine and the Greek system, known as the Unani system in India, both use gems. Practitioners of these systems have studied gems and their distinctive effects on the human organism, because gems are minerals in pure crystalline form and our body is composed of the same materials.

Ayurvedic and Unani systems possess an easy key—in the form of elements and humors—by which to explain the causes of imbalance in body chemistry and to help the healing process within the organism to overcome the imbalance. Western medicine also had this key, but somehow it became obsolete and lost its value. The system of the three humors in the Ayurvedic and Unani systems helps in diagnosis and in making prescriptions. The three humors (wind, bile, and mucus) are active agents of the five elements— earth, water, fire, air, and akash (ether). The five elements create the matrix for energy to operate through the organism, which itself is a product of these basic building blocks of the universe. The elements produce dhatus (discussed in the beginning of the book) and the humors allow the play of energy in a regular and harmonious sequence of assimilation, incorporation, and elimination. They play a crucial role in regulating the organism and its growth and preservation. The three humors, or doshas, must be properly understood, for they are the best friends and worst enemies of the human organism. One can witness their ceaseless interaction in the region between the heart and navel, in the digestion, assimilation, and distribution of nutrient material, and in elimination of toxins with waste products.

1. *Wind* is the principle of movement. It is said in Ayurvedic texts that bile and mucus are crippled and cannot move by themselves; they need wind, the principle of movement. This humor of wind governs all biological movements and is thus related to all subtle changes in metabolism.

All expansion and contraction, movement of nerve impulses, neuromotor signals (sensory and motor functions), breathing, excretion, secretion, cell division, pulsation, vibration, and speech functions are performed with the help of wind.

Wind (vata or vayu) has two kinds of movements—upward (urdha) and downward (adho). Upward movement of wind creates problems like breathlessness and acidity, while its downward movement is healthy and cleansing. Intestines (large and small), the pelvic cavity, bones, skin, ears, and thighs are seats of vata. Wind accumulates in these areas when it is aggravated. Fear, anxiety, nervousness, pain, tremors, and spasms are caused by vata. Wind is known as pranic force.

2. *Bile* is the principle of the fire element. It consumes the food we eat and converts it into heat energy. Bile provides the heat necessary to keep the pranic force moving inside the organism. It can be felt as body temperature, and it aids digestion, absorption, and assimilation. Bile provides lustre to the eyes and a glow to the skin. It is concentrated in the small intestines, stomach, sweat glands, blood, fat, eyes, and skin. Anger, hatred, and jealousy are produced by the humor of bile (pitta) when it is aggravated.

3. *Mucus* is the principle of the water and earth elements. Water and earth are the material content of the body. Humor of mucus (kapha) is dominated by water and serves as a lubricant for the joints and as a building material. It moistens the skin, strengthens the life force, saves the body from dehydration, and provides resistance, vigor, and stability. It is present in the body everywhere, but especially in the throat, chest, head, sinus, nose, mouth, stomach, and intestines. Mucus produces emotional at-

tachment and greed when aggravated and accumulates in the chest region.

Masters of Ayurveda studied gems and observed their properties in balancing the three humors and curing aggravated wind, bile, and mucus. For curing the three humors, or doshas, powders (pishthi) and oxides of gems were administered orally with honey or cream of milk (malai). We have already discussed this with the descriptions of the gems, but the following table may be helpful for gem therapists:

Gem	Dosha (Humor)	Energy	Color emitted	Oxide/ Pishthi
Ruby	pitta (bile)	minus	red	both
Pearl	kapha (mucus)	plus	orange	both
Coral	pitta (bile)	minus	yellow	both
Emerald	kapha (mucus)	plus	green	both
White sapphire	vata (wind)	neutral	sky blue	both
Yellow sapphire	vata (wind)	neutral	yellow	both
Diamond	kapha (mucus)	plus	rainbow, blue, and ultraviolet	only oxide
Blue sapphire	vata (wind)	neutral	violet, blue	both
Hessonite	kapha and vata (mucus and wind)	neutral	yellow	both

Gem therapists of the Ayurvedic system also use gem water and alcohol treated with gems in their therapy as well as ashes (oxides or bhasma) and powder (pishthi). Oxides and powder we have already discussed in detail with the descriptions of gems. Now we will discuss gem water and alcohol prepared from gems.

GEM WATER

To make gem water, the gems are placed in a copper or silver pot overnight. Before using the gems they are purified by washing them in cold, unboiled cow's milk and then in rainwater, spring water, or Ganga-water.

In the morning, the gem water is divided into three parts and given to the patient three times a day: in the morning, at noon, and in the evening.

Gems, as we have discussed, are electrolytes, and water is the best conductor of heat and electricity. The water is ionized by the gem and this helps the body's electromagnetic system and brings electrochemical balance. The water also absorbs rays of colored light emitted by the gems. Since colors are also chemicals in the form of frequencies, the water is changed chemically by the gems' light. As the water cannot be stored for a long time, fresh gem water must be made each time and given to the patient. Use of metal (copper or silver) also charges water with life-giving negative ions, which help the body chemistry.

ALCOHOL MADE FROM GEMS

Vaidyaraj Shri Radha Krishna Navetia, in his introduction to *Ratna Pariksha* by Shri Thakkar Pheru, describes a method of preparing alcohol from gems for use in gem therapy. He believes that the rays of light emitted by gems are absorbed by alcohol. Gem water cannot be stored for a long period of time and it requires twelve hours of time to prepare, so gem therapists prepare alcohol from gems. This alcohol can be stored easily for a long period of time and can be used whenever required.

The use of gem water, alcohol, oxides, and powder are all based on the same principle. This principle—which forms the backbone of Ayurvedic healing—involves detecting imbalance in the three humors of the body and reestablishing chemical balance by subduing the aggravated humor.

To prepare medicinal alcohol the therapist should use 90 to 100 percent rectified spirit (alcohol) of the type generally used for preparing homeopathic remedies. The alcohol should be kept in a glass jar or bottle. The use of a metal pot is not suitable for making alcohol from gems because the metal would not allow rays of light to penetrate the pot. Light is necessary for preparing the remedy. The gem should be purified by the method described in the preparation of the gem water. After purification, the gems should be allowed to dry and then placed in a glass jar containing alcohol. This jar should then be kept in a room where there is enough light, but never in direct sunlight. The preparation of alcohol from gems requires daylight, whereas for making gem water the gems are kept in water overnight. After twelve hours the gem may be removed from the alcohol, cleaned in fresh water, and stored for future use. The alcohol, which is now a medicine, should be stored in a cardboard box (which has either a white lining or a lining of the same color as the gem) in a cool and dry place.

Dosage: 10 to 12 drops of alcohol in a quarter of a cup of pure water once or twice a day as required.

The therapist should also consult the table that gives the relationship of gems to the nine dhatus and different parts of the body (see page 7). This information, along with the detection of imbalance of humors, will provide the therapist with a key to using gem water, gem alcohol, gem oxide, and gem powder.

THE ROLE OF COLOR IN GEM THERAPY

The use of color in curing illnesses—chromotherapy—is based on the understanding that the endocrine system works like a mediator of behavior through light. The chain reaction of hormonal secretions from the pineal, pituitary, and hypothalamus glands affects the body's chemistry, and one feels a kind of chemical environment inside, which is interpreted by the brain as a particular kind of feeling or mood.

Colors are frequencies of light that influence the endocrine glands directly and influence our body chemistry.

Colors are chemicals and, through a sympathetic response, influence our chemical system.

Everything in the universe is color-sensitive. Everything has a color of its own, including the planets, which influence human beings through different color frequencies they emanate and we readily absorb. Each planet has a color, and the light emitted by it forms the environment of our planet, the Earth. At the moment of our birth a pattern in our body chemistry is set, which is directly related to the position of the planets at that particular moment. It is our chemical nature, which we experience as moods and feelings. The position of the planets in relation to our placement at the moment of our birth determines our chemical nature. Each planet is related to a particular gem through color, and the color of the planet is reflected by the gem. Because the gems are cut to turn light back into the observer's eye, the gems (especially the cut gems) refract or bend light. The lustre of the gem also helps the absorption, reflection, and refraction of light by the gem's surface. Our body absorbs reflected rays and vibrations that come to us filtered through the gem we wear and through it our body chemistry is influenced. If a planet is emitting light (that is, color) frequencies that are not suited to our system, a gemstone that could counteract these frequencies would help the body chemistry and the unfavorable influence of that planet would be averted.

The Earth and man are inseparable, and Earth and the solar system to which it belongs are inseparable. The human body, like Earth, is a combination of minerals. Minerals are the bricks that constitute the Earth. They are inorganic chemical elements or compounds found in earth and man in the same way and, to an extent, in similar proportions. According to ancient seers, the human body performs all its activities in accordance with rays of cosmic light, which it receives through the colors and frequencies of light emitted by the planets. The position, angle, and alignment of planets is therefore of great importance to us. We can, with knowledge, add the missing frequencies of cosmic rays and vibrations by using the gemstone that provides the energy of the debilitated, wrongly posited, or conjunct planet. We can also accelerate the frequencies of any exalted or favorable planet to gain more strength, the same way we use glasses when our eyes become weak. All gemstones are crystals that have electrical properties, with the exception of coral and pearl. All gemstones are minerals, or chemicals, and they absorb and transmit—according to their chemical combination—the rays of light, electrical charges, and color frequencies that are changed into their chemical form inside the body. Gemstones absorb radiation and transform them in a constructive way to make them suitable for the body. According to *Agasthyamat* (in the opinion of sage Agasthya, whose text on gems is known by this name), they release positive vibrations and absorb negative vibrations. That is why they are supposed to have healing effects and healing qualities. Gems serve as saviors and protectors, just as rubber boots protect the feet from mud and water. They help us achieve our desired goals by giving us more strength of will, inspiration, and necessary insight to refine our latent potential. Possession of a beautiful and precious stone makes one happy. The fluorescent quality of gemstones receives a good deal of our attention, their shape, their lustre influence the wearer visually and emotionally. Colors also induce significant changes in emotional state and help to create positive emotional states in the mind of the wearer. Each color has its own area of influence in the body and produces physical and mental responses in that area. For example:

- **Red** is hot and stimulates the adrenals. It has a vitalizing effect and is magnetic and positive; it drives poison out of the body.
- **Orange** is warm, stimulates the gonads, has a cheering, inspiring effect that makes one more optimistic; it is positive and magnetic.
- **Yellow** is hot. It stimulates the brain and the nerves, saves one from insects, inspires one to gain knowledge, and produces optimism. Yellow is magnetic-positive.
- **Green** is refreshing and cool. It invigorates the blood chemistry, produces calmness, has a restful effect on the eyes, and is neutral.
- **Blue** is cold and acidic. It creates insecurity, pessimism, and serenity. It also cures spinal troubles, burns, poisonous bites, hysteria, and dry cough.
- **Sky blue** is cold and has a calming effect on the nervous system. It reduces heat in the system, cures burns, poisonous bites, headaches, and heart palpitations.
- **Violet** is cold. It acts as a germicide, creates antibodies, increases the body's resistance, and provides gentle heat to the body.

Gem therapists even prescribe the same stone in a different color to their clients considering their Moon sign and the color of the gem. For example:

- **Reddish agate** for Moon in Aries or Scorpio.
- **White agate** for Moon in Taurus or Libra.
- **Green agate** for Moon in Gemini or Virgo.
- **Transparent agate** for Moon in Cancer.
- **Orange agate** for Moon in Leo.
- **Yellow agate** for Moon in Sagittarius or Pisces.
- **Bluish black agate** for Moon in Capricorn.
- **Dark blue agate** for Moon in Aquarius.

The base of the gemstone must contact the skin of the wearer in such therapy. Transparency, lustre, and color combined with the electrical property of the gem exerts a powerful influence on the human body and psyche.

GEMS AND MERIDIANS

Some therapists use gemstones—quartz crystals—on the acupuncture points or meridians to induce electrochemical balance without considering the client's ascendant or Moon sign. It would be more effective if they considered their client's Moon sign and ascendant in selecting a stone. In any case, however, the gem's contact with the patient's electromagnetic field will help the electrochemical balance.

For getting the full benefit of the gemstone, it should be regularly worn as a ring or pendant. The presence of the gemstone on the body will provide an increased number of negative ions, and it will influence the electrolytic salts present in every cell of the body. Gems also contain chemical compounds that interact with the body through the gem's contact with the skin.

TALISMANIC VIRTUES OF GEMS

Gems are nature's storehouse of energy. Their beneficial uses have been mentioned in the Vedas and scriptures of Ayurveda as well as in books on astrology. They are supposed to have hidden powers, and their use as talismans has been popular in both the East and the West. It is said that Roman women wore the blue sapphire to improve conjugal relationships. Amethyst was worn for valor, chastity, and safety. Coral was used against lightning, whirlwind, fire, shipwreck, sorcery, and poison. Ruby was supposed to be an antidote for poison. It also saved its wearer from sorrows and evil thoughts. Diamond was used as a talisman for victory over enemies in the battlefield.

We have already mentioned many such qualities of gems when we discussed precious and semiprecious gems. Now we will discuss the preparation of talismans from precious and semiprecious stones. According to Tantra, special power can be induced in gems and metals if they are selected at a particular time, and if power is invoked in them by worship, the use of a mantra, and rituals.

In preparing a talisman the gemstone should be selected, bought, worshiped, and worn under the influence of the nakshatra favorable to the gemstone. The day of the week and the time of day also should be in accordance with the ruling planet of the gemstone.

A talisman can be prepared by any of the following methods:

1. Inscribing the yantra of the ruling planet on the gemstone.
2. Inscribing the mantra of the ruling planet on the gemstone.
3. Inscribing the yantra or mantra on the metal related to the ruling planet and then setting the gemstone in the inscribed metal.
4. Setting the gemstone on a metal plate that is formed into a shape related to the shape of the yantra of the gemstone's ruling planet.
5. Setting the gemstone on a metal capsule, inside which a yantra of the ruling planet has been stored after the proper rituals and worship are completed.

When the talisman is finished, grains and metal related to the ruling planet should be donated to a priest. After receiving his blessings, wear the talisman as a necklace or armband.

For the nakshatras favorable to gemstones and planets, see the discussion in chapter 2 and the nakshatra charts on pages 22 and 24. The yantras and mantras for each planet also have already been given in the chapters on the precious gems. There, the time of the day and the weekdays related to the planets are also discussed, and the same information holds good for semiprecious stones used as substitutes for precious stones.

INSTRUCTIONS FOR MAKING TALISMANS

Talisman of Ruby

Ruby should be set in the center of a circular plate made from a mixture of seven parts gold and one part copper. On the back of this plate, engrave the yantra of the Sun in the nakshatra favorable for ruby. The ruby should not weigh less than the prescribed

weight—2½ carats. A spinel ruby, star ruby, or lalri can be sub-
stituted if necessary. It is better to engrave the yantra (the numerical
yantra) and set the ruby, spinel, or lalri in such a way that the
back of the gemstone is in the central square of the yantra and
the gemstone can touch the skin.

The yantra should be worshiped for twenty-seven days. On the
twenty-eighth day one should donate gold, an iron rod, jaggery, an
unrefined brown sugar made by boiling cane juice, an orange
blanket, sesame seeds, ghee, and salt with some money to one's
priest. On the twenty-ninth day one should feed a brahmin (or
one's teacher) and offer him or her red clothes, red sandalwood,
wheat, saffron, red flowers, and some money. Then wear the talisman
for the first time on a Sunday morning before 10:00 A.M.

This talisman protects from fear, sorrow, and disaster and gives
a respectable position in the society if a ruby or star ruby is used.
If a lalri is used, this talisman makes one religious, gives one the
desire to travel to holy places, gives strength to the body, and
protects one from possession by ghosts and evil spirits. Ruby talisman
makes its owner prosperous and fortunate and saves him from
ghosts and evil spirits.

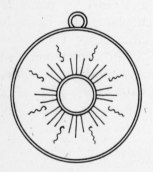

*Front view of ruby or lalri
talisman*

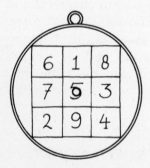

*Back view of ruby or lalri
talisman*

Note: The numbers should be engraved in the square as described in the
Yantra of Sun.

Talisman of Pearl

A pearl should be set in the center of a crescent moon made of silver. On the back of the plate the Yantra of Moon should be engraved. The pearl should not weigh less than the prescribed weight of 2, 4, 6, or 11 carats. Instead of a pearl, a moonstone, a brilliant cut crystal of quartz, white sapphire, or white topaz could also be used. The setting should allow the back of the gemstone to touch the skin, and the stone should be set in the central square of the yantra engraved on the back of the talisman.

The yantra should be worshiped for three or nine days. On the ninth day one should donate a conch, camphor, rice, ghee, yoghurt, sugar, and silver with some money to one's priest. Then one should feed a brahmin (or one's teacher) and offer him or her white clothes, white sandalwood, white flowers, and some money. Then wear the talisman for the first time on a Monday after 10:00 A.M.

This talisman gives freedom from negative thoughts and depression and brings happiness. It strengthens the heart, keeps one away from emotional high and low tides, increases love, makes one charming, prosperous, and gives one a happy conjugal life. It is supposed to protect women from widowhood.

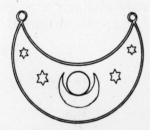

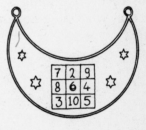

Front view of pearl, moonstone, white sapphire, or white topaz talisman

Back view of talisman

Talisman of Coral

A nice red coral should be set in the center of a triangular shape made of copper, or three parts gold and four parts copper. The weight of the coral should be not less than six carats. The setting should allow the back of the coral to touch the skin of the wearer. The Yantra of Mars should be engraved on the back. The special Yantra for Mars given below is supposed to make the most effective talisman. If the yantra is engraved on the coral itself, the power of the talisman becomes much more than an ordinary talisman engraved on the metal. A numerical yantra is also good and could be used without any problem.

The yantra should be worshiped for one day. This should be a Tuesday during a favorable nakshatra (i.e., Chitra, Anuradha, Dhanishtha). One should donate jaggery, wheat, red lentils, red sandalwood, saffron, a red blanket, and some money to one's priest. Then one should feed a brahmin (or one's teacher) and offer him or her red clothes and red flowers with some money. After this one should wear the talisman on a Tuesday morning after 11:00 A.M.

This talisman makes one courageous, saves one from nightmares, sorcery, storms, thunder, fear of getting struck by lightning, fire, and fear of getting wounded. It gives victory on the battlefield and protects one from enemies and fits of anger. It is believed that it saves women from widowhood, like the pearl talisman, and also helps them in finding a life partner. It saves children from the evil eye, whooping cough, teething problems, and evil spirits.

Front view of coral talisman

Back view of coral talisman

Special Yantra for Mars

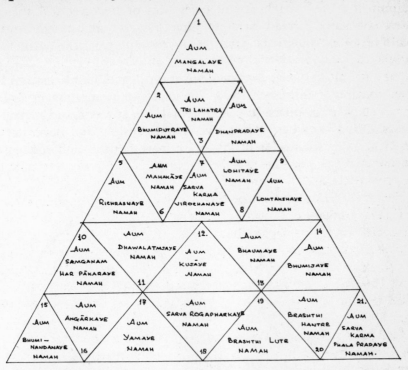

Note: There is no substitute for coral—coral alone must be set.

Talisman of Emerald

A nice green emerald should be set in the center of a circular piece of metal—on which a bow and arrow is carved—which is either pure silver; ten parts silver and one part gold or platinum; or bronze. The weight of the emerald should be no less than 3 carats. Instead of an emerald one could use bloodstone (heliotrope), turquoise, aquamarine, or green jade of good quality. The Yantra of Mercury should be engraved on the back of the circular plate and the emerald set so that the back of the stone touches the skin of the wearer.

The yantra should be made and worshiped in a suitable nakshatra, as given in the chart on page 24. It should be worshiped for sixty-four days (the time for worship each day is after 11:00 A.M.). On the sixty-fifth day one should donate gold, musk, bronze, rice, and some money to one's priest. On the same day, one should feed a brahmin (or one's teacher) and offer him or her green clothes, green vegetables, green or light blue flowers, and money and obtain his or her blessings. After this one should wear the talisman on a Wednesday.

The emerald talisman bestows wisdom, peace, happiness, and strength, and it improves one's financial situation. It saves one from snakes, evil spirits, ghosts, the evil eye, sorcery, and mental illness. One who wears it preserves good eyesight and never suffers from wet dreams. It makes one's mate faithful and reduces sensuality.

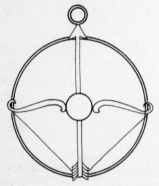

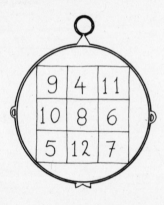

Shape No. 1:
Front view of emerald talisman   *Back view of emerald talisman*

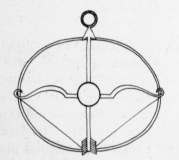

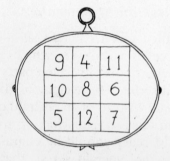

Shape No. 2:
Front view of emerald talisman   *Back view of emerald talisman*

Note: One may set turquoise and other substitutes for emerald together with the emerald in one talisman.

Talisman of Yellow Sapphire

A good specimen of yellow sapphire should be set in a circular piece of gold plate on which an eight-petal lotus is drawn, with the gem set in the center of the lotus. The weight of the gem should weigh no less than 3 carats. Instead of yellow sapphire, yellow topaz, citrine, or amber of a nice yellow color could be used, but it is advised that yellow sapphire or yellow topaz are the only stones that make the talisman valuable. Other stones could be set in the same talisman with yellow sapphire or yellow topaz or both.

The yantra should be engraved on the back side of the plate and the gem set in the central square so that it touches the skin of the wearer.

The Yantra of Jupiter should be worshiped on a Thursday during a favorable nakshatra between sunrise and 11:00 A.M. After the worship, which is recitation of mantras as prescribed, one should donate gold, turmeric root, yellow beans (gram dal), a yellow blanket made of wool, and some money to one's priest. On the same day one should feed a brahmin (or one's teacher) and offer him or her yellow clothes made of silk, yellow flowers, yellow sandalwood, and saffron and obtain his blessings. Then one should wear the talisman. All this worship and ritual should be done on a Thursday before 11:00 A.M.

The talisman bestows courage, health, wealth, wisdom, honor, and fame. It protects from evil spirits, accidental death, and schizophrenia; it helps young women to obtain a suitable match and removes obstacles that delay marriage.

Front view of yellow sapphire
talisman

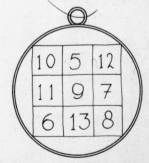

Back view of yellow sapphire
talisman

Talisman of Diamond

A piece of flawless diamond should be set in a metal plate made of silver, white gold (ten parts silver and one part gold), or platinum. The weight of the diamond should be no less than 1½ carats. Instead of a diamond, transparent white tourmaline, white zircon, or white achroite may be used.

The plate should be of the shape of an eight-pointed star (two squares intersecting each other). The yantra should be engraved on the back side of the metal plate and gemstone set in the center of the plate should touch the skin of the wearer.

The Yantra of Venus should be worshiped on a Friday during a favorable nakshatra (see the Nakshatra Chart on page 24). The worship should continue for forty-nine days. On the fiftieth day one should donate gold, silver, milk, yoghurt, rock sugar candy (white, transparent), and white sandalwood to one's priest with some money. Then one should feed a brahmin (or one's teacher) with rice, yoghurt, and rock sugar candy, offer him or her white clothes and white flowers with some money and obtain the person's blessings.

This talisman bestows wealth, good manners, patience, purity, fearlessness, victory over enemies, respect, luxuries, success. It protects from accidental death, sorcery. Increases will power, power of discrimination and promotes insight into secret science and occult knowledge. Saves from insecurity, insanity, fear of darkness and fear of getting struck with lightning.

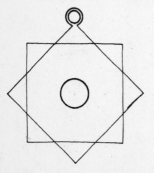

Front view of diamond talisman

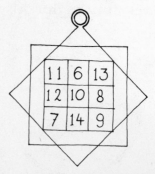

Back view of diamond talisman

Talisman of Blue Sapphire

A flawless blue sapphire should be set in an iron or steel plate or a mixture of iron and silver, shaped like a sword. The gem should weigh no less than 5 carats. The Yantra of Saturn should be engraved on the back of the metal plate, allowing the blue sapphire to touch the skin of the wearer through the square in the center. Instead of a blue sapphire one may use lapis lazuli, amethyst, black opal, black tourmaline, and so forth.

The yantra should be worshiped two hours before sunset on a Saturday for only one day. After worship one should donate black beans, mustard oil, black sesame seeds, or iron to one's priest with some money. Before sunset one should feed a brahmin (or one's teacher) and offer black clothes, violet, deep blue or dark flowers and some money and obtain the person's blessings.

A mixture of one part gold, two parts silver, three parts lead, one part copper, and five parts iron may also be used to make the metal plate for the talisman.

The blue sapphire talisman bestows favor from wise men and noble (royal) people as well as courage, peace, and happiness. It protects one from sorcery, the evil eye, ghosts, evil spirits, imprisonment, and evil thoughts. This talisman increases one's radiance and improves eyesight, promotes better conjugal relationships, and removes obstacles that cause delay.

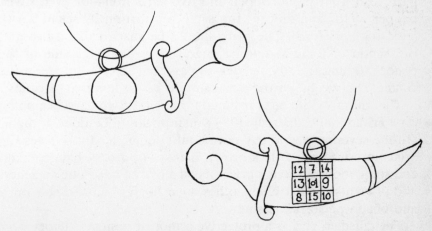

Shape No. 1:
Front view of blue sapphire
talisman

Back view of blue sapphire
talisman

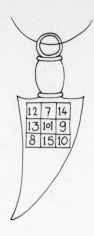

Shape No. 2:
Front view of blue sapphire
talisman

Back view of blue sapphire
talisman

Talisman of Hessonite

A nice honey-colored hessonite should be set in the metal plate made from a mixture of one part gold, two parts silver, three parts lead, four parts copper, and five parts iron—or iron, silver, copper, gold, and zinc in the same proportion as stated above (zinc replaces lead). The plate should be shaped like a fish and the Yantra of Rahu should be engraved on the back side of the plate, allowing the stone's back to pass through the square in the center. The weight of the stone should be no less than 5 carats.

The yantra should be worshiped for seventy-two days, beginning on a Friday or Wednesday. The worship should be done at night. On the seventy-second day one should donate lead, black sesame seeds, mustard oil, a dark brown blanket or a dark blue blanket, and some money to one's priest. Feed a brahmin (or one's teacher) and offer him or her blue clothes, blue flowers, and some money and obtain person's blessing.

The talisman acts as a protective armor; it bestows victory over enemies, gives health, wealth, and peace of mind. It saves one from poison and lightning and calms the nerves. In males, it increases masculine energy. It cures diseases that cannot be diagnosed.

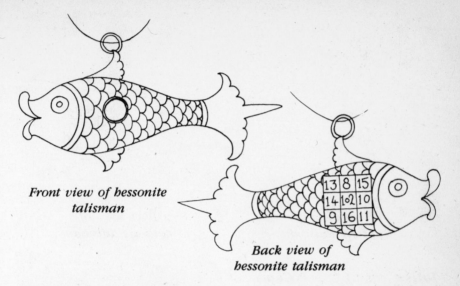

*Front view of hessonite
talisman*

*Back view of
hessonite talisman*

Talisman of Cat's-eye

A cat's-eye should be set in a metal plate made from the same
mixture of metals as prescribed for the hessonite talisman. The
metal plate should be given the shape of a flag and the Yantra
of Ketu engraved on its back. The gemstone should be allowed to
touch the skin of the wearer, as in the case of other talismans.
The weight of the cat's-eye should be no less than 5 carats.

The yantra should be worshiped an hour after sunset on a Wednesday. After the prescribed number of mantras are done (see chapter
11) one should donate a knife, musk, black sesame seeds, mustard
oil, iron, a black blanket, and some money to one's priest. Then
one should feed a brahmin (or one's teacher) and offer him or her
black clothes, black flowers with some money and obtain the
person's blessings. Then one should wear this talisman.

The talisman bestows happiness, health, wealth, and victory over
enemies. It protects from evil spirits and the evil eye, gives radiance
to the body, and saves one from financial loss and fear of drowning. This talisman increases speculative powers and intuition and
removes fear of accidental death.

Note: Turquoise can also be set with cat's-eye in the talisman to increase
its power against scorpion bites, evil spirits, lightning, and wounds caused
by sharp weapons.

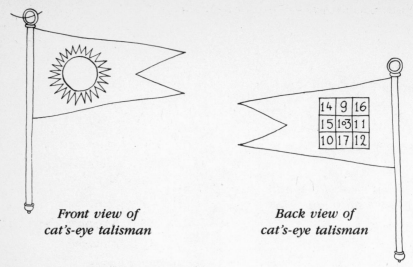

Front view of
cat's-eye talisman

Back view of
cat's-eye talisman

Talismans of Other Gems

Talismans of amethyst, aquamarine, bloodstone, carnelian, garnet, jade, lapis lazuli, sardonyx, and turquoise alone also can be made, using the yantra and mantra of the planet to which they are related. The nine-gem pendulum is the best talisman because it does not require worship, a yantra, or a setting in which the stones touch the skin of the wearer. It creates a power field of its own, which helps the wearer. It bestows good luck, peace, and prosperity, saves one from evil spirits and the evil eye and protects one from enemies, poisons. It calms the agitated mind, brings success and honor, and helps in the evolution of one's consciousness. For worship of a talisman one should consult the sixth chapter of my book *Tools for Tantra* and use the Shodashopchar method. The mantras are the same as those for the worship of Ganesha, the god with an elephant head, only the japa (or repetition of the mantra) is of the mantra of the ruling planet of the gem.

Jawahar Mohra

This is a special mixture of gem powders for use as a general tonic for weak people or old people. There are many formulae for making jawahar mohra in Ayurvedic texts. Here we are giving a formula from *Vaidyaraj Triloki Nath,* by Sahukara Bareilly. It has been made and used by the author himself.

Jawahar Mohra—Prescription No. 1:

pearl	25	grams
ruby	25	grams
white or yellow sapphire	25	grams
emerald	25	grams
blue sapphire	25	grams
coral branch	250	grams
agate	25	grams
musk	1.5	grams
amber	1.5	grams
silver leaf	50	in number (large size)
gold leaf	10	in number
zahar mohra (serpentine)	10	grams
abe resham (cocoon of silkworm)	5	grams

The gems should be cleaned and powdered with rose water. Small balls the size of a black peppercorn should be made while the paste is still in wet paste form and has not become dry powder.

As a general tonic one pill should be taken with one glass of boiled milk to which a pinch of ground saffron is added when the milk boils. Dates can be used for sweetening the milk. The remedy should be taken for at least two weeks.

In cases of heart trouble, heart palpitations, or irregular heartbeat, the pill should be powdered before use and given with powdered saffron and honey for at least forty days.

It works on the electrochemical system and provides strength to the heart and cures ailments of the heart.

Jawahar Mohra—Prescription No. 2, for summer:
Source: *Ratna Prakash* by Shri Raj Roop Tank, page 105

pearl	4	grams
emerald	6	grams
white or yellow sapphire	2½	grams
ruby	7	grams
coral	8	grams

Talisman Chart

Name of the Planet	Gems and Substitute Gems for Talisman	Minimum Weight Required	Metal Required	Mantra to be Recited	Prescribed Quantity for Japa (mantra repetition)	Yantra to be Engraved
Sun	1. Ruby 2. Garnet 3. Star Ruby 4. Red Spinel 5. Red Zircon 6. Red Quartz 7. Red Tourmaline	2½ carats	7 parts gold 1 part copper	ॐ ह्रीं हंस सूर्याय नमः ॐ AUM HRIM HANSA SURIYAYE NAMAH AUM	7,000 times	6 1 8 7 5 3 2 9 4
Moon	1. Pearl 2. Moonstone 3. Agate 4. Quartz 5. White Sapphire 6. White Tourmaline	2, 4, 6 or 11 carats	Silver	ॐ सों सोमाय नमः ॐ AUM SOM SOMAYE NAMAH AUM	11,000 times	7 2 9 8 6 4 3 10 5
Mars	1. Coral 2. Red Agate 3. Carnelian 4. Red-Jasper	6 carats	3 parts gold 4 parts copper	ॐ मों मंगलाय नमः ॐ AUM BHAUM BHAUMAYE NAMAH AUM	10,000 times	8 3 10 9 7 5 4 11 6
Mercury	1. Emerald 2. Aquamarine 3. Peridot 4. Green Agate 5. Jade 6. Green Zircon 7. Green Tourmaline	3 carats	Silver, white gold, platinum, or bronze	ॐ बुं बुधाय नमः ॐ AUM BUM BUDHAYE NAMAH AUM	4,000 times	9 4 11 10 8 6 5 12 7

Planet	Gems	Carats	Metal	Mantra	Repetitions	Yantra
Jupiter	1. Yellow Sapphire 2. Topaz 3. Citrine 4. Yellow Pearl 5. Yellow Zircon 6. Yellow Tourmaline	3 carats	Gold	ॐ बृं बृहस्पतये नमः ॐ AUM BRIM BRAHASPATAYE NAMAH AUM	19,000 times	10 5 12 / 11 9 7 / 6 13 8
Venus	1. Diamond 2. Zircon 3. White Sapphire 4. White Tourmaline	1½ carats	Silver, white gold, or platinum	ॐ शुं शुक्राय नमः ॐ AUM SHUM SHUKRAYE NAMAH AUM	16,000 times	11 6 13 / 12 10 8 / 7 14 9
Saturn	1. Blue Sapphire 2. Blue Zircon 3. Blue Spinel 4. Amethyst 5. Lapis Lazuli 6. Blue Tourmaline 7. Neeli	5 carats	Gold, 1 part silver, 2 parts lead, 3 parts copper, 1 part iron, 5 parts iron	ॐ शं शनिश्चराय नमः ॐ AUM SHAM SHANAISHCHARAYE NAMAH AUM	23,000 times	4 9 8 / 3 5 7 / 8 1 6
Rahu	1. Hessonite (Zircon) 2. Hessonite Garnet 3. Jacinth	5 carats	1 part gold, 2 parts silver, 3 parts zinc, 1 part copper, 5 parts iron	ॐ रां राहुवे नमः ॐ AUM RAM RAHUVE NAMAH AUM	18,000 times	13 8 15 / 14 12 10 / 9 16 11
Ketu	1. Cat's-eye 2. Turquoise	5 carats	1 part gold, 2 parts silver, 3 parts zinc, 1 part copper, 5 parts iron	ॐ कें केतवे नमः ॐ AUM KAIM KETAVE NAMAH AUM	17,000 times	14 9 16 / 15 13 11 / 10 17 12

(Prescription No. 2, continued)

turquoise	2½ grams
zahar mohra (serpentine)	12 grams
lapis lazuli	7 grams
yashav (white jade or Chinese jade)	12 grams
agate (yellow)	3 grams
agate (red)	3 grams
amber (in raw form)	3 grams
bansh lochan (calcium bamboana)	12 grams
gold leaf	3 grams
silver leaf	12 grams
white sandalwood powder	12 grams
black pepper	6 grams

The same process of cleaning and making a paste and gem pills should be repeated as in the case of the formula No. 1.

The dosage is about the weight of two grains of rice with honey or malai. It can be used as a general tonic with saffron milk, and for heart diseases with honey or a special syrup prescribed by a vaidya, or medicine man.

Jawahar mohra—Prescription No. 3, for winter:
Source: *Ratna Prakash* by Shri Raj Roop Tank, page 106

pearl	4 grams
emerald	8 grams
yellow or white sapphire	4 grams
turquoise	4 grams
zahar mohra (serpentine)	20 grams
coral branch	8 grams
lapis lazuli	8 grams
yashav	12 grams
ruby	8 grams
agate (yellow)	4 grams
agate (red)	40 grams

(Prescription No. 3, continued)

amber	4 grams
river coconut	12 grams
bansh lochan (calcium bamboana)	12 grams
white sandalwood powder	12 grams
musk	4 grams
momiayee (available only from Unani pharmacies)	8 grams
balsa oil	12 grams
pistachio oil	15 grams
gold leaf	4 grams
silver leaf	14 grams

Clean, powder, and shape as for the previous prescriptions.

Dosage: Take the weight equivalent of two grains of rice with honey or malai. To use it as a tonic, mix with milk and a pinch of saffron. For heart disease, mix it with the syrup prescribed by the vaidya, or medicine man.

SOURCES OF SUPPLY

1) Gem powders can be obtained through Ayurvedic companies in India that supply their products to the West.

2) Gem talismans, gem powders, and nine-gem pendulums can be ordered from:
   Mr. Dinesh Johari
   368, Govindpuri. Pincod: 249403.
   Haridwar, U.P.
   India

Note: Because these are not readily available, one must wait after placing the order. When ordering, please give your complete address; the day of the week, date, time, and place of birth. For information please write with prepaid postage.

Nine-gem pendulums can also be ordered in the United States from:

Harmat Enterprises Ltd.
50 West 34th Street
Suite 23 C10
New York, NY 10001

Glossary

amla murabba: jam of the amla fruit *(Emblica officenalis).*

bansh lochan: calcium bamboana.

bedmusk: Salix caprea, a distillate of cane.

bimb fruit: Coccinia indica.

chyavan prash: a compound with amla fruit as the basic ingredient. Amla is known as *Emblica officenalis.* Used as a general tonic; very rich in vitamins, especially Vitamin C. Available in Indian spice shops.

ghee kunwar: Aloe vera, liliaceae, *Aloe veshandensis;* it purifies blood and removes swelling.

hartal: yellow arsenic (As_2S_3) found in mines in Iran and China.

japa: repetition of a mantra.

jawakhar: Hordeum vulgare linn.

kajjali: a mixture of mercury and sulfur (HgS_3).

kateli (small): Solanum xanthocarpum.

kateli (large): Solanum indicum.

kulthi beans: Dolichos biflorus.

manphal: rubiaceae, *Randia dumetorum lam.* Its English name is emetic nut. It is the best drug to induce vomiting without causing any trouble. The seeds are the most powerful, but the skin is also used.

mansel: arsenic rubrum (As_2S_2).

neel grass: Indigofera tinctoria linn. Used to extract indigo color that acts as a whitener.

neem leaf: Azadirachta indica; only its tender leaves and flowers are used.

palash: leguminosea, *Butea monosperma,* bastard teak.

papadkhar: Ficus lacor buch-ham.

phala deepika: ancient scripture on astrology.

pipal: Pipar longum linn., from the family of *Piperaceae.*

pippli plant: Pipar longum. It makes mucus come out easily without loss of strength. Its fruit and roots are useful in medicines.

rattika: 1 rattika = .59 metric carats.

roli: mixture of turmeric and a very small amount of calcium hydroxide.

rudraksha: Elaeocapus ganitrus berry.

sarpgandha powder: Rauwolfia serpentina. It is the best medicine for high blood pressure.

sarva samput: two clay pots, joined together, in which the tablet of a gem oxide is fired.

shilajit: black bitumen, a mineral pitch. In summer, this mineral-rich liquid comes out of the mountains by the heat of the sun.

sitopiladi choorna (recipe):

    16 grams powdered rock sugar candy
     8 grams powdered calcium bamboana
     4 grams powdered pipal
     2 grams powdered white cardamom
     1 gram powdered cinnamon

sohaga: metal that is mixed with gold to provide lustre.

tilak: mark put on the forehead with roli or sandalwood paste.

triphala choorna: a powdered mixture of three fruits: harad or haritika, *(Terminalia chebula),* bahada *(Terminalia belerica),* and amla *(Emblica officenalis).*

Note:

The classification of gems into castes is not based on the caste to which one belongs by birth but on the classification that divides nakshatras in four categories.